BETWEEN PHILOSOPHY AND LITERATURE

BETWEEN PHILOSOPHY AND LITERATURE
BAKHTIN AND THE QUESTION OF THE SUBJECT

DAPHNA ERDINAST-VULCAN

STANFORD UNIVERSITY PRESS

STANFORD, CALIFORNIA

Stanford University Press
Stanford, California

©2013 by the Board of Trustees of the Leland Stanford Junior University. All rights reserved.

No part of this book may be reproduced or transmitted in any form or by any means, electronic or mechanical, including photocopying and recording, or in any information storage or retrieval system without the prior written permission of Stanford University Press.

Library of Congress Cataloging-in-Publication Data

Erdinast-Vulcan, Daphna, author.
  Between philosophy and literature : Bakhtin and the question of the subject / Daphna Erdinast-Vulcan.
      pages cm
  Includes bibliographical references and index.
  ISBN 978-0-8047-8582-2 (cloth)--ISBN 978-0-8047-8583-9 (pbk.)
 1. Bakhtin, M. M. (Mikhail Mikhailovich), 1895-1975--Philosophy. 2. Bakhtin, M. M. (Mikhail Mikhailovich), 1895-1975--Contemporaries. 3. Subject (Philosophy) in literature. 4. Continental philosophy. 5. Philosophy, Modern--20th century. I. Title.
  PG2947.B3E73 2014
  801'.95092--dc23   2013028147
   ISBN 978-0-8047-8839-7 (electronic)

Designed by Bruce Lundquist

Typeset at Stanford University Press in 10/14 Palatino

CONTENTS

Preface and Acknowledgments — vii

Abbreviations — xi

Introduction — 1

PART ONE: HOMESICKNESS, BORDERLINES, AND CONTRABAND

The Architectonics of Subjectivity — 23

The Poetics of Subjectivity — 50

The Shattered Mirror of Modernity — 76

PART TWO: THE EXILIC CONSTELLATION

Introduction — 101

The Dead End of Omniscience:
Reading Bakhtin with Bergson — 107

In the Beginning Was the Body:
Reading Bakhtin with Merleau-Ponty — 135

From Dialogics to Trialogics:
Reading Bakhtin with Lévinas — 166

Coda: A Home Away from Home   197

Notes   211

Bibliography   237

Index   255

PREFACE AND ACKNOWLEDGMENTS

The Humanities are that form of knowledge in which the knower is revealed. All knowledge becomes humanistic when this effect takes place, when we contemplate not only a proposition but also the proposer, when we hear the human voice behind what is being said.

Charles Frankel, "Why the Humanities?"
ACLS Newsletter 30 (1979): 15–16

This project dates back to the summer of 1992, when I began reading M. M. Bakhtin's *Art and Answerability*, then newly translated. Having earlier read his *Problems of Dostoevsky's Poetics* and *Rabelais and His World*, standard fare for any self-respecting academic in the humanities in the 1980s, I was entirely unprepared for Bakhtin's long essay "Author and Hero in Aesthetic Activity," which is overtly metaphysical in orientation and soaked through with religious rhetoric and sentiment. This essay seemed to be diametrically opposed to the standard view of what Bakhtin was all about, and unless one chose to dismiss it as a piece of juvenilia, it had to be taken on board as evidence of a profound, unresolved, and—to me—intriguing ambivalence in Bakhtin's thought. Having read and reread the essay throughout that summer and in the following years, I have come to believe that the fault line, so clearly visible between "Author and Hero" and *Problems of Dostoevsky's Poetics*, ought to be acknowledged and negotiated through a broader perspective; that Bakhtin's philosophical quest is closely related to what is currently labeled "continental," but perhaps—as Richard Rorty suggests—should more aptly be designated "conversational" philosophy; and that the strength of Bakhtin's work lies, not in its neat dovetailing with postmodernist buzzwords, but in its self-conscious threshold position.

This study will, therefore, eschew the routine assertions of the crisis, or the downright demise of the subject, which all too often become mere rhetorical tokens in discussions of postmodernity, along with pronouncements of the "death of the author." In the case of Bakhtin, the question of the subject is not only historically and concretely relevant but also acutely personal, inasmuch as Bakhtin—the real person writing under the long shadow of political state terrorism, enforced exile, physical pain, and material deprivation—must have experienced his own position as a "subject in process" (in the French juridical sense of being on trial as well), and the ethical question "How to be?" as blood-chillingly literal and urgent. The radical chic of dispensing with the notion of agency and responsibility and of stripping the subject of all powers of resistance would have been a disempowering, self-defeating gesture that he and his associates could hardly afford.

The author is not quite dead, then. And if he seems to be naïve at times, this is not the sheltered naïveté of the historically privileged West. Where the personal stakes are so high, and questions of how to be become very real—nonacademic, one might say—and have to be acted upon, there is an added gravitas that invites the reader to do some honest thinking. And so, while this is not a biographical study in any conventional sense, it is nonetheless produced with a powerful sense of Bakhtin, the speaker, revealing himself. And what he has to say on the question of ethics and subjectivity deserves to be listened to.

. . . .

As indicated above, this book took many years to mature, but it could not have been otherwise. As the years went by, the writing became a spiraling process: whenever I went back to a section I thought long completed and done with, I discovered that there was actually a lot more, or a lot else, to be said at that point, and thus often found myself beginning anew, taking on board what I had learned or unlearned in the meantime. Not the best way to get to the end of any project, for sure, but perhaps not the worst either.

If I had to find some justification for this long process of maturation, I would cite Lionel Trilling's profound discovery that the nature of the reader's engagement with certain texts is that of being read by them. "I have been read," he wrote in his essay on teaching the modernists, "by Eliot's poems and by *Ulysses* and by *Remembrance of Things Past* and by *The Castle* for a good many years now, since early youth. Some of these books at first rejected me; I bored them. But as I grew older and they knew me better, they came to have more sympathy with me and to understand my hidden meanings. Their nature is such that our relationship has been very intimate" ("On the Teaching of Modern Literature," 7). I believe that this insight may be extended to the nature of Bakhtin's work, whose very open-endedness invites the reader to evolve within an ongoing conversation. Perhaps, then, the intimacy of the relationship is a good enough justification of the time taken to be understood by the text.

The reading and rereading I needed to do in order to outgrow earlier conceptions of the project and to take it in different directions would not have been possible without the material support of the Research Authority staff at the University of Haifa, who have invariably been helpful and kind; a generous research grant from the Israel Science Foundation (ISF); and a research fellowship granted by the Center for Advanced Studies (CAS) in Oslo, Norway, where I spent some of the best months of my working life as a member of an international research team on Modernism and Narrative Theory. These months produced three collections of essays and some lifelong friendships. I would, therefore, like to acknowledge the assistance of these institutions with much gratitude and, on a more personal note, to thank my friends at CAS, Anniken Greve, Jeremy Hawthorn, Jakob Lothe, J. Hillis Miller, Jim Phelan, Susan Rubin Suleiman, Beatrice Sandberg, Annette Storeide, and Anne Thelle, for having been there to share ideas and feelings, to talk and listen to. As readers of Bakhtin know, human discourse is always implicitly addressed to an interlocutor, present or absent, nearby or far off. This is, of course, also true of academic conversations, and I would like to acknowledge my indebtedness to four of my implicit interlocutors—Michael Gardiner, Ken Hirschkop, Michael Holquist, and Sue Vice—for the articulated and unarticulated dialogues we held over these years and for their unfailing friendly and generous support. As the project came to its conclusion, I had the enormous benefit of assistance from Sergeiy Sandler, a young scholar of truly encyclopedic knowledge, who did his best to keep me on the straight and narrow with respect to Russian sources and translated some of Bakhtin's lesser-known texts for this book. I am very grateful to Professor Sergeiy Bocharov, Bakhtin's disciple and the literary executor of his estate, who has kindly given me permission to have these texts translated and to quote them. And, almost needless to say, I would also like to express my deepest gratitude to Jim Phelan, Anthony Steinbock, Meir Sternberg, Leona Toker, and other editors of academic journals where some of the work that makes up this volume was initially formulated and given voice.

Most and first of all, I am indebted to my lifelong partner, Achick, and to my children, Maya and Yonnie, for their sometimes amused but always fond tolerance of my philosophical obsessions, for the joy of being together, and for the generosity of their love, which is the very bedrock of my life.

ABBREVIATIONS
DESIGNATING M. M. BAKHTIN'S WRITINGS

Year(s) in parentheses following the title indicate the approximate time of writing.

AA	"Art and Answerability" (1919)
AH	"Author and Hero in Aesthetic Activity" (ca. 1922–24)
BSHR	"The *Bildungsroman* and Its Significance in the History of Realism" (1936–38)
DN	"Discourse in the Novel" (1934–35)
EN	"Epic and Novel: Toward a Methodology for the Study of the Novel" (1941)
FTC	"Forms of Time and the Chronotope in the Novel" (1937–38)
Mirror	"The Man at the Mirror" (ca. 1943)
N70–71	"From Notes Made in 1970–1971"
PCMF	"The Problem of Content, Material, and Form in Verbal Art" (1924)
PDP	*Problems of Dostoevsky's Poetics* (1929; 2nd ed., 1963)
PGP	"The Problem of Grounded Peace: A Lecture by M. M. Bakhtin" (1924–25)
PSG	"The Problem of Speech Genres" (1952–53)

PT	"The Problem of the Text in Linguistics, Philology, and the Human Sciences" (1959–61)
Rhetoric	"Rhetoric, insofar as it is false ..." (ca. 1943)
RW	*Rabelais and His World* (1940/1965)
SC	"On the Questions of Self-Consciousness and Self-Evaluation" (ca. 1943–46)
TMHS	"Towards a Methodology for the Human Sciences" (1974)
TPA	*Toward a Philosophy of the Act* (1919–21)
TPF	"Towards the Philosophical Foundations of the Human Sciences" (ca. 1940–43)
TRDB	"Toward a Reworking of the Dostoevsky Book" (1961)

DISPUTED TEXTS

CV	I. I. Kanaev, "Contemporary Vitalism" (1926)
FM	P. N. Medvedev, *The Formal Method in Literary Scholarship* (1928)
MPL	V. N. Voloshinov, *Marxism and the Philosophy of Language* (1929)

INTRODUCTION

THIS BOOK IS ABOUT HOMESICKNESS. It offers a portrait of Mikhail Mikhailovich Bakhtin (1895–1975) under Western eyes, as it were, as a thinker grappling with the question of ethics on the ruins of both the Cartesian and the metaphysical traditions; impelled by the movement of his own interrogation into an engagement with literature as another way of knowing; and straddling an unbridgeable divide between ideological secularity and a profound temperamental religiosity. Premised on a nomadic, deterritorialized conception of subjectivity, this reading of Bakhtin's exilic philosophical sensibility does not end in a "homecoming festival" (TMHS, 170).[1] It leads, at most, to a provisional home away from home, a precarious foothold rather than firm anchorage.

The book is also an attempt to put a Bakhtinian approach to the humanities into practice, to follow the modes of textual engagement explicitly or implicitly suggested by his work, and to take the liberties—risky but unavoidable—required to amplify and flesh out both his philosophical outlook and the method it generates. "Understanding," Bakhtin writes, is a "correlation [of the given text] with other texts and reinterpretation in a new context (in my own context, in a contemporary context, and in a future one)." The task of commentary is, then, to reach out and enable the work to exceed its own boundaries through interaction with other, remote texts and contexts (TMHS, 161).[2] I believe that this conception of the interpreter's work should be taken as a directive for reading Bakhtin's own writings on their borderlines, as it were, in contact with and through other texts, unknown to him, but responsive to the same anxieties addressed by his work.

This study thus aims to reconstruct a coherent Bakhtinian theory of subjectivity by tracing some conceptual strands through the various phases of his work, weaving them into an ongoing philosophical conversation with the contemporary European thinkers Henri Bergson, Emmanuel Lévinas, and Maurice Merleau-Ponty. These four thinkers, I suggest, set out from similarly "exilic" points of departure and move along parallel and sometimes intersecting philosophical itineraries, and a reading of their works with and through each other may highlight both their respective insights and their impasses.

If the value of philosophizing lies, as Michael Theunissen writes, in its risking failure by "venturing upon the unthought"; and if it is the hallmark of this kind of venture to be less than whole and sometimes riddled with ambivalence or inconsistency, it may make a virtue out of necessity by "[drawing] the interpreter more deeply into its movement than a complete, unequivocal doctrine ever could" (*The Other*, 363–64). Bakhtin's work, radically unsystematic and often apparently at odds with itself, is truly philosophical in this sense, and its "internal open-endedness," of which he is fully and unapologetically aware (accounting for it in terms of his "love for variations and for a diversity of terms for a single phenomenon. The multiplicity of focuses. Bringing distant things closer without indicating the intermediate links" [N70–71, 155]),[3] should thus be seen, not as an obstacle to neat theorizing, but as an open invitation. This very "unreadiness" calls for an answering note, an acknowledgment of a task—philosophical midwifery—to be undertaken on the part of the responsive reader.

But midwifery is a labor fraught with both risk and excitement. On the risk side, it should be said at the outset, Bakhtin does not propose a theory of the subject of ethics, or, for that matter, any other grand theory, and the difficulties of distilling a coherent theory out of his eclectic surviving essays are inherent in his work, inasmuch as a suspicion of system-building is built into his philosophical/anthropological outlook. Bakhtin does not attempt to subsume various projects under broader conceptual frameworks. He rarely cites his own previous writings, and he is, above all, overtly skeptical about traditional philosophical "theoreticism," as he called it. This antipathy to system-building may account for the apparent shifts of focus or position between his essays, his tendency to use different terms for ostensibly similar concepts, the looseness, not to say fuzziness, of his neologisms, and the internal inconsistencies that loom large over any attempt to homogenize his work. More frustratingly still, Bakhtin himself is thought to have been singularly cavalier about the physical preservation of his own work: the now-famous vignette about him smoking away the manuscript of the book on the *Bildungsroman*, which may or may not be pure myth, is symptomatic of the kind of lore that developed (and may have also been, at least to some extent, cultivated) around his life and his work.

These temperamental and ideological difficulties are compounded, of course, by Bakhtin's historical and biographical circumstances; the turbulence of exile, illness, and war; life under brutal state censorship and terror, where any and all articulations—what could be written and what could only be gestured at, what had to be carefully clothed in Aesopean language, and what had to be covered up by other voices—were literally a matter of life and death. Some of his work was probably lost, destroyed, or simply unpublished; some of it may have been published under different names or as a collaborative effort; and some may have been written "under a mask," overlaid by a protective and inevitable layer of Soviet-style political correctness. It is no wonder, then, that Bakhtin's work could generate diametrically opposite ideological readings and be happily endorsed by readers who position themselves in fiercely opposing ideological camps. Given these difficulties, it is the task of this Introduction to account for the sense of excitement that has made the risk of midwifery worth taking.

▪ ▪ ▪ ▪

While a full survey of the history of Bakhtin's reception in the West would be both cumbersome and redundant, a brief comment may serve to foreground the approach offered in this volume. The 1980s canonization of Bakhtin as an early prototype of the late twentieth-century cultural regime, heralded by Julia Kristeva's introductory essays in 1969 and 1970, was inspired by texts chiefly written by Bakhtin over a period of approximately twelve years, between 1929 and 1941. Ostensibly concerned with poetics, but ranging far wider into a territory of their own, the thrust of these works, which have yielded the Bakhtinian concepts of dialogue, polyphony, heteroglossia, and the carnivalesque, is, to use his term, "centrifugal"—radically anti-authoritarian, anti-theological, and anti-closural. Read out of context, they appear to anticipate some of the philosophical parameters of the postmodernist pantheon to which they admitted Bakhtin, with its focus on discursivity, militant de-authoring of meaning, and debunking of master narratives.

This wholesale assimilation was dearly purchased. The most obvious loss, unsurprisingly lamented by Russian scholars, was the specificity of Bakhtin's historical and cultural embeddedness: "critical theory inspired by Mikhail Bakhtin has rapidly outpaced the identification of the historical subject who lived from 1895 to 1975," Nicholas Rzhevsky writes.[4] But not only the vexed issues of authorial presence and historical context were at stake in this process of conceptual domestication. Even if one grants the legitimacy of historical decontextualization, which may, after all, yield surprising and suggestive conceptual synergies and is quite in keeping with the Bakhtinian imperative of linking remote texts, it seems that in the case of Bakhtin's early reception, the appropriative embrace was enabled by a silencing of Bakhtin's other, "centripetal" voice, which so clearly emerges from the earlier papers, written between 1919 and 1924, but published in the Soviet Union only in the 1970s and 1980s (following Bakhtin's rehabilitation and the publication of the later works), and translated in the West only in the early 1990s.

The translation of the earlier essays into English and their publication in the West initially met with what can only be described as scholarly silence. And while there may have been a number of reasons for this delayed response—the notorious slowness of academic publication mechanisms, or a certain waning of the Bakhtinian vogue in the academic marketplace—it seems that there was more to the avoidance than these relatively trivial explanations would account for. Indeed, these texts, and particularly "Author and Hero in Aesthetic Activity," appeared to be diametrically opposed to what had been accepted at the time as the Bakhtinian outlook, and much less compatible with the spirit of postmodernity. Readers who had formed their view of Bakhtin in light of his published works on Dostoyevsky and Rabelais may well have found the early works profoundly embarrassing.[5]

The response to these early texts finally came through at the International Bakhtin Conference in Moscow in 1995, which marked a watershed in Bakhtin's reception, since it triggered a shift from a literary to a philosophical engagement with his work, rekindled the issue of the "disputed texts," and opened up a whole new arena for conflicting interpretations and new sets of opposing ideological camp formations. Most of these ideological conflicts seem to have lost momentum and exhausted themselves by now, and I do not attempt to rehearse or resuscitate them here, but it is still worth noting that the elasticity, or apparent fuzziness, of Bakhtin's thinking, his loose use of his own neologisms, and his temperamental aversion to theoretical systems have enabled the endorsement of his work in the name of postmodernist, humanist-liberal, neo-Marxist, and Orthodox Christian thought. Perhaps it is also this very elasticity that accounts for the waning of interest in Bakhtin—at least as far as can be gleaned from counting academic articles and books—since around the turn of the twenty-first century.

What is offered in this study, then, is the work of a latecomer in more than one sense, and it definitely has its own agenda. While the difficulties, both internal and external, of distilling or reconstructing a coherent reading of Bakhtin's oeuvre cannot and should not be swept aside, I believe that he is neither a maverick nor the "broken thinker" to whom Anthony Wall alluded in 1998, and that his approach to the humanities should also be followed in engaging with his own texts. Through the various phases of his work, Bakhtin seems to return to the same persistent and overarching questions in various guises, but there is no apparent sequential evolution or a grand synthesis of these phases. Indeed, he is a thinker who is not interested in plots, and still less so in master plots. Hence, neither the teleological model nor any of the other homogenizing paradigms, whether "structural" or "embryonic," noted by Gary Saul Morson and Caryl Emerson in their study *Mikhail Bakhtin: Creation of a Prosaics* (4–9) would serve as an apt description of the organizing principle of this book. We should, indeed, keep in mind that for Bakhtin, the road not taken invariably remains in sight as a viable option. But (as Morson and Emerson's own work suggests) Bakhtin's aversion to system-building does not rule out the search for a different, nonsystemic type of cohesion in his work. Rather than follow the different phases of a journey, this study is concerned with a profound ambivalence that lies at its very core. I believe that listening to Bakhtin's voice through other voices and relating his interrogation of ethical subjectivity to the quest of his contemporaries in the West may help us take on board both his nostalgia and his invincible drive for freedom and bring us a little closer to our own immanent alterity.

THE SUBJECT IN QUESTION

Engagement with subjectivity, rather than with "the Subject," as announced in the title of this book, may invite the charge of a certain confusion of terms, but it is, I believe, mandated by the issues at stake. The turn from abstract philosophical formulations of the human subject to the concrete dynamics of subjectivity—the actual experience of embodied personhood, in and of this world—is premised on the conception of the subject as a being that questions itself, whose very mode of being is interrogative. If philosophy is "a struggle over pronouns," to borrow Maurice Natanson's wise aphorism ("The Schematism of Moral Agency," 13), it is, I suggest, precisely the struggle in which Bakhtin's work engages by turning from philosophy to literature, where self-interrogation may be best heard and performed. Like similar constructions of the genitive, the "question of the subject" is riddled with ambiguity: is it the subject as an entity that is discussed and questioned, or the subject as s/he who is asking the question? Far from accidental, this ambiguity is precisely what is at stake in Bakhtin's work on the subject of philosophical and literary discourse.

Lest this sound like an opening gambit in a postmodernist project, it must be noted at the outset that the "question of the subject" was on the table long before the mid-twentieth century, certainly as early as or perhaps earlier than Saint Augustine's "I have become a problem for myself" (*Confessions*, 222–23). To understand the philosophical tradition in which Bakhtin's work is embedded, we need to engage for a moment, if only sketchily, with this remote but entirely relevant context.

The Cartesian Subject, resident ghost of so much twentieth-century thinking, is so thoroughly familiar by now that it seems almost redundant to rehearse the standard account of this powerful and ubiquitous presence—almost, but not quite, for Descartes had his own specters to contend with, most notably that of Michel de Montaigne, the last of the great Renaissance humanists. Rather than repeat the received (and probably mostly justified) view of Descartes as a standard fixture or bouncing board for postmodern thinking, we may do well to look backward for a moment and listen to the irrepressible voice of Montaigne, whose looming presence Descartes had set out to exorcise in his own work. Both Montaigne and Descartes ostensibly embark on projects of introspection and self-narration, but the gap between them is nowhere wider than at the point where they try to offer these accounts of themselves, facing each other from the opposing sides of what I call here the "great divide."

Montaigne's point of departure may sound like an echo of Augustine's interrogation of selfhood, but the subsequent itinerary is very different: the Augustinian homecoming, the resolution or the nullification of the question in the embrace of religion, is no longer available to Montaigne, who insists: "I study myself more than any other subject. That is my metaphysics; that is my physics" (*Essays*, 821). The "question of the subject," the need for self-grounding is forcefully and persistently reiterated: "It is a thorny undertaking, and more so than it seems, to follow a movement so wandering as that of our mind, to penetrate the opaque depth. . . . There is no description equal in difficulty, or certainly in usefulness, to the description of oneself" (273). Positioned between the metaphysical reassurances of the medieval thinker and the secularized metaphysics of the early—or first—modern philosopher, Montaigne insists on facing the question of the subject as a concrete, singular, internally multiple, and embodied being, and his *Essays* offer a restless exploration of ungrounded subjectivity. But it is a quest that precludes any homecoming. The project does not end on a note of arrival, and there is no option of conversion that would put an end to the erring of the subject in either the literal-physical or the figurative-metaphysical sense. Rather more than an opening gambit, Montaigne's interrogative stance cannot be resolved into any foundational certainty beyond itself. Ever wandering, ever wondering, it can find no terra firma to offer it a resting place.

Montaigne's *Essays* thus constitute an autobiographical project that self-consciously revolves on its own "failure": monumental as it is, the project cannot fully contain, explain, and represent the writing subject, which remains a question to itself. Unable to attain a point of self-grounding, either metaphysical-theological (as Augustine did when faced with the same question) or metaphysical-rational (as Descartes would do in the following century), Montaigne resigns himself to the contingency of any self-definition, to the protean nature of subjectivity, to its inner diversity and inconsistency, and—to use the Bakhtinian formulation—to the absence of any authoritative external *point d'appui* (AH, 31) that would allow him to see himself as a coherent whole. As Jean Starobinski has beautifully put it, Montaigne's "hunger for being, the ontological hope, had for want of anything better withdrawn into the book once it became clear that the metaphysical quest for essence was doomed to failure." Even the relative stability of the self-portrait that emerges from the book is "still too much compared with the evanescence that it is the author's sole aim to capture, with the flux to which we are allowed to yield. Being proved to be inaccessible" (*Montaigne in Motion*, 220–21). Indeed, Montaigne himself relates to this "failure," which becomes the motor of his work: "If my soul could gain a firm footing," he writes, "I would not essay myself, I would resolve myself." Rather than a portrayal of his "being" in the shape of a stable representation of a coherent and cohesive selfhood, the *Essays* are a portrayal of "passing"; not an attempt to stake out a territorial enclosure of the *I*, but a persistent "essaying," questioning, trying, evaluating an ever-elusive subjectivity, which is "always in apprenticeship and on trial" (611).

But the ontological hunger, the need for the grounding of subjectivity, is hard to dismiss. Grappling with the same question a century later, Descartes would take another route up the same slippery slope, get to the top, and dominate the philosophical scene—in spite of the opposition sounded by thinkers like Pascal and, later, Kierkegaard, to name just two (out of not many more) voices of dissent—well into the twentieth century. Descartes's project of resolving the "question of the subject" offers a different mode of grounding, providing what appears to be a permanent home for the errant and erring subject portrayed by Montaigne. In fact, as has been noted by more than one astute reader, Descartes's entire work reads like a determined attempt to exorcise Montaigne, to rewrite or at least to "re-territorialize" the ungrounded subject that had emerged from the *Essays* and turn it into "its own foundation—its own home, in an absolute sense," as Hassan Melehy puts it (*Writing Cogito*, 103, 122; see also Judovitz, *Subjectivity and Representation*, passim).

The difference between the respective autobiographical undertakings of Montaigne and Descartes is accordingly vast. Whereas Montaigne offers an account of himself as an embodied, concrete, singular, and inherently heterogeneous being, firmly positioned in his time and place, Descartes offers a version of subjectivity where the autobiographical subject is conflated with the philosophical construct, setting itself up as pure thought, absolute knowledge, overriding the contingencies of the living, historically situated person called René Descartes. The conflation of these two entities within the quasi-autobiographical text is a rhetorical exercise, blatantly strategic, as Dalia Judovitz demonstrates, allowing Descartes's decontextualized, disembodied, abstracted, and capitalized Subject to become a transcendental stand-in for humankind in general.

What enables this universal representative quality is the homogenization and disembodiment of the autobiographical subject. The ostensible autobiographical subject "exists in the most abstract sense as an axiomatic entity of a discourse that affirms its own power to speak" (Judovitz, *Subjectivity and Representation*, 83–84). The first person narrative is thus tautological in that it is both premised on the universality of the Cartesian subject and designed to induce the readers into an acceptance of this premise. The emerging entity is a formal, self-contained, and schematic being, emptied of "any content other than that of thought" (87). Unlike the protean and contingent subject of Montaigne's essays, the Cartesian subject can become transcendental representation of all human subjects precisely because it has been stripped of context, body, internal multiplicity—everything that has made it human.

If the Cartesian project marks the beginning of secular inwardness, it does so by a subtle drifting apart from, rather than a complete and open breach with, its own metaphysical premises, and the autobiographical account Descartes offers as a counterweight to Montaigne's is, in fact, quite similar to that of Augustine: both are projects of "conversion" that culminate in a metaphysical apotheosis of the subject, and thus relegate the "discourse of the self" to redundancy (Riley, *Character and Conversion*, 73). Their ostensibly antithetical paradigms notwithstanding, the affinity between the Augustinian and the Cartesian resolutions is, as Patrick Riley astutely notes, compelling and profound: Augustine's autobiographical mode of writing ends with a conversion that delegitimizes the discourse of the self, the realization of the "futility of representing the worldly self, given its lack of autonomous being and its destination in the divine" (75); and Descartes's personal narrative gives way to "the ascendancy of the *universal* subject, purged of its individual characteristics, a logical consequence of the *cogito*" (74). It is a "silent transformation of the *moi* of self-referential discourse to the *je* of philosophical discourse. Like the enunciation of the Eucharistic formula, the pronouncement of the *cogito* effects an invisible metamorphosis in which the language employed to refer to the *moi* becomes the language of all possible selves" (74). In both Augustine and Descartes, "autobiographical discourse serves as means of arriving at a point beyond which autobiography is no longer necessary" (84).

The logical grounding provided by Descartes for the establishment of this autonomous and sovereign thinking entity, fully knowable and coherent to itself by virtue of its own rationality, still leans on a thoroughly metaphysical scaffolding: "Although the content of God's creation has been assimilated into the Cartesian project, God is still needed in order to provide the transcendental grounding for the axiomatic, guaranteeing its *a priori* status" (Judovitz, *Subjectivity and Representation*, 94–95). But the status of that metaphysical guarantee, or first axiom, is problematic, as Pascal, for one, realized when he allegedly wrote: "I cannot forgive Descartes. He would have liked to do without God everywhere in his philosophy, but he could not avoid allowing Him a flick of the fingers to set the world in motion. After that, he had no further need of Him" (*Pensées* [1670], 77). Grounded in its own ineluctable and circular logic, the Cartesian Subject has, in fact, assimilated and absorbed the metaphysical foundation within its own structure. It would not take long before the Age of Reason, with its innocent hubris, came into its own, and Laplace, when asked by Napoleon why he had not referred to God in his cosmology, would simply reply: "Your Highness, I did not need that hypothesis."

For a while—about three hundred years, following the Cartesian formula of subjectivity—it may have looked as though the conundrum had finally been resolved and could be laid to rest. The human subject—disembodied, generalizable, fully coherent and known to itself—had become generic, and the Cartesian apparent resolution of the question of the subject would lay out the foundations of philosophical modernity for the next three centuries. But Pascal, it seems, was amply vindicated after all. The metaphysical scaffolding could not easily be kicked off once the Cartesian edifice was in place. Paradoxically, perhaps, the drive toward self-validating subjectivity, the first step away from metaphysics and toward the creation of the Enlightenment Subject—rational, autonomous, and coherent—ended with the collapse of the subject of humanism in the post-Nietzschean century. It was not only the death of God that was finally announced by the sound of Nietzsche's philosophical hammer, but the "end of his murderer" as well, to quote Michel Foucault (*The Order of Things*, 385). The ultimate dependence of the Enlightenment conception of the subject on metaphysical premises, recognized and articulated by Heidegger in his "Letter on Humanism," by Foucault in *The Order of Things*, and by Derrida in "The Ends of Man," has generated a cultural project—loosely known as postmodernism—driven by the attempt to get away from both metaphysics and humanism; to do, as it were, without either God or "Man."

At the turn of the twenty-first century, the emancipatory thrust of the anti-Cartesian drive seemed to have reached a dead end. Notwithstanding their diversity and incompatibilities, most anti-humanist versions of subjectivity have turned out to be as abstracted from life and concrete embodiment as the philosophical discourse they were trying to evade; more disturbingly, most of them still leave us with the problem of ethical responsibility, which seems to have been poured down the drain with the murky bathwater of metaphysics and Enlightenment subjectivity. The deposition of the foundational Cartesian Subject, the exposure of its vulnerability to and dependence on ideological, cultural, and discursive systems has, it appears, all but disabled the empowering concepts of moral reflexivity and agential action. I suggest that this dead end is where the Bakhtinian "architectonics of subjectivity" becomes supremely relevant.

THE METHOD IN QUESTION

Substance and method are closely interwoven, and Descartes's search for certitude about the question of the subject is at the same time "the search for an idea of language, one where truth can be equated with propositional correctness and where language itself ceases to exist materially as discourse" (Judovitz, *Subjectivity and Representation*, 20). And so, at the risk of belaboring the obvious, it should be stressed that the Cartesian moment laid out the path of Western philosophy from the mid-seventeenth century on, not only in terms of the question of the subject, that is, the object of its inquiry, but also in terms of the tools of its trade, its foundational postulates, and its very discourse. It determined the conception of what philosophy should be.

This is the moment of the great divide between philosophy and literature. Plato did not quite manage to banish the poets from his republic (being something of a poet himself), but the Cartesian line of demarcation has turned out to be much more effective. Henceforth, philosophy would labor under the laws of abstraction, formalization, and logic, to the exclusion of the phenomenal world, sensory experience, and the constitutive diversity of the human subject. Here, as Stephen Toulmin writes, is where "the failure of understanding between Science and the Humanities" is rooted, at the point "when Descartes persuaded his fellow philosophers to renounce fields of study like ethnography, history, or poetry, which are rich in content and context, and to concentrate exclusively on abstract, decontextualized fields like geometry, dynamics, and epistemology" (*Cosmopolis*, x). Following the Cartesian line, modernity has adopted "an intellectual and practical agenda that set aside the tolerant, skeptical attitude of the 16th-century humanists, and focused on the 17th-century pursuit of mathematical exactitude and logical rigor, intellectual certainty and moral purity," which have led Europe "both to its most striking technical successes and to its deepest human failures" (x).

As a theory of knowledge that takes mathematics for its norm, philosophy can be firmly and solidly rooted in logical and formal abstractions, free of the messiness of specific contexts. With the replacement of the Platonic cave by the metaphor of the window, which becomes the foundation for the entire Cartesian philosophical project (see Judovitz, *Subjectivity and Representation*, 106–7), the question and mode of representation—language, discourse, style—become "pure," that is, transparent and irrelevant to substance. None of the hallmarks of Montaigne's *Essays*—concreteness, singularity, embodiment, ambiguity—has any claim to legitimacy in this line of inquiry, which sets itself up as pure thought, absolute knowledge overriding the contingencies of the living human body. Indeed, for about three centuries, the virtual monopoly of the Cartesian paradigm in philosophy relegated Montaigne to the messy realm of literature, the excluded "other" of philosophy. From Descartes on, the ancient quarrel between philosophy and literature has been resolved through a territorial division, as rational philosophical discourse set itself apart from and beyond the literary, demarcating its proprieties and property rights on the side of abstract theorizing, strict adherence to formal logic, and claims to universal validity. What has remained in the twilight zone, carefully excluded from the discourse of philosophy, is "merely literary": concrete, singular, embodied, and inherently riddled with ambiguities and contradictions.

The highway of philosophy was thus laid out by Descartes, broad and clear, along parallel tracks: as regards method, it stipulated strict and exclusive adherence to abstract theorizing and laid claims to universal, timeless, and decontextualized validity; as regards style, it mandated formal logic and "noiseless" language; and as regards substance, it concerned itself with the human subject as disembodied, abstracted, and universally standardized. The story is too well known to rehearse here, and, whatever our misgivings about the tendency to suppress nuances, shadings, and sometimes even more major differences in any attempt to draw a panoramic picture, this has been the standard account of the Cartesian moment.

But alongside that highway, there were winding alleyways and side roads that led elsewhere, and these alternative routes converged, starting about 1900, into a challenge to the legitimacy of the Cartesian heritage, which seemed to have come to a dead end. The resurgence of interest in Montaigne since the 1970s is thus not surprising.[6] Read "proleptically," as it were, he is often perceived as an early precursor of late twentieth-century attempts to break away from the Cartesian paradigm. Montaigne's "skepticism about grand theories" and his reliance on "concrete experience rather than abstract, universal, and timeless propositions"; his keen sense of the "kaleidoscopic diversity and contextual dependence of human affairs" (Toulmin, *Cosmopolis*, 26–27); his "almost postmodern awareness of the impossibility of providing an absolute theory of representation" (Judovitz, *Subjectivity and Representation*, 188); and his tolerance of ambiguity, plurality, and lack of certainty—the very qualities of thought and temperament that had relegated him to the category of literature—turned him into an early beacon for a line of thinkers who were to challenge the proprieties and property rights of Cartesian philosophy centuries later.

STRADDLING THE GREAT DIVIDE

Bakhtin's work seems at times to be thoroughly embedded in this counterphilosophical tradition. His project, like those of various European contemporaries of his, has followed the side roads opened up by late Renaissance humanists, philosophers, and poets—Erasmus and Rabelais, Montaigne and Shakespeare—at the time when these two modes of thinking were still at peace with each other. This is certainly true when he works in the "centrifugal" or the "unfinalized" (to use Morson and Emerson's favored term) mode, as he does, to take the most obvious case, in invoking Montaigne's ghost through the Rabelaisian body through the concept of the carnivalesque.[7]

But Bakhtin cannot be easily read as a latter-day reincarnation of Montaigne (or as a postmodernist *avant la lettre*), and the cultural significance of his work lies not in its neat dovetailing with the "postmodern" line of thinking or with its premodern precursors, but in its unique threshold position, its anxiety, and its inherent ambivalence. His work, I suggest, is uneasily suspended between a critique of the transcendental subject, a position founded on the singularity, concreteness, and embodiment of all human experience, and an equally compelling recognition of metaphysics as a constitutive vector of subjectivity. Side by side with his recognition of the ultimate open-endedness, fluidity, and inner diversity of actual human experience, there is a deep current of nostalgia for the narrative coherence of subjectivity, for some form of authorial grounding, a "centripetal" need, which is just as compelling and real as the "centrifugal" desire.

The anxiety generated by this double awareness and the "question of the subject" as it emerges from Bakhtin's work is, first and foremost, related to ethics, because the "struggle over pronouns" becomes critical when we address the apparent paradox of universal singularity. The core question of ethics concerns the relation between the singular, concrete, embodied human being and the generalized, generic "subject" who features in the scripts of Cartesian and Kantian philosophy, in political science and in law. From the Kantian vantage point—predicated on a commonality that runs deeper than any individual differences, and on the Cartesian model of rational, abstracted, and generalized subjectivity—the experience of singularity is at best an illusion and at worst an obstacle to a universalist conception of ethics. The need to navigate between the equally untenable alternatives of the kind of universalism that flattens the subject into a mere abstraction and a relativist view of subjectivity that does not offer an axiological horizon beyond that of the individual is the prime challenge facing any version of postmodern ethics. Translated into the tug-of-war between the centripetal and the centrifugal, between a profound temperamental religiosity, which may be diagnosed as a metaphysical homesickness, and a powerful need to break free of any form of external containment, the challenge becomes most acute in the case of Bakhtin.

The underlying thesis of this study is that Bakhtin recognizes the fallacy of extending the presumption of Cartesianism—logic-bound, systemic, abstracted from all particularities and contexts—to ethics. But he also knows that contingency is a double-edged sword and is fully aware of the danger of relativism or nihilism lurking at the other end: like his hero Dostoyevsky, he knows that if God—the authorial other—is dead, everything is allowed. This, I believe, is the most persistent source of anxiety in his work, the need to find the missing link between the universal and the particular; between a set of principles, Kantian or other, and the concrete and singular human act; between our abstract awareness of the "ought" and our commitment to acting it out. This study contends that the recognition of that missing link that emerges—or can be extrapolated—from Bakhtin's work is predicated on the analogy between the dynamics of *intersubjectivity* and the workings of *intrasubjectivity*.

Part One of this book, titled "Homesickness, Borderlines, and Contraband," follows Bakhtin's quest of the "forgotten path" leading toward an alternative, non-Cartesian "first philosophy." The first chapter, "The Architectonics of Subjectivity," focuses on the watershed of Bakhtin's work—the complex relationship between "Author and Hero" and *Problems of Dostoevsky's Poetics*. Making a detour through questions of self-representation, narrative identity, and autobiography, this chapter offers a reading of the Bakhtinian subject of ethics as it evolves out of the tensile relation between a "centripetal" vector—the need for grounding, form, and coherence—and a "centrifugal" drive toward the transgression and transcendence of any and all given boundary lines. The second chapter, "The Poetics of Subjectivity," shifts the engagement with the Cartesian divide from substance to discourse and method, focusing on the transition from philosophy to literature, which, I would argue, is mandated by and evolves from Bakhtin's disillusionment with traditional philosophy and formal ethics, as well as his unacknowledged affinity with the formalists. Making a detour through the psychoanalytic work of Wilfred Bion, D. W. Winnicott, and Christopher Bollas, the second part of this chapter seeks to highlight the relation of text and psyche through the "poetics of subjectivity" that underlies the intersection of philosophy, literature, and psychoanalysis. The third chapter, "The Shattered Mirror of Modernity," sets out from Bakhtin's apparent transition from an ocular to an auditory structuring metaphor, and offers the trope of "refraction" as a potentially more nuanced and productive alternative to the visual-auditory dichotomy, which is all too often taken as representative of the modern-postmodern divide. Following the discussion of structuring metaphors, the second part of this chapter makes a case against the postmodernist appropriation of Bakhtin's work and relates it instead to that of the literary modernists, much closer in time, and closer still, I would argue, in spirit.

DOTTED LINES AND CONSTELLATIONS

Part Two of the book, "The Exilic Constellation," offers a reading of Bakhtin with and through the work of three continental thinkers—Bergson, Merleau-Ponty, and Lévinas—philosophers whose itineraries run parallel to and sometimes intersect with Bakhtin's. These readings aim to chart the modulations of the philosophical project in which—independently of one another and in very different circumstances—these fellow travelers were all engaged. Working on the boundaries of their respective endeavors, this Bakhtinian reading may offer some resolutions to the still-unanswered questions of these thinkers and open up some of the philosophical impasses of their itineraries. The most cogent articulation of what is attempted here as a method for delineating this exilic constellation is Bakhtin's own description of Dostoyevsky's work:

> As an artist, Dostoevsky uncovered in the image of a given idea not only the historically actual features available in the prototype . . . but also its *potentialities*. . . . [He] placed the idea on the borderline of dialogically intersecting consciousnesses. . . . He extended, as it were, these distantly separated ideas by means of a dotted line to the point of their dialogic intersection. In so doing, he anticipated future dialogic encounters between ideas which in his time were still dissociated. (*PDP*, 91)

This drawing of dotted lines, as Bakhtin recognizes at a later phase of his work, is not the exclusive prerogative of the artistic project. Distinct Dostoyevskian echoes are heard in the late notes, where Bakhtin extrapolates his conception and turns it into a working principle: like the human subject who has "no sovereign internal territory" (TRDB, 287), who lives on its own boundary lines and occasionally transgresses them in the interaction with other subjects, "each word (each sign) of the text exceeds its boundaries. Any understanding is a correlation of a given text with other texts." And the text, he writes, "lives only by coming into contact with another text (with context). Only at the point of this contact between texts does a light flash, illuminating both the posterior and anterior, joining a given text to a dialogue" (TMHS, 162).

Having described this project as a labor of midwifery, I would therefore suggest that this maieutic metaphor can be validated by Bakhtin's own view of the human sciences, since it is through the drawing of dotted lines, bringing texts into contact with other texts, and contexts into a relation with other contexts, that the "potentialities" of a philosopher's thought may be delivered, come to light, and take flesh. What is proposed here, following the Bakhtinian imperative, is an attempt to study a cultural phenomenon as an "organic unity: open, becoming, unresolved and unpredetermined, capable of death and renewal, transcending itself, that is, exceeding its own boundaries" (N70–71, 135). This self-transcendence can only be attained by the "interrelation and interaction of 'spirits'" (144), in the contact of two or more "meanings that meet and accompany one another" (146), and through the inclusion of future, ever-growing, and "unfinalized context" (TMHS, 160), inasmuch as the "event of the life of the text . . . always develops *on the boundary between two consciousnesses, two subjects*" (PT, 106). Working on these boundaries between the Bakhtinian project and those of his fellow exiles, the study will thus attempt to tune in, not only to the "said," but also to the "unsaid" in Bakhtin's work (TMHS, 163); to its "potentialities," elicited through encounters and intersections with others' thought; and to its contextual meanings, understood in relation, not only to the past or to immediate contemporary contexts, but also to future, unanticipated conversations.

Not surprisingly, a similar approach to philosophical labor is proposed in Merleau-Ponty's introduction to an essay on Husserl:

> We cannot define a philosopher's thought solely in terms of what he has achieved. We have to take account of what at the very end still he was struggling to think. Naturally this unthought thought [*impensé*] must be shown to be present through the words which circumscribe and delimit it. But then these words must be understood through their *lateral implications* as much as through their manifest or frontal significance. ("The Philosopher and His Shadow," 160; emphasis added)

Much of Merleau-Ponty's own work was left "unthought," or at least unwritten, at the time of his sudden death in 1961, and the labor of articulating its lateral implications has been taken up by subsequent philosophers and interpreters. But I would suggest that the philosophical task—this particular version of midwifery—of reading the "unthought" can be performed, not only within the works of a single philosopher, but also between several philosophical projects, as in the case of Bakhtin, Bergson, Merleau-Ponty, and Lévinas, who resonate and echo one another's concerns and are actually synergized by being read through one another.

These affinities, the nuclei of the constellation, call for both a prospective inquiry and a retrospective study of formative influences and vicarious contacts. Reading Bakhtin with and through the work of his continental contemporaries allows, I believe, for extensions, elucidations, and articulations of the "unthought," or at least the "unsaid" in his unfinished philosophical project, enabling us to move beyond his explicit theses, such as they are, toward what Merleau-Ponty called the "movement of his thought" ("On the Phenomenology of Language," 84). The labor of philosophical midwifery attempted here is meant to bring out the potential implications of what has remained understated or latent in Bakhtin's writings through a dialogic encounter with his fellow exiles.

Other dotted lines, other relations, could obviously have been drawn, so it is one of the tasks of this volume to bring home to the reader the philosophical productivity of this particular constellation and the reasons why it is, to my mind, so compelling. What justifies the clustering, I would argue, is a common exilic sensibility in more than one sense. These thinkers—a Catholic, an assimilated Jew, a religious Jew, and a Russian Orthodox Christian—were all spiritual exiles, laboring out of a profound temperamental religiosity in a post-metaphysical world, and with a similarly powerful need to resist their own nostalgia, their own metaphysical homesickness. Working from within a profound liminal sensibility, they were all looking for a home away from home. But they were also exiles in another sense, related to the ancient quarrel between philosophy and poetry. Their common territory is also the state of voluntary vocational exile of thinkers who have taken themselves out of the Platonic-Cartesian regime of traditional philosophy and into the wildness of poetry, and are therefore impelled to look for an alternative mode of philosophizing.

Part Two of this study explores the work of this constellation by drawing dotted lines between Bakhtin and his fellow exiles. The staged encounters that form the nuclei of the discussion are concerned with the particular issues at stake at each of these conceptual intersections. The first chapter, "The Dead End of Omniscience," offers a reading of Bakhtin's work with and through the Bergsonian project of temporalization, and focuses on the ethical and literary significance of the transition from space to time. The second chapter, "In the Beginning Was the Body," follows the parallel itineraries of Bakhtin and Merleau-Ponty, who set out from a study of concrete somatic experience and then move on to what is conceived by both as the analogous realm of the semiotic and the dynamics of transcendence in discourse. The third chapter, "From Dialogics to Trialogics," relates to the convergences and the divergences between Bakhtin and Lévinas, their recognition of the potential danger of relativism entailed in the dyadic or the dialogic relation of self and other, and their respective gestures of triangulation. The coda to this volume "A Home Away from Home," focuses on the Bakhtinian attempt to restore "new philosophical wonder" and formulate his nontheological or nonmetaphysical religiosity in terms of what I would call "lateral transcendence."

In following the itineraries of these thinkers through the conduit of Bakhtin's work, this second part of the study returns to some of the central passages discussed in Part One. Unavoidably, there is some overlap between the conceptual nuclei around which these chapters are structured and some repetition of key passages that bring out these affinities. But the prospect of the exilic sensibility, I hope, also fans out and gains some enhancement through the conversations staged in the process. The kind of cohesion that may emerge from this reading-through is thus neither teleological nor unequivocal. It may best be described, perhaps, in Gertrude Stein's words, as "beginning again and again."

PART ONE
HOMESICKNESS, BORDERLINES, AND CONTRABAND

THE ARCHITECTONICS OF SUBJECTIVITY

> The search for the ultimate foundation is as much an unremovable part of human culture as is the denial of the legitimacy of this search.
>
> **Leszek Kołakowski, *Metaphysical Horror***

ONE OF BAKHTIN'S EARLIEST SURVIVING FRAGMENTS, translated and published in the West as *Toward a Philosophy of the Act*, reads like the beginning of a monumental project. What is announced at the outset is a sense of disillusionment with what Bakhtin calls "fatal theoreticism" (27), the Cartesian legacy of formal rationalism, objectivism, and abstraction, which has set the direction for Western philosophy:

> It is an unfortunate misunderstanding (a legacy of rationalism) to think that truth [*pravda*] can only be the truth [*istina*] that is composed of universal moments; that the truth of a situation is precisely that which is repeatable and constant in it. Moreover, that what is universal and identical (logically identical) is fundamental and essential, whereas individual truth [*pravda*] is artistic and irresponsible, i.e., it isolates the given individuality. (*TPA*, 37)

It is this legacy, Bakhtin says, "that leads philosophical thinking, which seeks to be on principle purely theoretical, to [the] peculiar state of sterility, in which it, undoubtedly, finds itself at the present time" (18–19).

Bakhtin's point of departure appears to be epistemological, but his view of the sterility of philosophy is most evident in what he describes as the failure of formal Kantian ethics with its "essential and fundamental abstraction from the fact of my unique being and from the moral sense of that fact—'as if I did not exist'" (9). His critique of philosophy focuses explicitly on its inability to address the question of the concrete ethical event, the moment of actual choice, the singularity and uniqueness of the context:

> Formal ethics (which developed exclusively within the bounds of Kantianism) . . . theorizes the *ought*, and, as a result, loses the individual act or deed. And yet the *ought* is precisely a category of the individual act; even more than that—it is a category of the individuality, of the uniqueness of a performed act, of its once-occurrent compelledness, of its historicity, of the impossibility to replace it with anything else, or to provide a substitute for it. (25)

Rather than a structure of normativity, Bakhtin proposes to study the "moral *subiectum*," the concrete and unique individual facing a moment of ethical choice and answerability (6). Like some of his continental contemporaries, to whom we shall turn later on, Bakhtin sets out to replace the formal, abstract, and universalist Kantian system with an alternative phenomenological conception of ethics, to explore the actual "ethical moment," both in the sense of a vector within a dynamic event and as that point in time when the encounter with the other takes place.

In defiance of what he calls "epistemologism," that is, the Cartesian postulate of generalization and abstraction, Bakhtin claims: "Man-in-general does not exist; I exist and a particular concrete *other* exists—my intimate, my contemporary (social mankind), the past and future of actual human beings (of actual historical mankind)" (47). Rather than a "system" or a "systematic inventory of values," he proposes to provide "a description of the actual, concrete architectonic of value-governed experiencing of the world—not with an analytical foundation at the head, but with that actual, concrete center (both spatial and temporal) from which valuations, assertions, and deeds come forth" (61). Rather than a normative model or an ethical system, he offers an "architectonics," a dynamic conception of the embodied subject in the ethical event. Notwithstanding the use of the Kantian term, Bakhtin's project is, in fact, a new departure. The ambitious task outlined in this fragment is the beginning of an alternative "first philosophy," which proceeds, not by "constructing universal concepts, propositions, and laws," but by offering "a phenomenology" of the "answerably performed act," taking the experience of the concrete, historically situated and fully embodied subject as its point of departure (31).

The Bakhtinian architectonics of the subject is thus profoundly anti-Cartesian in that it offers a view of the human subject as fully embodied, singular rather than generic, and always in the process of becoming, taking the experience of the concrete, historically situated person as its point of departure. But, though much closer to Montaigne in this sense, Bakhtin, as we shall see, can neither fully revert to nor remain content with the open-endedness of Montaigne's quest. Being both temperamentally religious and deeply concerned about the danger of ethical relativism, so closely attendant on the loss of metaphysical moorings, Bakhtin must struggle to produce his own version of subjectivity. His "architectonics," however, is not a structure made up of the building blocks of theory: it is a relational process, a "meeting of *two* movements on the surface of a human being that consolidates or gives body to his axiological boundaries" (AH, 91). The precise nature and the dynamics of these "two movements" are not explicitly articulated in Bakhtin's subsequent work, but it is arguable that they correspond to what he elsewhere called the "centripetal" and the "centrifugal" forces (DN, 270–73) in reference to historical formations of language and culture. I suggest that these forces are just as active *within* the human psyche as they are in the socio-linguistic sphere, and the dynamics of this architectonic conception may be troped as the visual puzzle of a Möbius strip, where the two sides of the band are clearly distinguishable, yet seem to fold back and reverse their positions as they intersect.

This first chapter focuses on the two texts that most explicitly articulate the "centripetal" and the "centrifugal" modalities of subjectivity, but it is important to note at the outset that, notwithstanding the apparent predominance of the former in "Author and Hero in Aesthetic Activity" and the latter in *Problems of Dostoevsky's Poetics*, it is not the transition *between* these texts and their respective modalities of subjectivity, but the internal contradictions, the irreducible ambivalence and equivocation *within* these texts, that generate the "architectonics" of the subject: the tensile relation between the "centripetal" and the "centrifugal"—between Descartes and Montaigne, as it were—is translated in Bakhtin's work into a tug-of-war between a critique of the transcendental subject and an equally compelling recognition of metaphysics as a constitutive vector of subjectivity.

HOMESICKNESS: THE CENTRIPETAL VECTOR OF SUBJECTIVITY

"Author and Hero in Aesthetic Activity," probably written in 1922–24,[1] offers an oddly anachronistic prescription for the "relationship" between the author and the fictional hero (both invariably designated as masculine).[2] Within the aesthetic framework, the relationship is predicated on the author's "outsideness," his "transgredient" position beyond and above the characters, which allows for an "excess of seeing" and, thus, of knowledge: the author can contain the hero in a field of vision far wider than that of any of the characters themselves; he can know what the hero is in principle incapable of knowing. This excess of knowledge enables the author to "consummate" the hero, to see him in his wholeness, to gather the hero's moment of birth, the moment of his death, his background, the environment against which he acts (which, from the hero's vantage point, is a mere "horizon"), and the axiological "rhythm," the pattern of his life, which can only be perceived against its totality: "The organizing power in all aesthetic forms is the axiological category of the *other*, the relationship to the other, enriched by an axiological 'excess' of seeing for the purpose of achieving transgredient consummation" (AH, 189).

Oddly, though, this thesis, which seems almost trivial when we bear in mind the different ontological status of author and character (the "real" and the "fictional" are, after all, ontologically distinct at the most commonsensical level), evolves into a treatise on human subjectivity in blatant disregard of ontological distinctions, conceptual boundary lines, and fundamental categories of philosophical conceptualization. The essay is premised on an analogy between the fictional "hero" and an "I-for-myself" mode of being (that is, the lived experience of the phenomenal, embodied subject)—terms used interchangeably throughout the text, as if there were no distinction to be made between a character in a work of fiction and the living subject. Conversely, the term "author" is often replaced by "other" with the same disregard for ontological or epistemological distinctions.

Dispensing with all forms of rhetorical or logical mediation, establishing an unproblematic continuum between the real and the fictional, Bakhtin moves back and forth between these two sets of conceptual categories with alarming ease. The essay, which relegates itself to the safety of aesthetic theory and reads like an apologia for authorial omniscience, is thus also—primarily, perhaps—a thesis on the constitution of human subjectivity, premised on a constant slippage and extrapolation between these two conceptual sets.[3] There is no recognition of boundaries or seam lines; no attempt to mediate the shift either logically or rhetorically. The aesthetic theory seems to blend into a philosophical theory of the subject, and vice versa. Bakhtin himself is not unaware of his own engagement in philosophical contraband: "It is true," he blandly admits, "that the boundary between a human being (the condition for aesthetic vision) and a hero (the object of aesthetic vision) often becomes unstable" (AH, 228).[4] There is not a shade of apology in this admission.

What enables this slippage is the analogy of relational structures. True to his programmatic statement in *Toward a Philosophy of the Act*, Bakhtin sets out from the experiential situatedness of the human subject.[5] There is, he argues, an essential asymmetry between the perceptual experience of "I-for-myself" and "I-for-the-other." Experiencing myself from within, I cannot produce an autonomous and whole representation of my self; my own boundaries are structurally inaccessible to my perception and consciousness: I cannot directly perceive the top of my head, see myself from behind, observe myself as fully positioned within my surroundings, or consciously experience the moment of my own birth and my death. This phenomenological observation of the perspectival finitude and limitations of the embodied subject, who cannot perceive its own spatial and temporal boundary lines is, as Michael Holquist points out ("The Role of Chronotope in Dialog"), directly related to Kant's *Critique of Pure Reason* and does not offer a new insight in and of itself. But the perceptual experience of being invisible to oneself is also translated in this early essay—far less trivially, I contend—into axiological terms:

> A human being experiencing life in the category of his own *I* is incapable of gathering himself by himself into an outward whole that would be even relatively finished. The point here is... the absence in

principle of any unitary axiological approach from within a human being himself to his own outward expressedness. (AH, 35; see also 59, 91)

Hence, says Bakhtin, "a human being's absolute need for the other, for the other's seeing, remembering, gathering, and unifying self-activity—the only self-activity capable of producing his outwardly finished personality. This outward personality could not exist, if the other did not create it" (35–36). The other—whether fully internalized or external to the subject—is analogous to the author, "the living bearer and sustainer of this unity of consummation," who is transgredient to the hero and therefore able to "collect the hero and his life and to complete him to the point where he forms a *whole* by supplying all those moments which are inaccessible to the hero himself from within himself" (14). Just like a hero authored by a writer of fictional narratives, the living human subject is "authored," configured, contained, and rendered whole by an internalized other. In precisely the same way, the human subject's sense of itself is always confined to a partial "internal" perspective, which can only be transcended through an external vantage point. "I myself cannot be the author of my own value, just as I cannot lift myself by my own hair" (55), or, as we might say, by my own bootstraps.

NARRATIVE IDENTITY AND
THE IMPOSSIBILITY OF AUTOBIOGRAPHY

The cultural and temporal remoteness of the Bakhtinian vocabulary, compounded by his partiality for idiosyncratic word formations, should not obscure the relevance of this early essay to the "narrativity paradigm" that has informed so much of the work done in the humanities and the social sciences during the last two decades of the twentieth century.[6] Translated into the philosophical frames of reference offered by thinkers such as Paul Ricœur (1992), David Carr (1986, 1991), or Alasdair MacIntyre (1981), for instance, Bakhtin's views of the aesthetic relationship and the concomitant conception of subjectivity are clearly associated with the same human need for emplotment, configuration, and narrativization of life into a coherent whole.[7] It is the same need for a unifying "transgredient" perspective, a definable structure, a plot, as it were, that generates the narrative coherence we call the self, since the "aesthetic validity" of the subject can only be obtained through the framing gaze of the authorial other (AH, 59, 188–89).

No other moment of writing so clearly brings out this question of boundary lines as the moment when the living subject tries to become both author and character in his/her own narrative. It is hardly surprising, therefore, that Bakhtin should be interested in the generic distinctiveness of autobiography, which is a point of intersection between narrative framing and the constitution of subjectivity. One of the books known to have been in Bakhtin's possession is the first volume of Georg Misch's *A History of Autobiography in Antiquity* (1907), a very early and forward-looking study of the genre as an interpretation of experience that is, to a large extent, culturally, socially, and ideologically constructed. The challenge of discerning a pattern in the diversity of autobiographical writings, Misch writes, is not only related to "the infinite natural multiplicity of individual life but also [to] the historically determined multiplicity in its forms of presentation" (5). Misch seems to anticipate much later studies of the genre when he allows for the presence of "unconscious" elements in the narrative of self-consciousness (8), or when he concedes that the self-possession implied in the autobiographical act may well be illusory:

> A skeptical observer of the world of men will . . . smile at the way men talk as a matter of course of their "self" or "ego." He recognizes that it is owing to the self-awareness peculiar to man that the individual with his bodily frame feels himself and is felt by others to be a person; but he smiles at the naïve idea that places an ego at the back of that psychic phenomenon, as a solid and concrete thing that remains constant in spite of the changes of life from birth to death. (9–10)

However, for all his historicist sensibility and his nod toward skepticism, Misch is still very much the Enlightenment scholar in his insistence on the ultimate possibility of self-knowledge and the "truth" that emerges from the "creative objectification of the autobiographer's mind" (12). The "philosophical dignity" of autobiography derives from the full and panoramic vantage point available to the autobiographer alone:

> The man who sets out to write the story of his own life has it in view as a whole, with unity and direction and a significance of its

own. In this single whole the facts and feelings, actions and reactions, recalled by the author, the incidents that excited him, the persons he met, and the transactions or movements in which he was concerned, all have their definite place, thanks to their significance in relation to the whole. He himself knows the significance of his experiences, whether he mentions it or not; he only understands his life through the significance he attaches to them. This knowledge, which enables the writer to conceive his life as a single whole, has grown in the course of his life out of his actual experience, whereas we have the life of any other person before us as a whole only *ex post facto*; the man is dead, or at all events it is all past history. (7)

Bakhtin would take the very opposite view. Autobiography—the attempt to name and appropriate oneself, to establish what is proper to the self and to stake out the boundary lines of its territory—is foredoomed at the outset. This is where we face our foundational heteronomy, because the psychic modality that Bakhtin calls *I-for-myself* can never become a given object for itself, can never coincide with itself, must always reach out beyond itself as "yet-to-be":

> I can remember myself, I can to some extent perceive myself through my outer sense, and thus render myself in part an object of my desiring and feeling—that is, I can make myself an object for myself. But in this act of self-objectification I shall never coincide with myself—*I-for-myself* shall continue to be in the *act* of this self-objectification, and not in its product. . . . I am incapable of fitting all of myself into an object, for I exceed any object as the active *subiectum* of it. (AH, 38)

The "speaking" subject (the agent of the speech-act, to update the terms) and the "spoken" subject (the grammatical subject of the utterance) can never coincide. The hiatus separating them is the very same gap between the subject of the *énonciation* and the subject of the *énoncé* that Émile Benveniste would elaborate some four decades or so afterward. But far beyond the syntactic impossibility, it is the axiological dimension, perceived by Bakhtin as analogous to the parameters of both space and time, and just as real, that underlies the utter impossibility of autobiography: "No act of reflection upon myself is capable of consummating me fully, for, inasmuch as it is immanent to my sole answerable consciousness, it becomes a value-and-meaning factor in the subsequent development of that consciousness. My own word about myself is in principle incapable of being the last word, the word that consummates me" (142–43).

This excess of the subject in relation to any and all of its own articulations is precisely why, according to Bakhtin, "there is no clear-cut, essentially necessary dividing line between autobiography and biography, and this is a matter of fundamental importance. . . . Neither in biography nor in autobiography does the *I-for-myself* (my relationship with myself) represent the organizing, constitutive moment of form" (150–51). Nearly forty years later, Bakhtin would get back to the impossibility of autobiography and reassert the heteronomy of the subject who "has no internal sovereign territory," who is "wholly and always on the boundary." The project of autobiography, or "self-nomination" is "imposture," Bakhtin says. Trying to see itself as a whole, the subject "looks *into the eyes of another* or *with the eyes of another*" (TRDB, 287–88).

In this recognition of the impossibility of autobiography, Bakhtin is much closer to Montaigne than to Descartes, who, as Dalia Judovitz perceptively writes, had "left out that which is the defining essence of man—language" (*Subjectivity and Representation*, 25), purging the conception of truth from the materiality of discourse to the point where language itself came to be seen as transparent. Montaigne, however, recognizes that "the character of the self is mediated by the fact that both observation of and action upon it pass through the conduit of the same linguistic and representational medium" (11); and his "process of self-scrutiny results in the affirmation of alterity and a pluralization of selves through the act of representation. As both subject and object of his own inquiry, Montaigne recognizes the impossibility of knowing and understanding himself as a definite entity" (12).

Indeed, Montaigne is explicit on the essential doubleness of subjectivity: "We are, I know not how, double within ourselves" (*Essays*, 469); the syntactic split that seems to allow the separation of the subject-narrator and the subject-character in our autobiographical projects, whether written or simply lived through, is the inscription of a profound split within the human subject, whose desire for self-containment is ineluctably doomed to deferral. As Montaigne had observed, our relation to ourselves cannot ever be purged from our experiential being: "I do not love myself so indiscriminately, nor am I so attached and wedded to myself, that I cannot distinguish and consider myself apart, as I do a *neighbor* or a *tree*" (720). This is the same asymmetry between *I-for-myself* and *I-for-the-other* that Bakhtin takes as his own point of departure.

To make a temporal leap and bring this closer home, we should turn for a moment to Derrida who frankly acknowledges both his own autobiographical desire, the "obsessive desire to save in uninterrupted inscription, in the form of a memory, what happens—or *fails to happen*," and his ambivalence about it. Unable to dismiss this need to gather up and totalize (or "consummate," as Bakhtin would have it) the self as a "lure," he asks, "isn't this what keeps me going?" And then, in an uncannily Bakhtinian idiom, he tells his interviewer the "idea of an internal polylogue . . . was first of all the adolescent dream of keeping a trace of all the voices which were traversing me—or were almost doing so—and which was to be so precious, unique, both specular and speculative" (Derrida, "This Strange Institution," 35).

We should pause at this point for a moment. What we have to reckon with is not only the constitutional inability of the subject to represent itself to itself, but a powerful and exclusively human desire or a need to accomplish this self-representation. It is the unfulfilled "hunger for being" that Starobinski diagnoses in Montaigne's *Essays* and the need for self-possession and metaphysical grounding that has generated the Cartesian subject. Different as their itineraries are, Augustine, Montaigne, and Descartes—figureheads for the medieval, Renaissance, and Enlightenment conceptions of subjectivity—are motivated by the same autobiographical desire, the same hunger for being. The human subject, to put it briefly, is a creature that needs to have a sense of its own boundary lines, to represent itself to itself, and the project of autobiography is the direct expression of that need for self-enclosure and grounding. If we are all storytelling animals, it is due to the need to lift ourselves by our bootstraps, to observe ourselves even as we participate in our own lives. To satisfy our ontological hunger, we must have a narrator—an internalized authorial figure—to endow our lives with a sense of wholeness and coherence.

THE PROBLEM OF AUTHORING

Read as a thesis on aesthetics, "Author and Hero" is an oddly anachronistic, prescriptive theory of authorial omniscience. As a theory of subjectivity, it is a profoundly disturbing work: granted the structuring power of plotlines and our apparently built-in need for storytelling, it is all the more crucial to consider the potential cost of subjectifying ourselves in and through the eyes of the internalized other, who may be less than benevolent, and the "master narratives" within which our self-narratives are embedded are not necessarily conducive to the good life, however defined. Considering the implications of the "narrative identity" thesis, the question of voice, of "who is telling the story," becomes far more important than the narrative itself.

Here, precisely, is where we encounter the problem of grounding. In "Author and Hero," Bakhtin seems to be oddly oblivious at times to the potentially dangerous role of the authoring other (oddly and ironically, because he himself was only a little later directly victimized by an institutionalized, political form of "authoring").[8] He appears to accept and approve of the need for the constituting gaze of the other, since he gives an unqualified blessing to the dyadic, reflexive, "aesthetic" relationship it produces. The operative force in this relationship is definitely "centripetal," because the privileged, "transgredient" position of an authorial other in relation to the subject/hero produces a form of axiological validation and offers a sense of coherence that is not available to the subject from within. Understandably, then, when "Author and Hero" was published in an English translation in the West in 1990, it met with a certain degree of uneasy reticence or embarrassment among readers who had formed their views of Bakhtin in light of the later texts (translated and published about a decade earlier). The early "aesthetic" conception of subjectivity, highly problematic both in its implicit assumption of the subject's passivity under that "consummating" authorial gaze of the other and in its seemingly naïve trust in the other's benevolent "authoring," could not be easily reconciled with the familiar Bakhtinian tags that have made him so congenial to Western readers in the thoroughly secular climate of postmodernity: polyphony, dialogism, heteroglossia, and the carnivalesque.[9]

What emerges in full force from this early essay is a "hunger for being," a need for metaphysical grounding, which can only be assuaged within a religious frame of reference. If God is the ultimate other, "the heavenly father who is *over me* and can be merciful to me and justify me where I, from within myself, cannot be merciful to myself and cannot justify myself in principle" (AH, 56), the I—with its partial perspective, its immanent inadequacy, its incompleteness—may be offered a resting place, a "powerful *point d'appui* outside itself . . . some genuine source of real strength out of which I would be capable of seeing myself as another" (31). The aestheticization of the subject is a response to the need for "a firm and convincing position (convincing not only outwardly, but also inwardly, with respect to meaning) *outside* my entire life" (86). The hypothesis of a loving "consummation," an authorized justification of one's life which is premised on trust in a divine providential Being, is a promise of homecoming.

"Author and Hero" can be read as a treatise that "one could call Bakhtin's theology in the form of aesthetics or his aesthetics resolved in theological terms," as Sergei Bocharov aptly puts it ("Conversations with Bakhtin," 1018). Whatever the differences of scale and gradation, it is the same relational structure that underlies both the religious and the aesthetic relationship:

> An aesthetic event can take place only when there are two participants present; it presupposes two noncoinciding consciousnesses. . . . When the other consciousness is the encompassing consciousness of God, a *religious* event takes place (prayer, worship, ritual). (AH, 22)

> A whole, integral human being is the product of the aesthetic, creative point of view and of that point of view alone. . . . A whole, integral human being presupposes an aesthetically active *subiectum* situated outside him (we are abstracting from man's religious experience in the present context). (83)

Indeed, the aesthetization of the subject, the gift of selfhood, is conceived as a form of grace, "the bestowal—from outside—of lovingly merciful acceptance and justification of the given. . . . In himself, a human being can only repent; and only the other can give absolution" (57). Entirely uninhibited in his use of devotional rhetoric, Bakhtin models the "aesthetic relationship" on a quasi-medieval metaphysical paradigm: "Aesthetic grace . . . bestowed [upon the soul] . . . [is] a lovingly merciful justification of its being that is impossible from within the soul itself" (67). "Aesthetic love," "transgredient aesthetic form" is "the relationship of a gift to a need; of an act of freely granted forgiveness to a transgression; of an act of grace to a sinner" (90). The human author derives his authority from the transcendental Auctor Mundi, as the "divinity of the artist consists in his partaking of the supreme outsideness.... Aesthetic activity collects the world scattered in meaning and condenses it into a finished and self-contained image... it finds an axiological position from which the transient in the world acquires the axiological weight of an event, acquires validity and stable determinateness" (191). If this equation appears to be simple to the point of naïveté, that does not seem to trouble Bakhtin, who explicitly links this "consummation" to a state of passive acceptance of a gift of selfhood bestowed by the transgredient other.

No matter what view one takes of the precise shade of Bakhtin's religious inspiration and the nuanced affinities and sympathies that might have influenced his work, the passionate conviction of the metaphysical analogy that structures "Author and Hero" cannot be overlooked. The recourse to the discourse of religion is neither a residual stylistic mannerism nor a conceptual aberration in Bakhtin's work: it is, in fact, inherent in the aesthetic conceptualization of the subject, which requires authoring or grounding from without. It is only the convergence of aesthetics and metaphysics that allows for the slippage between "author" and "other," for what is at stake is nothing less than the naked need for a master narrative and a master narrator. With this gesture of what I would call "radical naïveté," Bakhtin seems at this point to throw a metaphysical blanket over the question of the subject.

But Bakhtin is not an Augustinian or even a Cartesian philosopher. He knows that the conflation of aesthetics, metaphysics, and self-representation can retain its validity only so long as the human act of authorship is a delegation of transcendental authority. This is a matter of trust, that "deep trust in the highest level of authority that blesses a culture— ... trust, that is, in the fact that there is another—the highest other—who answers for my own special answerability, and trust in the fact that I do not act in an axiological void" (AH, 206).[10] As we shall presently see, this deep trust is no longer easily available to Dostoyevsky, who bears witness to the demise of aesthetic culture as his tormented characters teeter and reel on the verge of that "axiological void." When the metaphysical scaffolding collapses, the aesthetic paradigm no longer holds. Dostoyevsky's abdication of authorial jurisdiction anticipates the awakening of the modernist consciousness, the consciousness of an essentially secular world, where neither the fictional nor the historical subject can refer to an authorial Being—outside and above the self—for comfort and confirmation (203–4).[11]

Temperamentally profoundly religious, Bakhtin recognizes both the power of autobiographical desire, an ontological hunger that is so fundamentally human, and the inability to produce a hypostasis of subjectivity without recourse to some metaphysical foundational premises. Being a citizen of the post-Nietzschean world, he is no longer able to revert to the kind of naïveté that is needed for the acceptance of "consummation" by an authorial other, either divine or human. This, I would suggest, is what makes him an exile, straddling both territories and homeless in both.

BORDERLINES AND CONTRABAND: THE CENTRIFUGAL VECTOR OF SUBJECTIVITY

Having followed the "centripetal" vector of the Bakhtinian architectonics as far as it goes in "Author and Hero," let us now turn to the "centrifugal" vector. It is *not*, to reiterate my initial claim, a question of alternating and distinct "phases," a pendulum movement, as it were, in Bakhtin's work: what makes his architectonics so productive is rather the tensile relation of these vectors, their simultaneity and friction, which generate both the ambivalence and the energy of Bakhtin's work. Even in "Author and Hero," with its apparent endorsement of the aesthetic/metaphysical analogy, Bakhtin positions the subject of ethics beyond the pale of aesthetic containment, beyond the seductions of "consummation" by the authorial other. Ethical subjectivity, constituted by the *I-for-myself* mode of being, is that which actively resists and subverts the narrativization or the aestheticization of the subject.[12]

Against the "whole, integral human being" produced aesthetically by the transgredient other, Bakhtin positions the "ethical *subiecum*," which is "in principle nonunitary," inasmuch as it resides in the gap between "is" and "ought" (AH, 83; see also 118), where the only sense of its own wholeness is no more than a "unity yet-to-be" (126). Bakhtin relates to the ethical subject in the very same terms he uses to describe the yet-unconsummated hero, who "orients his actions within the open ethical event of his lived life" (12); who is "the bearer of the open unity of the event of a lived life—a unity incapable of being consummated from within itself" (14).

But unlike the fictional hero who is simply unaware of his containment within the aestheticizing, transgredient authorial gaze, the ethical subject must always be "unconsummated," must transgress the narratives that frame its life in order to be free to choose and to act. Bakhtin is explicit on this point: "Ethical freedom ('freedom of the will') is not only freedom from cognitive necessity (causal necessity), but also freedom from aesthetic necessity" (119):

> If I am consummated and my life is consummated, I am no longer capable of living and acting. For in order to live and act, I need to be unconsummated, I need to be open for myself—at least in all the essential moments constituting my life; I have to be, for myself, someone who is axiologically yet-to-be, someone who does not coincide with his already existing makeup. (13)

> The ethical *subiectum* is present to itself as a task—the task of actualizing itself as a value, and it is in principle incapable of being given, of being present-on-hand, of being contemplated: it is *I-for-myself*. (100)

Significantly, Bakhtin uses the concept of "rhythm" as a synonym for the narrative pattern, that "plot-bearing significance" of a biography—not to be confused with a "life" (112)—which can be established and ratified only retrospectively from a position of transgredience through the containing, aestheticizing gaze of the authorial other. This, says Bakhtin, is not possible from the perspective of I-for-myself: "my own existence is devoid of aesthetic value, devoid of plot-bearing significance, just as my physical existence is devoid of plastic-pictorial significance. I am not the hero of my own life" (112). Rhythm is "the axiological ordering of what is inwardly given or present-on-hand." It "presupposes an 'immanentization' of meaning to lived experience itself. . . . a certain predeterminateness of striving, experiencing, action" (117).

But when life is predetermined, enclosed in a set rhythm or narrative pattern, there is no room for free will and agency. Rhythm becomes "a distortion and a lie," however, when we operate in the ethical modality, Bakhtin says, because the moment of ethical choice and action is one of "fundamental and essential dissonance," a moment that "does not submit to rhythm—it is in principle extrarhythmic, nonadequate to rhythm"; "a moment where that which *is* in me must overcome itself for the sake of that which *ought to be* . . . where *is* and *ought* mutually exclude each other" (118). Free will, responsibility, and agency are in principle "incompatible with rhythm" and "cannot by rhythmicized" (119). Translated into our own terms, this "predeterminateness" means that there is an inverse relation between the degree of narrative coherence (rhythm) in our self-perception and our freedom of choice and action. In order to live, to make choices and to act, the ethical subject, "I-for-myself," must always slip out through a "loophole," transgress the boundaries of the narrative frame. "I myself as *subiectum* never coincide with me myself; I—the *subiectum* of the act of self-consciousness—exceed the bounds of this act's content. [It is a matter of] an intuitively experienced *loophole* out of time, out of everything given, everything finitely present-on-hand" (109).[13] It appears, then, that the inability of the subject to produce a whole representation of itself to itself is not necessarily just a perceptual limitation to be overcome through the prosthesis-gaze of the other; it is also—primarily, perhaps—the enabling condition of action and agency.

We shall return to this point in Part Two of this book. For now, let us look back to Montaigne, whose own autobiographical project is the articulation of a rejection of some of the very premises of autobiography. Montaigne, too, realizes that the narrative pattern imposed on a life is only valid within the realm of aesthetics, leaving it to artists "to arrange into bands this infinite diversity of aspects, to check our inconsistency and set it down in order" (*Essays*, 824–25). Art, he implies, is "that part of ourselves accessible to the gaze of others, the deliberate work that we interpose between ourselves and the outside world" (Starobinski, *Montaigne in Motion*, 90–91), and its task is the imposition of "form, constancy, stability, solidity—all qualities invoked earlier to define essences." For Montaigne, as Starobinski notes, all of these qualities are merely illusions manufactured to "attribute a unique and stable identity to that which has a thousand faces" (85). No artwork is exempt from this rule; "even good authors are wrong to insist on fashioning a consistent and solid fabric out of us. They choose one general characteristic, and go and arrange and interpret all a man's actions to fit their picture" (Montaigne, *Essays*, 239). Montaigne himself does not strive for this artful and artificial self-consistency. Rather than attempt to portray "being," he would portray "passing" in the minutest detail, at the highest resolution: "not the passing from one age to another, or, as the people say, from seven years to seven years, but from day to day, from minute to minute" (867). His own sense of himself as a subject, he says, is "always in apprenticeship and on trial" (611). It is not the "rhythm" but the "loophole" that is the ultimate truth of subjectivity.

To conclude, then, the centripetal-aesthetic mode of being—that sense of wholeness, pattern, and rhythm, which is produced by the authorial other—is inherently incompatible with the centrifugal-ethical mode of being, which cannot be contained, enframed, and rhythmicized: "The *subiectum* of lived life and the *subiectum* of aesthetic activity which gives form to that life" are, Bakhtin asserts, "in principle incapable of coinciding with one another" (AH, 86). This sounds like an echo of the distinction made earlier in *Toward a Philosophy of the Act*, where Bakhtin writes of the irreducible difference between aesthetic seeing (based on "outsideness") and the "world that is correlated with me" (I-for-myself), which is "fundamentally and essentially incapable of becoming part of an aesthetic architectonic" (TPA, 74). Significantly, Bakhtin writes of the "temptation of aestheticism," the temptation to act out a conception of oneself through the eyes of the other, which must be resisted by the intensely situated, participative, and answerable subject (18).[14] The nostalgia for the culture of boundary lines, the desire to be cocooned and consummated within an authoritative master narrative is checked by the awareness that the aesthetic may get dangerously close to the anesthetic.

CONTRABAND

In *Problems of Dostoevsky's Poetics*, the centripetal modality of "Author and Hero" appears to be displaced by a thoroughly centrifugal position. The scopic-aesthetic sensibility of the early essay seems to give way to an auditory/oral frame of reference, based on the concepts of voice, polyphony, heteroglossia, and dialogue—the hallmarks of what became known in the West up to the early 1990s as the Bakhtinian spirit and turned him into a prototype for the postmodern zeitgeist. The touchstone of this shift is, of course, the different perception of Dostoyevsky's work.

In "Author and Hero," viewed against the metaphysical-aesthetic postulate, Dostoyevsky is treated as a maverick, an author who has (regrettably) failed to sustain the position of transgredience. Dostoyevsky's failure of transgredience enables the hero to "[take] possession of the author," who then becomes "unable to find any convincing and stable axiological point of support *outside* the hero" (AH, 17), unable, in other words, to "consummate" the hero. This type of aesthetic loss, writes Bakhtin, "includes almost all of Dostoevsky's heroes" (20). Relating to the refusal of Dostoyevsky's heroes "to accept a possible judgment by God or by man," Bakhtin writes that these "anthropomachic" and "theomachic" elements (i.e., the hostile positioning of the other) "preclude aesthetic concord, preclude the concord intrinsic to prayer" (146; see also 130).

In *Problems of Dostoevsky's Poetics*, the maverick becomes the standard-bearer of a new cultural era, the author of a "small-scale Copernican revolution" (PDP, 49). The second chapter of this treatise, titled "The Hero and the Position of the Author with Regard to the Hero in Dostoyevsky's Art," is diametrically opposed to the conception of the relationship presented in "Author and Hero," and the polyphonic principle that structures Dostoyevsky's work—"*a plurality of independent and unmerged voices and consciousnesses*" (PDP, 6)—is presented as a radically "new artistic model of the world" (Bakhtin's preface to the 2nd edition, 1963, PDP, 3). The fundamentally different relationship between author and hero that makes for this revolutionary model turns the Dostoyevskian hero into "the author of a fully weighted ideological conception of his own," rather than the object of Dostoyevsky's "finalizing artistic vision." The hero is now "a fully valid, autonomous carrier of his own individual word" (PDP, 5); and the fictional characters are no longer contained within the benevolent authorial vision: they are not "objectified images" but "*pure voice*[s]" (39, 53), making themselves heard as loud as the voice of the author, refusing to be enframed and "consummated" in his vision. Dostoyevsky's abdication of "transgredience," the privileged aesthetic position that would have allowed him to "consummate" the characters, is now presented as a paradigm shift of Copernican magnitude.

The Dostoyevskian revolution, as Bakhtin conceives it, is inextricably related to the collapse of the metaphysical outlook that was, as we have seen, the enabling condition of Bakhtin's aestheticized conception of subjectivity. In "Author and Hero," Bakhtin laments this collapse, which has led to "an attempt to force an admission from within self-consciousness, which is possible only through the other; an attempt to do without God, without listeners, without an author" (AH, 181). The references to that lost aesthetic/metaphysical culture are distinctly elegiac: it is, he writes, "a culture of boundaries," which "presupposes that life is enveloped by a warm atmosphere of deepest trust.... [and is premised on] the existence of a firm and secure position outside of him. ... [and] presupposes an essential axiological consolidatedness of the enveloping atmosphere" (203–4). Dostoyevsky is positioned, according to Bakhtin's conception, at the graveside of "aesthetic culture," where boundary lines are no longer recognized and all forms of transgredience are refused (203).

This cultural diagnosis of Dostoyevsky's position at the conclusion of the secularization process remains consistent in *Problems of Dostoevsky's Poetics*, where Bakhtin again links it to what he had earlier called the "crisis of authorship," the "immanentization" and the "psychologization" of God, and the loss of "faith in the essentialness and kindness of the power that gives form from outside" (AH, 203). In the absence of an Auctor Mundi, the human author loses his share of that "supreme outsideness," the transgredient position, the "excess of seeing" that has enabled him to "consummate" the hero. However, Dostoyevsky's abdication of the transgredient authorial position is now perceived, not as a symptom of a cultural failure, but as a bid for freedom. If, "from the viewpoint of a consistently monologic visualization and understanding of the represented world ... Dostoevsky's world may seem a chaos" (*PDP*, 8), it is now the very chaos that serves to enable autonomy and agency. For Bakhtin, this freedom from authorial finalization, the characters' "capacity to outgrow, as it were, from within and to render *untrue* any externalizing and finalizing definition of them" (59), is the very essence of the ethical mode of being.[15] The shift of attitude has not escaped Bakhtin's translators: the word *zavershenie*, rendered in the translation of "Author and Hero" as "consummation," an operation of loving containment, has been translated—just as rightly—as "finalization," a violent act of closure, in the Dostoyevsky book.[16]

As in the centripetal mode of "Author and Hero," the literary frame of reference slides into a philosophical conception—centrifugal now—of human subjectivity: like the Dostoyevskian hero, "a living human being cannot be turned into the voiceless object of some secondhand, finalizing cognitive process" (*PDP*, 58). "As long as a person is alive he lives by the fact that he is not yet finalized, that he has not yet uttered his ultimate word" (59). The foundational principle of human subjectivity is now perceived as a "non-coincidence" of the subject—fictional/literary or historical/real—with itself, or rather, with any "secondhand," "finalizing" definition of itself:

> A man never coincides with himself. One cannot apply to him the formula of identity A≡A. In Dostoyevsky's artistic thinking, the genuine life of the personality takes place at the point of non-coincidence between a man and himself, at this point of departure beyond the limits of all that he is as a material being, a being that can be spied on, defined, predicted apart from its own will, "at second hand." (*PDP*, 59)

Far from a mere artistic transition, the "revolt" of the Dostoyevskian hero against his literary "finalization," the capacity to "outgrow, as it were, from within and to render untrue any externalizing and finalizing definition," evolves into a new paradigm of subjectivity. The ethical implications of this paradigm of non-coincidence with oneself become much clearer when we recall Bakhtin's earlier claim that "in order to live and act, I need to be unconsummated. . . . I have to be, for myself, someone who is axiologically yet-to-be, someone who does not coincide with his already existing makeup" (*AH*, 13; see also 16). The position of the subject at its own borderlines is the very condition of free ethical choice.

AT THE CROSSROADS

Reading "Author and Hero" and *Problems of Dostoevsky's Poetics* against each other, we seem to be offered two diametrically opposed views of human subjectivity and two equally irreconcilable cultural-ideological positions.[17] Did Bakhtin experience a "secular conversion" at some point between these two texts? This account of the transition from the "aesthetic/metaphysical" to the "ethical" modality of the latter would be entirely in keeping with Julia Kristeva's early introduction of the Russian thinker to the Western world as a poststructuralist *avant la lettre*, a proto-Derridean figure, who had anticipated and laid the ground for the conception of intertextuality and opened the gateway to a new radical epistemology. On Kristeva's passionate account, Bakhtin's prophet of "intertextuality" is Dostoyevsky, whose polyphonic novels are "built on that breach of the 'I,'" offering "a plurality of languages, a confrontation of types of discourse and ideologies, with no conclusion and no synthesis—without monologic or any axial point" ("The Ruin of a Poetics," 111). The unresolved confrontation of discourses of Dostoyevsky's characters, the fragmentation and pluralization of the speaking subject in the intertextual space, creates a "contrapuntal, polyphonic ensemble," which "lacks unity of speaker and of meaning," and which Kristeva sees as emancipatory, "plural, anti-totalitarian and anti-theological" (110). For Kristeva, the concept of dialogism, which, she argues "may well become the basis of our time's intellectual structure," is generated by the logic of transgression ("Word, Dialogue, and Novel," 89). The celebration of dialogism, of the carnivalesque, and of the polyphonic novel "challenges God, authority, and social law; insofar as it is dialogical, it is rebellious" (79).

Indeed, there is much in Bakhtin's work to warrant Kristeva's reading. Bakhtin's own references to Dostoyevsky as the standard-bearer of a new era certainly seem to celebrate an emancipatory plurivocality, a poetic revolution that is a concomitant of the secularization process. Divestment of the author's prerogative, abdication of transgredience, and dismantling of axiological sovereignty vis-à-vis the hero may well be, and have in fact been conceived as Bakhtin's contribution to the heterological tradition, the promotion of a nonidentitarian logic, and the persistent questioning of boundaries that are the hallmarks of postmodernist thinking. Bakhtin does celebrate the "radical change in the position of the author" and the "birth of a new form of novel (a new form of visualization and a new human being–personality; overcoming materialization)" (TRDB, 291). This, for Bakhtin, is more than an aesthetic revolution. Dostoyevsky's replacement of the monologic, reified model of the world by a dialogic one ushers in a new, polyphonic, secular cultural era (292–93).

But this "Copernican revolution," whatever its scale, does not offer a clean break with the Ptolemaic, centripetal outlook of Bakhtin's earlier texts. Noting the recurrence of religious phraseology, the "continual mention of the hero's 'soul' and 'conscience'" in *Problems of Dostoevsky's Poetics*, Kristeva relegates this counterevidence, with a distinctly apologetic tone, to the accidents of history, the inevitable sociological and cultural "theoretical limitations" of Bakhtin's text, which, though looking ahead of its time, is still fettered by the discursive framework of its historical context. Kristeva notes "the lack of any theory of the language-user" and the "unrecognized influence of Christianity in a humanist terminology" ("The Ruin of a Poetics," 106). Bakhtin's vocabulary, Kristeva concedes, is "furtively influenced by theology: the term 'conscience' may well occur more often than 'discourse', and the word 'voice' is not without some transcendental echoes" (110). To counter the embarrassment of these metaphysical echoes, what is called for is a distillation of the "advanced" contemporary "kernel" of Bakhtin's ideas from the "worn-out ideological husk which surrounds them" (107); a mining project that would clear the rhetoric of metaphysics out of the way and extract, from "beneath the layers of traditional Russian culture which impose these language-habits," the "new departure which Bakhtin's analysis introduces" (110). This salvage operation should, if we follow Kristeva's argument, turn Bakhtin into a "hitherto unknown precursor [of our age], unaware of [his] role" (107).

This is clearly not the case. If the religious rhetoric of *Problems of Dostoevsky's Poetics* may be dismissed as no more than embarrassing cultural baggage, it is much harder to explain away the fact that when Bakhtin himself allowed his editors to publish "Author and Hero" in the 1970s, well after the publication of his later writings, he apparently felt no need to disown this early still-unpublished essay so overtly predicated on a metaphysical paradigm. A distinct note of nostalgia creeps into his later work when he writes of the historical "expunging the other's . . . sacred and authoritarian word . . . with its indisputability, unconditionality and unequivocality" (N70–71, 132–33). The monologic novel is no longer possible when "the primary author . . . clothes himself in *silence*," and the human author's "quests for the authorial position" become at this point "the most critical problem of contemporary literature" (149). One cannot overlook the elegiac note of this commentary as Bakhtin looks back to the lost "earthly paradise" from which Dostoyevsky's heroes were expelled, and the privilege of naïveté denied them (139). This late "lapsarian" metaphor is identical to the conception of Dostoyevsky's world half a century earlier: the author's loss of his transgredient position leaves the hero on his own "in the light of to-be-attained meaning" where he "begins to see his own nakedness and to be ashamed, and paradise is lost" (AH, 172). Most poignantly, Kristeva's celebration of Dostoyevsky's polyphonic Copernican revolution may sound rather hollow when we learn that Bakhtin saw his book on Dostoyevsky as "morally flawed," because it could not openly deal with "the main questions . . . what Dostoevsky agonized about all his life—the existence of God" (Bocharov, "Conversations with Bakhtin," 1013).

Bakhtin's equivocation is not unlike the metaphysical ache of Dostoyevsky himself, whose work, even at its most "polyphonic," is energized by the tensile relationship between the persistent desire for grounding and the radically secular, ideologically centrifugal mode. In Bakhtin's "Toward a Reworking of the Dostoevsky Book," there is an oblique note on Dostoyevsky's conception of atheism as "a lack of faith in this sense, as indifference toward an ultimate value which makes demands on the whole man, as a rejection of the ultimate position." In the same paragraph, however, there is a comment on Dostoyevsky's "vacillations as regards the *content* of this ultimate value" (TRDB, 294). Indeed, when the need for a *point d'appui* outside the subject, the most fundamental metaphysical need, remains unanswered, the problem of grounding emerges in full force both in the constitution of the subject and in the constitution of the ethics. This has been the core question of Western ethics throughout the process of secularization: how is one to choose that "ultimate value" without recourse to an ultimate authoritative other? It is the very same question that lies at the core of Dostoyevsky's work, for even the most radically polyphonic of his novels still conclude on a note of extreme, if somewhat forced, piety.

Dostoyevsky's characters are fully aware of the axiological void that has opened up with the removal of the metaphysical anchor: "there is no virtue if there is no immortality"; "If God is dead, everything is allowed" (*The Brothers Karamazov*, 77–78, 156; see also ibid., 273–75, 294–309; and Bakhtin, *PDP*, 86, 89, 144, 152). On this issue, too, one would have to question Kristeva's claim that "the remark of old Karamazov, 'God is dead, everything is allowed', seems to have been decoded as what it becomes, if one goes just a step further towards what he refrains from saying, 'God is dead, everything is interdiction'" (Kristeva, "The Ruin of a Poetics," 115). There is just one small word between that formulation and the Bakhtinian/Dostoyevskian text. The ideological struggle among the Karamazovs revolves on a much more tentative formulation: "If God is dead, everything is allowed." That "if" is precisely what is at stake here. The removal of the ultimate narrator, the unmooring of the subject, and the uncoupling of ethics from metaphysics has left an impossible legacy for the following century. Living on the threshold of a secularized civilization, Dostoyevsky himself was surely aware of the need for ethical grounding and of the wound left gaping with the removal of the metaphysical anchor. What seems to emerge here is clearly more than a form of recidivism. These are not merely twinges of nostalgia for a lost world or worn-out rhetorical tics, as Kristeva would have them, but a genuine and profound equivocation, which cannot be evaded.

Another, much later aporetic moment with which we must reckon occurs in "The Problem of the Text," written toward the very end of Bakhtin's career, where the concept of the "superaddressee" is introduced:

> The author of the utterance, with a greater or lesser awareness, presupposes a higher *superaddressee* (third), whose absolutely just responsive understanding is presumed either in some metaphysical distance or in a distant historical time (the loophole addressee); In various ages and with various understandings of the world, this superaddressee and his ideally true responsive understanding assume various ideological expressions (God, absolute truth, the court of dispassionate human conscience, the people, the court of history, science, and so forth)....
>
> Each dialogue takes place as if against the background of the responsive understanding of an invisibly present third party who stands above all the participants in the dialogue. (PT, 126)

Bakhtin seems to be aware of the implications of this new addition, for he hastily adds that this superaddressee, who is "a constitutive aspect of the whole utterance," is not "any mystical or metaphysical being (although, given a certain understanding of the world, he can be expressed as such)" (126). This disclaimer notwithstanding, it is hard to conceive of this ultimate listener as anything but the "tertium non datur," the metadiscursive voice expunged by the conception of dialogicity, according to Kristeva ("The Ruin of a Poetics," 111). It does not take much philosophical acumen to realize that this late supplement actually hollows out the very notion of dialogicity and sterilizes its more radical implications. Does the late introduction of the superaddressee mark the return of the "supreme author" or "ultimate other" who stages his comeback through the back door? Leaving the question of the superaddressee for a later point in this volume, let us turn back to the "architectonics" of the Bakhtinian subject.

ARCHITECTONICS

The *I* that tells itself does not exist, says Derrida. We cannot have the last word, says Bakhtin. Whether it is a story where we attempt to capture the rhythm and stake out the boundaries of our life, or a story-shaped life (lived according to generic contracts that are all the more powerful for being implicit), our narrative identity is the parameter of subjectivity born out of the desire for emplotment, for a sense of coherence and wholeness that can only be granted within a well-framed story. But human subjectivity—psychological and ethical—emerges architectonically in and from the tensile relations of narrative and dialogue, rhythm and loophole, aesthetics and ethics—the "two movements" that meet in the human subject in an oppositional and complementary relationship (AH, 91). This immanent duality is directly linked, as Holquist points out, to Kant's distinction between the "empirical" and the "transcendental" *I*, between perception and apperception (Holquist, "The Role of Chronotope," 13), but for Bakhtin—positioned at the apparent end of the process of secularization, when the transcendental or the "transgredient" can no longer be taken for granted or easily synthesized with the perception of "I-for-myself"—the immanent split of subjectivity is even more poignantly felt as a problem, requiring, not only a new architectonic conception, but an entirely different "first philosophy."

The need to narrativize the self, to contain it within a pattern, a rhythm, a well-wrought tale, may be deeply embedded in human culture and part of our self-perception. But unlike some of our contemporary proponents of the narrative identity thesis, Bakhtin is well aware of the dangers of this desire for "consummation." Even as we recognize the incurable need to aestheticize the self, to secure it within a narrative framework, and to ground it in the authorial Word, we must also be fully aware of the contingency of our narratives in an authorless existence. Ever true to his suspicion of boundary lines and narrative frames, Bakhtin does not indulge in any utopian visions—humanistic or carnivalesque—of subjectivity. Having renounced the ontological proposition, the foundational claim of an essence, a substance, a solid kernel of being, he offers an "architectonics" of subjectivity, a view of the human agent as a character in an authorless narrative—fully embodied, inhabiting time and space, but having no sovereign inner territory, always facing the other, inescapably ethical. But this living-on-borderlines, which makes the subject so vulnerable and its sense of identity so precarious (and hence calls for the narrativizing perspective of the transgredient other), is not necessarily a weakness. Paradoxically, this non-self-sufficiency is also what constitutes and empowers the ethical subject, for it is precisely in this absence of the authorial other that we become fully responsive to and responsible for the other. We are, indeed, storytelling beings who desire to be framed and narrativized into coherence, to be characters in a novel, as it were. But it is our inability to remain cocooned within those narrative frames and our recognition of the permeability and the provisional nature of our autobiographies that, in turning us out of our metaphysical-aesthetic home, has turned us into ethical beings.

If we add up the points raised here, it becomes clearer that neither the centripetal nor the centrifugal mode of subjectivity is ethically viable in and of itself. If "Author and Hero" has left us wondering about the passivity of the subject who is axiologically enframed by an authorial other, *Problems of Dostoevsky's Poetics* leaves the subject unmoored in a space where everything becomes relative, without any point of grounding outside itself. It is just as clear that Bakhtin is well aware both of the need to account for loopholes in the rhythm of transgredient authoring, and of the desire for some sort of authoritative grounding that would resolve the problem of ethical relativism. What Bakhtin offers throughout his work is neither a confident metaphysical thesis nor an all-out subversion of metaphysical grounding. The tensile relation of the "centripetal" and the "centrifugal," the persistent framing and unframing, the seduction of rhythm and the necessity of the loophole, deconstructs the very concept of the thetic subject. Proud and self-conscious straddler as he is, Bakhtin looks back to the assurances for metaphysics even as he dismantles the metaphysical props of subjectivity. As Caryl Emerson rightly warns, he is not an "apostle of freedom who rejoices . . . in the undoing of rules, in centrifugal energy, in carnival clowning, in novels as loopholes, and in sly denials of authorship. . . . [He] is, if anything, an apostle of constraints" ("Problems with Baxtin's Poetics," 507).

Bakhtin is an exile. The persistent echo of Dostoyevsky's "If God is dead, everything is allowed" is an incurable homesickness, an ache that will not go away. But this desire for the authorial other, for ethical grounding in what is larger than one's self, though fully recognized as a constituent of human subjectivity, remains just that: a desire that is, by definition, doomed to deferral. Knowing only too well that there is no "internal sovereign territory" where the subject can name itself, that "self-nomination is imposture" (TRDB, 287–88), he is homesick for that prelapsarian region where "the organizing force of the *I* is replaced by the organizing force of God; my earthly determinateness, my earthly name, is surmounted, and I gain a clear understanding of the name written in heaven in the Book of Life—the *memory* of the future" (AH, 145). It is precisely this problem of grounding, this metaphysical vacuum, that, I would suggest, enables the return of the superaddressee, the ultimate other, into Bakhtin's last essays. Like his hero Dostoyevsky, he too was among the disinherited. A lapsed metaphysician or a nostalgic radical, Bakhtin recognizes the problem of ethics against the silence of the primary author and is fully aware of the "if" that many of his Western contemporaries have so casually suppressed. Straddling both territories, Bakhtin is not at home in either of them. It is that state of homelessness, he tells us, in which we have got to make our name.

THE POETICS OF SUBJECTIVITY

> Man can give himself in saying to the point of poetry—or he can withdraw into the nonsaying of lies.
>
> Emmanuel Lévinas, "Dialogue" with Richard Kearney

BAKHTIN'S INTELLECTUAL ITINERARY, we have noted, does not lend itself to any easy emplotment. While the chronology of his writings may suggest that he started out as a philosopher and then shunted his work into literary theory, the trajectory of his reception in the West was almost an inverse mirror-image of the apparent permutations of his work. Throughout the 1980s, he was one of the most-often cited theoretical sources in literary studies, and the prolific "Bakhtin industry," as it is somewhat impatiently dubbed, which drew almost exclusively on the texts written between 1929 and 1942, was primarily busy with rather loose "applications" of Bakhtinian terms in discussions of literary texts, with concepts like "carnival," "dialogism," and "polyphony" taking pride of place, usually in an adjectival position. The translation of the early essays into English in the early 1990s, and the Moscow conference of 1995 generated a surge of interest in Bakhtin's philosophical legacy and (I would argue) an all-too-easy dismissal of his literary writings as either merely illustrative or as an "Aesopean" mode of discourse, which does not need to be addressed in and of itself. It was broadly assumed that under the state terrorism of the Stalin era, writing about literature, philosophizing "under a mask," as it were, would have been one way of engaging in intellectual work with marginally better prospects of personal survival. The "literary Bakhtin" was henceforth shelved and relegated to the storehouse of ephemeral academic fashions.

Bakhtin's own retrospective view of his intellectual itinerary was unequivocal. In 1973, when asked by Viktor Duvakin if he had been "more a philosopher than a philologist" in the 1920s, he answered: "More a philosopher," adding "and such have I remained until the present day. I am a philosopher. I am a thinker. But in Petrograd we were all caught up in such concerns as: What is philosophy? Neither one thing nor the other. One had to be a specialist" (quoted by Emerson, "Prosaics and the Problem of Form," 36n18).[1] The ambiguous wording of this response is worth noting: for Bakhtin, philosophy seems to be a default option precisely because it is "neither one thing nor the other": "Our analysis," he elsewhere writes, "must be called philosophical mainly because of what it is not: it is not a linguistic, philological, literary, or any other special kind of analysis (study). The advantages are these: our study will move in the liminal spheres, that is, on the borders of all the aforementioned disciplines, at their junctures and points of intersection" (PT, 103).

Arguably, this self-conscious liminality offers an alternative to the conceptual opposition between literature and philosophy through its rejection of traditional disciplinary boundary lines and theoretical hierarchies. Indeed, what emerges from even the most cursory survey of Bakhtin's discontinuous project and its various permutations is a lifelong attempt to articulate a "philosophical anthropology" transcending the traditional demarcations of disciplinary territories and exploring the relation of the subject to its "other" (be it a particular human other in interpersonal, ethical, or psychological relationships; an authorial other in an aesthetic relationship; or an official other—the state, the church, official culture). The degree of ethical freedom enabled by the relation to the other is perhaps the most important aspect of this philosophical anthropology.

However, proud straddler as Bakhtin may have been, the question of disciplinary affiliation is by no means trivial. Given the fact that most of his work revolves around his readings of literature, can one view this lifelong preoccupation merely as a matter of political expediency, an Aesopean camouflage of philosophical ideas? The question becomes even more pressing against the note of disillusionment with philosophy that, as we have already seen, clearly sounds in Bakhtin's earlier surviving fragment. Bakhtin's condemnation of the "fatal Theoreticism" that is the bane of traditional philosophical thinking is a clean break with the Cartesian method. It is, to get back to the inaugural passage quoted earlier, an "unfortunate misunderstanding (a legacy of rationalism) to think that truth [*pravda*] can only be the truth [*istina*] that is composed of universal moments; that the truth of a situation is precisely that which is repeatable and constant in it. Moreover, that which is universal and identical (logically identical) is fundamental and essential, whereas individual truth [*pravda*] is artistic and irresponsible, i.e., it isolates the given individuality" (*TPA*, 37).

This is precisely where the two strands of the Cartesian divide converge, since the kind of abstract, quasi-mathematical thinking that has turned the subject into a disembodied abstraction or a generic entity is the enabling condition for formal theoretical ethics, as read by Bakhtin. The Cartesian-Kantian recourse to universalized abstractions, divorced from the concreteness, temporality, and particularity of human existence, "leads philosophical thinking, which seeks to be on principle purely theoretical, to [the] peculiar state of sterility, in which it, undoubtedly, finds itself at the present time" (18). "That is why this theoretical philosophy cannot pretend to being a first philosophy.... *Such a first philosophy does not exist, and even the paths leading to its creation seem to be forgotten*" (19; emphasis added).

And so Bakhtin, along with other contemporary philosophers, sets out to recover the forgotten path leading back to the philosophical tradition cut off by the great divide, and away from what he sees as the sterility of post-Cartesian philosophy, the legacy of rationalism, objectivism, and abstraction that has set the direction for Western philosophy (27). The path toward an alternative "first philosophy," or another way of knowing, would go through literature, or art, which "is closer than any of the abstract cultural worlds (taken in isolation) to the unitary and unique world of the performed act" (61). Bakhtin's preference for the "world" of literature—unique, relational, and unrepeatable—over the ostensibly transparent, pure, and abstract discourse of traditional philosophy is explicitly related to the greater truth claims of the former. The literary—that traditional other of philosophy—is another way of knowing that cannot be accessed through traditional philosophical theoretization.

Bakhtin is not alone. The disenchantment with traditional philosophizing and the turn to literature or art in search of truth is, in fact, definitive for the entire spectrum of what is called "Continental" philosophy, from phenomenology to deconstruction, whose "most persistent feature, through all its multiple mutations, is a commitment to the questioning of foundations," and the conception of meaning, not as "a metaphysical essence or substance," but as "a task of intersubjective and intertextual relations" (Kearney, *Continental Philosophy*, 2). Thus Heidegger's reply to his own question, "What does 'in truth' mean?" sounds uncannily similar to Bakhtin's:

> Truth is the essence of the true. What do we have in mind when speaking of essence? Usually it is thought to be those features held in common by everything that is true. The essence is discovered in the generic and universal concept, which represents the one feature that holds indifferently for many things. This indifferent essence . . . is, however, only the inessential essence." (Heidegger, "The Origin of the Work of Art," 50)

Heidegger, too, stands opposed, in the later phase of his work, to the conception of "propositional truth," the "agreement or conformity of knowledge with fact," which has reigned supreme since the time of Descartes (51), and looks to painting and, by extension, to art in general, as the place where truth "happens" as a concrete and singular event (56).[2]

The boldest response to Heidegger's call for "poetic thinking" is that of Derrida, who devoted most of his work to the transgression of the boundary lines between philosophy and literature. Unlike Bakhtin, Derrida insists on his own literary, rather than philosophical, affiliation: "[M]y most constant interest, coming even before my philosophical interest I should say, if this is possible, has been directed towards literature, towards that writing which is called literary" ("The Time of a Thesis," 37); "My 'first' inclination wasn't really towards philosophy but rather towards literature, no, towards something that literature accommodates more easily than philosophy" ("An Interview with Derrida," quoted in id., *Acts of Literature*, 2). Derrida is trying to reconnect to the mode of thinking and discourse that takes on board the singularity, concreteness, and embodiment of human subjectivity, the kind of philosophical discourse shunted off by the great Cartesian divide into the realm of the literary. His definition of deconstruction as a "coming-to-terms with literature" ("Deconstruction in America," 9) and his conviction that "the 'economy' of literature sometimes seems to me more powerful than that of other types of discourse" ("This Strange Institution," 43) set the stage for his own transgressive, flamboyant, and sometimes exasperating rhetorical practices.

True to his word, Derrida deploys a strategy of transgression in an overt defiance of theoretical proprieties, boundaries, and property rights. In his discussion of Nietzsche's *Ecce Homo*, addressing the questions of the borderlines between the system (the corpus of the work, the philosophical writings) and the subject of the system (the corpus of empirical accidents that constitutes the life of the philosopher), Derrida flatly refuses to make any concessions to the proprieties of traditional philosophical categories: "We say no to this," he writes, as he crosses and re-crosses the boundary lines between the "work" and the "life," the corpus of the text and the corpus of the subject, the semiotic and the somatic, philosophy and literature. It is precisely to the dynamics of this "borderline which traverses the two 'bodies'" that he addresses his work, "seeking out the edges, the inner walls, the passages" of the text and of the subject (*The Ear of the Other*, 5–6, 11).

Bakhtin, too, is a "philosopher of borderlines," overtly concerned with questions of framing, exploring the significance of liminality, transgression, and points of intersection. His inaugural act of philosophical contraband—the call for a shift from the "truth of philosophy" to another way of knowing—sets the scene for a blatant transgression of the most fundamental categories of philosophical conceptualization: the slippage from the semiotic to the somatic and back again; the pervasive interchangeability of "hero-author" and "self-other"; the smooth transition from the realm of art (the construct, the artifice, that which is made up) to the realm of immediate human reality may certainly be read as a self-aware deconstructive move, a strategic subversion of the founding metaphysical opposition between presence and signification, the primary and the derived, the real and the textual. This cavalier breach of theoretical decorum almost puts him in a league with Derrida.

But this is only the "centrifugal" vector of Bakhtin's work. As we have already noted, Bakhtin is profoundly ambivalent about the breach he seems to inaugurate and celebrate. The very same slippage between "hero" and "I-for-myself," between "author" and "other," may also be construed as enabled by an anachronistic, religious, or naïve frame of reference, a virtually medieval analogical chain of "transgredient" others: the other who authors the subject, the author who creates the hero, and the transcendent Auctor Mundi.[3] And so, while it seems that both Heidegger and Derrida set out from the same philosophical disenchantment and rupture, which Bakhtin, too, so keenly feels, it is equally clear that that their attempted deconstruction of the opposition between philosophy and literature and their own mode of "poetic philosophizing" would not have been equally congenial to Bakhtin, whose turn to literature is founded on the very stability of this distinction, and whose personal style of thought and discourse was rather more austere and much less self-conscious than theirs.

Most important, as we saw earlier, the distinction of Bakhtin's quarrel with the Cartesian paradigm lies in the specific and explicit *ethical* thrust of his critique, and his philosophical disenchantment is primarily grounded in the apparent failure of formal ethics to provide the missing link between the singular and concrete human act and the general, abstract ethical imperative. The task undertaken by Bakhtin is formidable. It is an attempt to set up a connection between ontology and ethics, a bridge between a set of formal principles, Kantian or other, and the concrete and singular human act; between our awareness of the "ought" and our commitment to acting it out. And the forgotten path he sets out to recover goes through literature, the exiled other of philosophy. The recognition that emerges—or can be extrapolated—from Bakhtin's work is that the discovery of that missing link is predicated on the analogy between the dynamics of *intersubjectivity* and *intrasubjectivity*, and that this analogy is most visible, not in the theses of philosophy, but in the workings of literature.

THE QUESTION OF LITERARINESS

It should be said at the very outset that for Bakhtin, literature is not an illustration or sublimation of philosophical concerns. He is remarkably unconcerned with the thematics of the literary works he examines, and rarely examines the viewpoints, perceptions, or ethical positions of the characters or the implied author in these texts. And if this indifference to thematics is problematic in obvious ways, particularly in Bakhtin's readings of Dostoyevsky, it is profoundly productive in approaching ethics, not as a set of formal principles but as *a mode of being*.

Already in Bakhtin's earliest known publication, "Art and Answerability" (1919), he writes: "I have to answer with my own life for what I have experienced and understood in art, so that everything I have experienced and understood would not remain ineffectual in my life. But answerability entails guilt, or liability to blame. It is not only mutual answerability that art and life must assume, but also mutual liability to blame" (1). This cryptic passage will gain meaning and depth in Bakhtin's subsequent work, *Toward a Philosophy of the Act*, where he predicates his critique of the "fatal Theoreticism" of traditional philosophical thinking, not on epistemological, but on ethical questions, and particularly on the issue of *answerability*. How, then, can literature, or art in general, open a gateway into ethics, a way of knowing that does not resort to the sterile abstraction and universalization of formal philosophical thinking?

One aspect of this relation has been highlighted by Ken Hirschkop, who perceives the relation of literature and ethics as predicated on the concept of "novelness," extrapolated from literature to language in general. The novel as perceived by Bakhtin, says Hirschkop, embodies "a distinctive *form* of intersubjectivity, a unique and unprecedented communicative structure," wherein the "'inter' separating subjects is not a limitation but the very condition of meaningful utterance" (*Mikhail Bakhtin: An Aesthetic for Democracy*, 5; emphasis added). The novel, and particularly the Dostoyevskian novel, is thus the vehicle for what Hirschkop perceives and welcomes as Bakhtin's leap "from philosophy to social critique" (5), inasmuch as it embodies and highlights "the dialogism intrinsic to language as such" (175). It is this "identification of the ethical and the linguistic," foregrounded in the Dostoyevskian novel (as read by Bakhtin), that "marks a break with Kantian moral philosophy" (198), and it is thus "not Dostoevsky's moral beliefs, but his *representational* achievements that impress Bakhtin" (199).

Undoubtedly, this Habermassian platform would have been entirely congenial to Bakhtin (with a possible reservation about the given nature of the grammar of human communication). But it seems to me that Hirschkop's thesis does not go far enough, in that, even though it discards thematics, its focus on intersubjective dynamics brings it too close to a paradigm of "enactment": the idea that "language itself embodies ethical reality as the secret of its operation" (175), though immensely attractive, is problematic in that it begs the obvious question: if language as such embodies the ethical by definition, and given the fact that all humans are natural language users (at least by most definitions), why aren't we all ethical beings in the same natural way? Another issue that remains unresolved in this account is the precise relation between literary (or "novelistic") and nonliterary uses of language. In what ways is the immanent dialogism of language amplified in and through literary discourse?

Surprisingly, perhaps, the answers to these questions may emerge from the ranks of Bakhtin's ostensible opponents, since the elusive quality of "literariness" (*literaturnost'*) was precisely what Bakhtin's formalist contemporaries had set out to explore.[4] The key to distinguishing literature from nonliterature, according to the formalists, is Victor Shklovsky's concept of "estrangement" (*ostranenie*), or "defamiliarization," as it is sometimes designated, which has become the foundational principle of the formalist project. Shklovsky's seminal essay "Art as Technique" (1917) is directed against the then-current conception of art as "thinking in images," which—like Western philosophy in the wake of the Cartesian moment—aims at presenting "the unknown in terms of the known."[5] Significantly, Shklovsky's point of departure—like that of Bakhtin in "Author and Hero"—is "the general laws of perception." As perception becomes habitual, it also becomes automatic and unconscious; our daily routines are based on "learning to ignore"—we hardly notice ourselves performing habitual actions; we no longer really see our surroundings; we go about our daily business almost as if we were blindfolded. We settle for partial, token indications of things rather than for the things themselves. This, Shklovsky says, "explains the principles by which, in ordinary speech, we leave phrases unfinished and words half expressed."

More significantly still, Shklovsky chooses the language of algebra to serve as the paradigm for this mode of language: "In this process, ideally realized in algebra, things are replaced by symbols. . . . By this 'algebraic' method of thought we apprehend objects only as shapes with imprecise extensions; we do not see them in their entirety, but rather recognize them by their main characteristics. We see the object as though it were enveloped in a sack. We know what it is by its configuration, but we see only its silhouette" ("Art as Technique," in *Russian Formalist Poetics*, 11). For Shklovsky, the exclusive use of language as a practical, automatic, and transparent vehicle of communication—what he (misleadingly, of course) calls "prose"—is deadening:

> The object, perceived thus in the manner of prose perception, fades and does not leave even a first impression; ultimately even the essence of what it was is forgotten. Such perception explains why we fail to hear the prose word in its entirety. . . . The process of "algebraization," the over-automatization of an object, permits the greatest economy of perceptive effort. . . . And so life is reckoned as nothing. (11–12)

This poignant last sentence, a quotation of Tolstoy's diary of 1897, is immediately followed by Shklovsky's own poetic formulation: "Habitualization devours works, clothes, furniture, one's wife, the fear of war. 'If the whole complex lives of many people go on unconsciously, then such lives are as if they had never been'" (12). When love, the significance of labor, aesthetic pleasure, or the fear of war are "devoured"—trivialized, devalued, flattened, and hollowed out of their meaning by habituation—life is not worth living. And art, says Shklovsky, "exists that one may recover the sensation of life; it exists to make one feel things, to make the stone *stony*" (12). This redeeming role of art is to "make-strange," "defamiliarize," de-automatize, and thus restore and revive the sensation and the value of life through a disruption of mechanical and habitual modes of perception.

> The author's purpose is to create the vision which results from that deautomatized perception. A word is created "artistically" so that its perception is impeded, and the greatest possible effect is produced through the slowness of the perception. . . . The language of poetry is, then, a difficult, roughened, impeded language. (22)[6]

Estrangement in art—the aesthetic practice of displacement, disruption, deconstruction—does not allow for the smooth assimilation and reduction of otherness; it calls forth that which is normally allowed to fade out of our field of awareness; it demands that we recognize an otherness in ourselves. For Shklovsky, then, the literary experience is thus profoundly ethical.[7]

Before we turn to Bakhtin's point of affinity with Shklovsky, we should note Bakhtin's own reservations (in "The Problem of Content, Material, and Form in Verbal Art," "Author and Hero," and his late notes) and give some consideration to the case made against formalism by Bakhtin's close associate and possible collaborator P. N. Medvedev.[8] References to Shklovsky's "Art as Device" (an alternative translation of "Art as Technique") appear in *The Formal Method in Literary Scholarship* (1928), attributed jointly to Medvedev and Bakhtin, in the section headed "the nihilistic slant of formalism," where terms like "making it strange" (*ostranenie*) are alleged to be "completely infused with this [nihilistic] tendency" and condemned for being merely "negative" rather than constructive. The crudely worded charge seems entirely perverse when we read it against Shklovsky's essay. The case in point is that of Tolstoy's "Kholstomer: The Story of a Horse," where, *The Formal Method* argues, the story is narrated by a horse in order to bring forth "a moral value, which against this background stands out all the more sharply and vividly precisely as a moral value" (60). This, of course, is precisely what Shklovsky himself says of the morally destructive effects of automatization that erode love, the value of work, and the fear of war. *The Formal Method* seems to be absurdly intent on a reductive and distorted reading of Shklovsky's text, producing a straw man for the sake of the ideological polemic. We should note, however, that even in this critical context, the value of the device itself—making it strange—is not in question, only its alleged negativism and abstraction from semantic and social contexts. This implicit recognition of "making it strange" as the underlying imperative of art is far more interesting than the ideologically motivated condemnation of its "nihilistic" usage.

Shklovsky is also indicted by *The Formal Method* for his "psychological subjectivism," inasmuch as his concept of "deautomatization" presupposes "a perceiving, subjective consciousness" (149). The focus on perception, the "subjective condition of consciousness" rather than the "objective datum of the work" (149), is condemned for being indifferent to ideology, "empty of all content" (150), and exclusively related to the individual rather than to history, ideology, and "real" social intercourse (152). Needless to say, these charges can be easily countered if we read Shklovsky closely, because subjective "perception" is certainly not confined to inanimate objects or physiological sensations alone, but is always inclusive of the social sphere. Furthermore, doesn't Bakhtin himself set out from the data of subjective individual perception in "Author and Hero"? Couldn't he, too, have been easily targeted for having recourse to "psychological subjectivism"?

To conclude the case for the defense, let us turn to Shklovsky's manifesto "The Resurrection of the Word" (1914), as quoted by Medvedev, which reads like an uncanny echo of Yeats's elegiac lines: "The old has died and the new is not yet born," he writes, "and things have died—we have lost the sensation of things: we are like a violinist who no longer feels the bow and strings; we have ceased being artists of everyday life; we do not like our houses and our clothes and we part easily with a life that is not perceptible to us. Only the creation of new forms can return the perceptibility of the world to man, can resurrect things and kill pessimism" (*The Formal Method*, 179n3). Here, then, is Shklovsky himself sounding the note of metaphysical exile. The "disenchantment of the world," the conclusion of its secularization that has hollowed it out of wonder, can only be reversed through the power of the poetic/literary.[9]

I would suggest that Shklovsky, too, is a member of the exilic constellation discussed at length in Part Two of this study. *Ostranenie*, the term he coined for the defining principle of art, suggests, Svetlana Boym astutely observes, "both distancing (dislocating, *depaysement*) and making strange. *Stran* is the root of the Russian word for country, *strana*, and the word for strange, *strannnyi*: the Latin and Slavic roots are superimposed upon one another, creating a wealth of poetic associations and false etymologies. It is not by chance that Shklovsky refers to Aristotle's observation that poetic language is always to some degree a foreign language. Foreignness here is of a poetic and productive kind, enticing, rather than alienating" (Boym, "Poetics and Politics of Estrangement," 586).

We may now be in a better position to see the profound relevance of the principle of "estrangement" for Bakhtin's conception of subjectivity and to his search for the missing link relating the moral code to the ethical act.[10] A good point of departure for establishing this link is an essay by Michael Holquist and Ilya Kliger, "Minding the Gap" (2005), which offers a "historical poetics of estrangement" beginning with Kant. The essay, which is mostly concerned with Wilhelm von Humboldt's linguistic translation of the Kantian split, concludes with brief comments on four Russian thinkers—including Shklovsky and Bakhtin—who followed von Humboldt's conception of language in their own work. Bakhtin's figure for his "vision of deeper estrangement" is the Dostoyevskian hero: "Not only is reality mediated through transcendental structures of our (authorial) consciousness, not only does it have to pass through the veil of language, but that veil itself is interwoven with an irreducible otherness, with heroes who persist in their refusal to be finalized. Under such conditions, synthesis is rendered highly problematic, and we are indeed reminded that unity, either of object or of subject, is no more than an image, a metaphor" ("Minding the Gap," 634). But while this is undoubtedly valid, it seems to me that it can be taken a step further. The fact that reality is mediated through structures of consciousness and through language, which itself is fraught with "otherness," does not equate with a conception of subjectivity that would either quench or obliterate the inborn, "centripetal" desire for coherence. If estrangement is "a view of life grounded in a division," and if the split within the individual subject is, as Holquist and Kliger engagingly write, "between some version of a core self and . . . something else" (614), it is precisely the ellipsis in this phrase that needs to be further explored.

Bakhtin's conception of the ethical subject is also premised on the encounter with "something else," with the alterity, not only of another person, but that inheres in the very concept of the subject. Intersubjectivity and intrasubjectivity are difficult to tell apart, because the human subject is an entity that lives on its own borderlines. In the fragmentary notes "Toward a Reworking of the Dostoevsky Book," there is an oblique reference to non-self-sufficiency. Self-consciousness, Bakhtin writes, is

> not that which takes place *within*, but that which takes place on the *boundary* between one's own and someone else's consciousness, on the *threshold*. And everything internal gravitates not toward itself but is turned to the outside and dialogized, every internal experience ends up *on the boundary*, encounters another, and in this tension-filled encounter lies its entire essence. (TRDB, 287)

To recapitulate briefly, Bakhtin insists on an essential asymmetry between the perceptual experience of "I-for-myself" and "I-for-the-other": the human subject's sense of itself is always confined to a partial "inside" perspective, which can only be transcended through an external vantage point, the view through the eyes of an authorial "other." Human subjectivity, in Bakhtin's view, emerges architectonically in and through the tensile relations of the centripetal and the centrifugal forces, "two movements" that are both oppositional and complementary. While the "centripetal" force allows the subject to see itself a coherent whole, positioned and integrated within a social, cultural, and ideological context, the "centrifugal" force is what turns the subject into an agent, free to make its own choices, transcend its own boundary lines, project itself ahead of its authored "self." The ethical subject is never adequate to itself: it is "in principle nonunitary" (AH, 83); "present to itself [only] as a task"; "incapable of being given, of being present-on-hand, of being contemplated" (100). The ethical mode of being offers a loophole out of all and any narrative rhythms and configurations of selfhood: "The *subiectum* of lived life and the *subiectum* of aesthetic activity which gives form to that life are in principle incapable of coinciding with one another" (86). The ethical moment is the moment when

> that which *is* in me must overcome itself for the sake of that which *ought to be*; where being and obligation meet in conflict with me; where *is* and *ought* mutually exclude each other. It is a moment of fundamental and essential dissonance, inasmuch as what-is and what-ought-to-be, what-is-given and what-is-imposed-as-a-task, are incapable of being rhythmically bound *within me myself* from within myself, i.e. they are incapable of being perceived on one and the same plane. (118)

Significantly, the structuring metaphor for the ethical moment is that of the loophole, a breach, an act of contraband transgressing given frames and borderlines. The "rhythm" of a life that can only be enabled in a state of aesthetic or religious naïveté, and is perceived only retrospectively from a position of transgredience, becomes "a distortion and a lie" when "I from within myself, participate in the unitary and unique event of being" (118). Against the gift of aesthetic wholeness, that integral rhythm of life, which is granted by the author-other, Bakhtin positions the ethical subject who must reach out through the loopholes, be free, undetermined, and unframed in order to act:

> I myself as *subiectum* never coincide with me myself: I—the *subiectum* of the act of self-consciousness—exceed the bounds of this act's content. . . . a loophole out of time, out of everything given, everything finitely present on hand. I do not, evidently, experience the *whole* of myself in time. (109; see also 119)

Bakhtin's juxtaposition of "rhythm" and "loophole" might well have been borrowed from or inspired by Shklovsky and given a more "prosaic" slant. But this is *not* to say that Bakhtin is a formalist: his entire work, we should remember, is founded on a rejection of the distinction between the literary and the nonliterary that lies at the core of the formalist endeavor, and I shall have more to say about this in Part Two of this book. To continue the present discussion, however, we should note that when Medvedev condemns Shklovsky's apparent disparagement of the "prosaic" and valorization of the poetic, he quotes the latter's distinction between "prosaic" and "poetic": the former is the regulating rhythm of work, which is "an automatizing factor"; the latter is "prosaic rhythm disrupted." It is "a disruption which cannot be predicted" and hence cannot be systematized or fully theorized (cited in *FM*, 90). But the "poetic," for Shklovsky, is obviously not a particular genre but a synonym for literature at large, whereas the "prosaic" is that form of discourse that is sedimented, smoothed out with usage, transparent, and purely instrumental. Regardless of his or his associates' reservations about formalism, Bakhtin's juxtaposition of "rhythm" and "loophole" in the experience of subjectivity is applicable to the workings of literature as Shklovsky conceives it. It is, in fact, yet another version of "making-strange," of the dynamics of literature, which wrenches its utterances from habitual formations and gives birth to itself through the transgression of regularity and the sometimes-violent de-automatization of practical communication.[11] The ethical subject is not fully identical with itself; it is never at home in its own skin.

TEXT AND PSYCHE

As the title of this study indicates, the "question of the subject" is positioned *between* philosophy and literature. But this question, as it emerges from Bakhtin's work, cannot be contained in either of these disciplinary territories. Bearing in mind Bakhtin's choice of liminality as his default position, the need to move "on the borders . . . at [the] junctures and points of intersection" of established disciplines that relate to the human sciences (PT, 103), I would suggest that the forgotten path from philosophy to literature goes through the work of psychoanalysis. From the foundational work of Freud, who explicitly attributed his insights to the work done by poets, playwrights, and writers of fiction many centuries before his time, but who was at the same time locked in an Oedipal struggle for mastery with the arts, the discipline of psychoanalysis has never, throughout its various permutations, disowned or severed its ties with literature. And it may well be this (often ambivalent) familial relation that has discredited psychoanalysis, at least in some circles, and relegated it to the slightly suspicious margins of academic psychology—a discipline that seeks to establish itself as rigorously on the side of science. This is, of course, yet another offshoot of the Cartesian divide. Psychoanalysis, more at home in departments of literature than in psychology, offers an approach to intrasubjectivity that cannot be empirically tested, measured, and quantified. Like other disciplines included by Bakhtin under the heading of the human sciences, its approach to the human psyche is primarily textual. I would suggest, therefore, that the underlying coherence of Bakhtin's engagement with the question of the subject may become more clearly visible if we extrapolate from his "architectonics" to his "poetics" of subjectivity by way of the less-traveled road of psychoanalysis.

Bakhtin's own professed hostility to what he called "psychologism" has probably had a great deal to do with the fact that, with few notable exceptions, the subject of his relation to or interaction with psychoanalysis has been relatively underexplored. The remarkable discussions addressing Bakhtin's relevance to psychology have mostly suggested that his intersubjective focus takes him closer to the theoretical formulations of L. S. Vygotsky or G. H. Mead than to Freud, or dealt with Bakhtin's dismissal of the unconscious, which is the very foundation of Freud's theory (see Emerson, "Outer Word and Inner Speech"; Pirog; Shotter; Shotter and Billig). While these are undoubtedly valid grounds of opposition, it would be relatively easy to refute them by claiming that Freudian theory, being so thoroughly and explicitly culture-oriented, is in fact deeply concerned with intersubjectivity, and thus not as remote from the spirit of the Bakhtin circle as V. N. Voloshinov, for instance, would have it;[12] and that the Freudian unconscious may actually be quite comfortably incorporated within Bakhtin's concept of the multi-voicedness of discourse and read as yet another term for any of the diverse vocal strands that make up the fabric of the human psyche.

I would suggest that the roots of Bakhtin's reservations about "psychologism" (rather than about Freudian psychoanalysis) may be traced to what he sees as its apparent indifference to what he is mostly concerned with, namely, the question of "how to be." In his discussion of the different perspectives that constitute the experience of selfhood, Bakhtin mounts a three-pronged critique. The first line of opposition, which was dealt with in the previous chapter, is the objection to the epistemological and philosophical premises of the Cartesian conception of an abstract, generalized, and disembodied subject that is entirely coherent, knowable, and identical to itself. The second line, more relevant to "psychologism," relates to what is perceived as a deterministic stance, the postulate of "psychological laws" governing the human psyche. And the third line, most significant here, is closely related to the former objections, but targets "psychology" directly, based on the claim that it studies the experience of selfhood without any reference to ethics:

> *What-is-mine* [i.e., the I-for-myself perspective] in the experiencing of an object is studied by psychology . . . in complete abstraction from the axiological weight of the *I* and the *other*—in abstraction from their uniqueness; psychology knows only a "hypothetical individuality". . . . The inward given is not something contemplated, but something investigated, without any value judgment, within the prescribed (to be attained) unity of a psychological regularity. (AH, 114)[13]

Clearly, then, what troubles Bakhtin here is what he reads as a complete lack of concern on the part of psychology with questions of ethics and value judgments. This charge is much harder to refute than either Freud's concept of the unconscious or his alleged exclusion of the social domain. Indeed, there does seem to be an odd non-relationship between the psychoanalytic and the ethical modes of inquiry into human subjectivity. The Freudian philogenetic and ontogenetic account of the process of socialization is implicitly based on a view of ethics as equated with submission to a moral code and relates to the pre-social subject as though it were ontologically and chronologically prior to the social subject. In Freud's metapsychological essays (*Civilization and Its Discontents, Totem and Taboo, Moses and Monotheism*), the individual's acquiescence to the social-moral code is conceived of as a necessary outcome of the need to survive within the group through the sublimation and suppression of instinctual, primary drives and atavistic desires, which are, by definition, asocial. This necessary adjustment, which follows the Oedipal phase, entails a sacrifice, often conceived of as a symbolic form of castration. Mental health, according to the Freudian narrative, is tantamount to an equilibrium between the opposing forces of the instinctual and the social, between desire and law. On this account, ethics is equated with a set of social norms and prohibitions that, rather than being fundamental to human subjectivity, form a secondary—though powerful—superstructure.[14]

For Bakhtin (and, as I shall show later, for thinkers such as Merleau-Ponty and Lévinas), the ethical and the social are not secondary formations, inasmuch as intersubjectivity precedes and constitutes subjectivity. Much has been written of Voloshinov's and Bakhtin's conceptions of the psyche as inner discourse, made up of many diverse voices, and Bakhtin's focus on the novel, which allows for a representation of this multi-voicedness and dialogicity, is almost self-evident (Morson and Emerson, *Mikhail Bakhtin: Creation of a Prosaics*, 192–220). As cogently argued by Gerald Pirog (1987; 1989), for instance, the equation of the psyche with "inner speech" means that intersubjectivity precedes and constitutes subjectivity itself; that the social is not a mere supplement to the individual; and that our very individuality emerges from the commonality of discourse. I would argue, however, that the conception of the psyche as an ongoing conversation, however sound, is not nearly sufficient to do full justice to the significance of Bakhtin's potential contribution to the study of subjectivity.

Closely related to this issue is the question of assumed knowledge that characterizes the traditional relations between analyst and analysand. In one of the passages that appeared in the 1929 edition of *Problems of Dostoevsky's Poetics*, but were omitted from the 1963 edition, Bakhtin writes:

> From the first to the final pages of his artistic work [Dostoyevsky] was guided by the principle: never use for objectifying or finalizing another's consciousness anything that might be inaccessible to that consciousness, that might lie outside its field of vision. . . . In Dostoevsky's works there is literally not a single significant word about a character that the character could not have said about himself (from the standpoint of content, not tone). Dostoevsky is no psychologist. (*PDP*, Appendix I, 278)

This goes back, of course, to Dostoyevsky's own apparently paradoxical disclaimer, quoted on the preceding page: "I am called a psychologist: that is not true, I am only a realist in the higher sense, that is, I portray all the depths of the human soul" (277; see also 60). Indeed, recent developments in psychotherapy that have focused on the relations between the analyst and the analysand tend toward a relational rather an omniscient approach, or—in Bakhtinian terms—are far closer to the Dostoyevskian abdication of the authorial "surplus of knowledge" as described by Bakhtin. Be that as it may, it is important to note that Bakhtin's suspicion of psychology stems from his profoundly ethical objection to the finalizing all-knowing gaze of the other—author, psychologist, or disembodied authority. Dostoyevsky, on this account, is certainly a better psychologist (*pace* his own disclaimer) precisely because he does not put himself in an all-knowing position.

As we have already seen, Bakhtin does not subscribe to the equation of ethics with a moral or social code (hence his opposition to Kantian formal ethics); for him, the question of ethics concerns not the code, but the particular act, or "signature" of a concrete and singular individual at the moment of ethical choice (*TPA*, 38). And while the authorial other of Bakhtin's "centripetal mode" may well be abstracted—as it is in both Freud and Lacan—into a set of cultural norms, the ethical subject in Bakhtin's work is related *not* to the centripetal, but to the *centrifugal*, I-for-myself mode of being, which allows the human subject a loophole out of the framing gaze of the authorial other, out of the rhythm of codes and conventions. The centripetal may delineate the territory of social existence, but the centrifugal—the only position that allows individual agency and responsibility—is what makes it possible to navigate freely as an ethical being within this territory. It may be argued, then, that Bakhtin's architectonic formulation reverses the paradigm of desire versus the law: the ethical is not equated with acquiescence to the containing framework of social/cultural and ideological authority, but—on the contrary—it is that which refuses to be contained, authored, and enframed.[15]

Paradoxically, then, Bakhtin's architectonic conception of ethical subjectivity, which entails a critique of the premises of psychoanalysis, takes us very close to the turf of post-Freudian psychotherapy. The first case in point is the work of Wilfred Bion, whose conceptual categories of the "container" and the "contained" lend themselves to a distinctly Bakhtinian translation.[16] Following his and Melanie Klein's work with psychotic and borderline psychotic patients, Bion writes of two opposed but interdependent emotional states within the human psyche: integration/containment, on the one hand, and fragmentation and splitting, on the other. Taken to their psychotic extremes—these states are analogous to the depressive (D) and to the paranoid-schizoid (PS) positions respectively. The former is characterized by excessive integration or "containment," and the latter by disintegration and fragmentation. If the D pole takes over, the self is subjected to emotional suffocation inside its container, which ultimately assimilates and annihilates it. If the PS pole takes over, the self disintegrates into chaos and psychosis. It "goes to pieces."

The container-contained paradigm has been further extended by Bion to a description of the human psyche as having two essential and complementary functions, which strive for a state of equilibrium.[17] The first function, related to a state of containment, secures the sense of a stable and consistent identity and is tagged the "continuous" aspect of personality; the second function is that which allows for change, for nonidentity with oneself, and is tagged the "emergent" aspect of personality.[18] This is a delicate balance, and a disruption of the equilibrium on either side is "catastrophic," as Bion describes it: if the continuous self takes over, the patients remain paralyzed, "unable to accommodate any change and growth for fear that their world would be shattered and their continuous self annihilated." The result of this rigid containment is a state of emotional suffocation.[19] The very same psychic mechanism that ensures a sense of stability and self-consistency may turn into a paralytic enclosure if it does not allow the emergence of any new and different aspects of selfhood. It is not difficult to relate this "malignant containment," as Ronald Britton calls it (112), to a potentially destructive authoring by the other as articulated in Bakhtin's work.

Conversely, if the "emergent" self takes over, unchecked and uncontained by any sense of continuous identity, the psychic result is equally catastrophic, and leads to a sense of fragmentation and emotional disintegration, when the patient loses the sense of a stable identity (Britton, 111–12). This is how one gets to the schizoid psychotic state. For a similar process in Bakhtin's work, we should look no further than the carnivalesque, where the body exceeds its own boundary lines and is extended, distended, and fragmented beyond any possibility of a consistent selfhood or subjective interiority. The absence of a psychic container is just as disabling as total containment: the former may lead to psychosis; the latter may lead to depression.[20]

Getting back to Bakhtin: the "continuous" and the "emergent" modes of self-experience are respectively evident in "Author and Hero," where the subject is aestheticized, "consummated," enframed, and totalized by the authorial other (the kind of containing bear hug that may lead to the depressive state as described by Bion), and in *Rabelais and His World*, where borderlines are transgressed to the point of obliteration, to the point where subjectivity disintegrates and approaches the schizoid pole. The point of equilibrium between these poles is to be found in Bakhtin's work on discourse in general and on literary discourse in particular. The "continuous" aspect of language is the structural system of laws that Saussure called *langue*, shared by the speakers of a language or by a cultural community, which enables it to function as a signifying system. As we know, however, the phenomenon of language is not confined to regularities of syntax, grammar, and denotation; it also allows for the articulation of an infinite number of wholly new utterances.

Taking this fundamental capacity of language to exceed itself, one might argue for the existence of two complementary modes of discourse: a "continuous" mode where communication becomes transparent in and through routine-formulations, instrumental conversation, formulaic interaction, and habituation; and an "emergent" mode of discourse, which allows for entirely new articulations. The utterances of individual speakers are often far more than mere instantiations (performance) of their linguistic competence: new utterances and idiosyncratic modes of expression are not a rarity, but an integral part of the reality of discourse. From the very regularities of language and its stock of grammar, syntax, and vocabulary, every child can produce an utterance that has never been heard before. This is the "emergent" aspect of discourse. Noam Chomsky's memorable example "colorless green ideas sleep furiously," intended to make the very opposite point, has always struck me as a good case of the creative (in a non-Chomskean sense)—or should it be "poetic"?—capacity that exceeds any notion of mere performance. This is how literature is made.

What becomes clear when we triangulate Bakhtin, Shklovsky, and Bion is that the continuous and the emergent modes of being—*I for the other* and *I for myself*; the rhythm and the loophole—are interdependent; that they cannot be synthesized and yet are simultaneous; that a takeover by either of them would be dearly bought. What is true of the development and sustenance of the healthy human psyche is also true of the subject of ethics. Human subjectivity requires a sense of its own continuity, its identity with itself over time, its internal coherence, and the plot-bearing rhythm of its life. But to be able to make free choices, which is, after all, what ethics is about, it should be able to free itself from that familiar rhythm, to emerge through a loophole and become a stranger to itself.

Another convergence of Bakhtin's architectonics with post-Freudian theory is offered by Winnicott's constructs of "true" and "false" selves, astutely highlighted and discussed by Beatriz Priel. Pointing to the interaction of interpersonal and intrapsychic dialogue, Priel suggests that Winnicott offers a "paradigmatic dialogical structure" (492) that informs the relation between mother and child and the subsequent psychic development of the child: "Winnicott's psychoanalytic point of view assumes an otherness in the self," she writes, and "both his concept of early maternal responsiveness to the infant's gesture and Bakhtin's assumptions about the basic modalities of children's appropriation of the mother's word indicate that dialogic processes are boundary processes that take place between voices" (493). Taking the idea of the self as a narrative construction (following Donald Spence, David Stern, Roy Schafer, Arnold Modell, and Stephen Mitchell), Priel offers a translation of Winnicott's paradigm into "a question of genre," modeled on the Bakhtinian juxtaposition of epic and novel. The monologic epic paradigm where "past time prevails as absolute, finished, complete" is premised on "one single point of view from which a coherent and monologic account evolves." "Novelness" conversely offers "a maximal contact with the open-endedness and inconclusiveness of the present"; it is a relativistic worldview marked by incompleteness, and the hero "always has unrealized potentials and unrealized demands" (495–96). Winnicott's false-self processes conform to the former in that they are monological, unitary, and relatively static; true-self processes are novelistic in that they are "dialogical, multivocal, and open to change and creative meaning" (496).

While this analogy may sound a little too neat and begs the question of whether these "selves" are indeed distinct enough to sustain this polarity, it is only the first step toward an investigation of the "generic transformation" that constitutes the psychotherapeutic process. Form and substance, as we have noted, are closely interwoven, and the intersection of literary and psychoanalytic thought is relevant to their modes of inquiry and discourse as well. The psychoanalytic process proceeds through free association "intended to subvert narrative laws, thus allowing for changes in genre to take place by means of the suspension of the basic narrative laws of coherence and continuity, free association allows incoherent or discontinuous hidden voices to be heard" (500). Although Priel does not relate this part of her work to Bakhtin's constructs, it is clearly relevant and analogous to the juxtaposition of "rhythm" and "loophole" discussed earlier. While the former offers a pattern of coherence and continuity, a mode of being that constitutes a sense of "selfhood," the latter allows the transgression that will enable the generic change and development of the subject. This is what Winnicott calls the "relaxation" of sense-making (or a "formlessness"), which makes it possible to step out of one's set boundary lines and explore a new territory of subjectivity. This is clearly a step beyond the true-self–false-self antinomy, as these two modes of being are clearly supplementary: "Paraphrasing Winnicott, it can be said that psychoanalytic change takes place in the intermediate area between narrativity and free association" (501–2), or—to get back to Bakhtin—between rhythm and loophole.

Perhaps the best case in point for Bakhtin's relevance to psychotherapy is that of Christopher Bollas, whose therapeutic work and theoretical formulations are, not unlike those of Freud himself, clearly enhanced and deepened by his keen receptivity to literature. Bollas writes of "the essential split between two subjective locations: the place of the initiating subject who reflects upon the self, and the position of the subject who is reflected upon, turned in a brief moment into the object of thought" (*Being a Character,* 13). These two modes of being are related to two interdependent modes of engagement: "immersive" (i.e., experiential and unconscious) and "reflective," synthesizing, objectifying function (14–15).[21] Put in Bakhtinian terms, I-for-myself and I-for-the-other. The importance of dream-work, according to Bollas, is in the simultaneous presence of both the "producer" and the "protagonist" modes of being. "When I enter the world of dreams I am deconstructed, as I am transformed from the one who holds the internal world in my mind to the one who is experientially inside the dramaturgy of the other. . . . To be in a dream is thus a continuous reminiscence of being inside the maternal world when one was partly a receptive figure within a comprehending environment" (14). Going back to Winnicott's idea that we all begin as "unintegrated, scattered islands of organized potentials," Bollas suggests that the dream is a return to "unintegration," to a "plenitude of selves." Waking up is a return to synthesis, a reintegration of these diverse selves into a reflective *I* (14–15). The oscillation between these two modes of engagement enables us to move freely in the "interplay between the movement of our idiom, driven by the force of our instincts, and the unconscious system of care provided by our mother and father" (17). Again, it is not difficult to relate this interplay of subjective dispersal and objectifying condensation to the Bakhtinian architectonics of subjectivity.

Significantly, "being a character," in Bollas's view, is tantamount to having a particular "idiom" of selfhood. Each of us, he says, is born with "a unique idiom of psychic organization that constitutes the core of our self" (51), and that, though subsequently modified by our relations with our parents, with the family, with the environment, remains "deeply known (profoundly us) yet unthought" (51). Similar to the Bakhtinian conception of character in terms of "voice," the discursive frame of reference is much more than a metaphor, as it is in and through language (including, as we shall shortly see, the language of the body) that the project of subjectivity comes into being. In response to the postmodernist view of the self as an illusion and the challenge to its phenomenological integrity, Bollas writes of the "lifting" of the self, the expression of the particular idiom of character that reveals our sensibility, that it is as though

> there is an other who is partly there and that other is the I. I have hundreds, thousands, by my death millions, of sequential self states arising from the dialectical meetings between my self and the object world, which release me to some conscious knowing of my life. Like my postmodernist cousins, however, I do not think of the self as phenomenologically unified. It cannot be, because in the first place, the true self is not an integrated phenomenon but only dynamic sets of idiomatic dispositions that come into being through problematic encounters with the object world. (29–30)

In a strikingly Bakhtinian idiom, Bollas expands on these encounters with objects or people that are evocations of the idiom of subjectivity:

> Any subject who receives the other's word and presence is open to evocations of self that cohere and then scatter in the disseminations ordered by the ego that processes the meanings of life. As such, any two egos know that to communicate with one another is to evoke each other, and in that moment, to be distorted by the laws of unconscious work. . . . To know the other and to be known is as much an act of unconscious evocation that parts the subjects and announces the solitude of the self as it is an act of intelligent comprehension in which one can put one's knowing of the self and the other into coherent thought and structure of language. (45)

What I find particularly moving and persuasive about Bollas's formulation is its fundamental emphasis on mental health rather than pathology, and its retention of subjective agency.[22] We are, he says, not only penetrated and inhabited by other people's voices: it is often these voices that allow us to release the particular idiom of our own subjectivity. To be a character is "to gain a history of internal objects, inner presences that are the trace of our encounters" through which the subjective idiom elaborates itself (59). And while some people are "spiritually impoverished" in that they are less capable of receiving those other presences, and others may be "spiritual imperialists, greedily moving through others, militantly affecting people in destructive ways" (Bakhtin's "authoritative word" comes to mind), there are also those—and Bollas does not shy away from the ethical and the spiritual implications of this—who can be "inhabited by the other" and "yet know the limit of any other to host us" (63). Bollas relates to the need for the idiom of subjectivity to articulate itself as an "aesthetic" need (65), an inborn creativity of spirit, and goes time and again to the testimonies of Wordsworth, Seamus Heaney, Czesław Miłosz, and Fernando Pessoa, to name just a few of the poets he enlists to support his theoretical constructs.

Considering these observations on the correlations between Bakhtin, Bion, Winnicott, and Bollas, we may be in a better position to understand why Bakhtin chose to articulate his conception of subjectivity through literature. In the architectonic paradigm offered in his work, the distinction between the social intersubjective and the psychic intrasubjective spheres loses much of its force, not only because the human psyche is constituted by inner speech, but because the two "architectonic" forces that operate in discourse in general are even more powerfully evident in literary discourse: the constituent regularity of communal language, and the built-in possibility of "making it strange." The creative principle of "estrangement" works in a way that is analogous to Bion's psychic dynamics of subjectivity and to Bakhtin's ethical architectonics. The "emergent self," as Bion calls it, or the subject of ethics who "does not coincide" with itself and is always "yet-to-be," as Bakhtin describes it, is that mode of self-experience that refuses containment in the sedimented language of habit and routine, which would always find a loophole out of the rhythm of codes and systems.[23] Bakhtin's philosophizing through literature is, then, not just an "Aesopean" strategy of survival under brutal state censorship, but a genuine choice of a medium that not only enables but actually incorporates the architectonics of subjectivity into its very dynamics. The

Bakhtinian subject is "poetic" through and through, in that it is thoroughly embedded in the infrastructure of commonality, the narrative rhythm that underlies a sense of continuity and coherence, but will always transcend and exceed it through loopholes of its own making. It is the healthy subject that is ethically bound to recognize and affirm the irreducible strangeness within itself.

THE SHATTERED MIRROR OF MODERNITY

"God sees everything," repeated Wilson.

"That's an advertisement," Michaelis assured him.

F. Scott Fitzgerald, The Great Gatsby

STYLE, THE SAYING GOES, IS CHARACTER. Discourse is an inscription of one's subject position and context, and the metaphors we live by, to borrow George Lakoff and Mark Johnson's title, are both constituted by and constitutive of our very outlook and ideological stance. Style, then, is neither supplementary nor incidental, and texts, both literary and philosophical, are not neatly divisible into contents and form, depth and surface, theme and rhetoric. If Bakhtin's fine attunement to the dynamics of language at work, even when read in translation, can teach us anything, it is a teaching that emerges from the nontransparency of his own discourse.

As we have already seen, Bakhtin's smooth assimilation into the canon of Western postmodernism, following Kristeva's inaugural essays in the early 1970s, is hardly surprising, given his own apparent valorization of the "centrifugal" and its derivatives—polyphony, heteroglossia, the carnivalesque—terms and concepts that are all too easily translated into postmodernist catchphrases and buzzwords. Indeed, it is immensely tempting to relate to Bakhtin's own "small-scale Copernican revolution," as a shift from a modern to a postmodern sensibility. This temptation becomes overpowering if we conceive of the shift of structuring metaphors from the predominantly visual rhetoric of "Author and Hero" to the auditory underlying metaphors of *Prob-*

lems of Dostoevsky's Poetics as a paradigm shift that neatly overlaps with the much vaunted scopophobic tendencies of the age. So let us begin by following this well-trodden path as far as it can take us.

To recall the earlier discussion, for Bakhtin, the "aesthetic" is not confined to textual or artistic production; it is also a powerful psychic modality, an *I-for-the-other* mode of being, which enables the subject to see itself as a whole, contained and framed by the eyes of an internalized author. Underlying this relation is the need for a sense of one's own boundary lines, an inner representation of "form" that the subject cannot attain from within its own bodily perspective.

> Form must utilize a moment or constituent feature which is transgredient to the hero's consciousness (transgredient to his possible self-experience and concrete self-valuation) and yet is essentially related to him, determining him from outside *as a whole*: the moment of the hero's "advertedness" outward, his *boundaries*, and his boundaries moreover, as boundaries of the whole that he is. *Form is a boundary* that has been wrought aesthetically. (AH, 90)

The derivation of this equation, in keeping with the rest of this early essay, is entirely visual and predicated on the concept of the authorial gaze and on the equation of vision and knowledge. As already noted, the author is defined in this essay as "a principle of seeing," the sum total of "the transgredient moments of seeing that are actively referred to the hero and his world" (207, 208). The "aesthetically productive" relationship of author to hero is founded on the author's "outsideness," tantamount to an "excess of . . . seeing" (12–14) or—translated into standard critical terminology—*the omniscient viewpoint*, which enables him to frame the hero, to "consummate" and render him whole, to contain him within his context, against his background, between the moments of his birth and his death (134).

What Bakhtin offers in this essay, to recall my earlier argument, is an uninhibited and explicit thesis on the metaphysics of subjectivity in relation to aesthetics. It is the same relational structure that underlies the religious and the aesthetic configuration. The inability of the subject to see itself whole, its constitutional noncoincidence with itself leads to the "essential referredness to God," and the "trust in absolute otherness" (144). In fact, this referredness to God becomes the precondition for the aesthetic relationship, defined at the outset by trust in a higher and formative alterity. The metaphysical blueprint is unmistakable: the ultimate, most encompassing gaze is God's viewpoint, and "the divinity of the artist consists in his partaking of the supreme outsideness" of the Auctor Mundi (191).

No wonder, then, that an accelerated process of secularization—the "immanentization" and the "psychologization" of God, the loss of "faith in the essentialness and kindness of the power that gives form from outside" (203–4)—should lead to a "crisis of authorship" (203). When the postulate of "a firm and secure position outside" is shaken, the aesthetic relationship is no longer possible, "[and] all stable transgredient forms begin to disintegrate (first of all in prose—from Dostoevsky to [Andrei] Bely)" (203). The collapse of the metaphysical-aesthetic edifice entails the collapse of boundary and form.

It is thus entirely in keeping with the conceptual shift celebrated in *Problems of Dostoevsky's Poetics* that the scopic-visual structuring metaphor of "Author and Hero" should give way to an auditory-oral frame of reference based on the concepts of voice, polyphony, heteroglossia, and dialogicity. This fundamentally new rhetorical modality is generated by the conceptual and ideological message of the "Dostoyevskian" revolution. Given Dostoyevsky's abdication of the authorial-scopic prerogative of "transgredience," the characters in his work can no longer be contained or "consummated" within his benevolent authorial vision. The hero is no longer an "image"—objectified, finalized, fully framed by the author—but a "voice," an opposition that is taken by Bakhtin to great (perhaps exaggerated) lengths. In Tolstoy's work, Bakhtin contends, "the total finalizing meaning of the life and death of each character is revealed only in the author's field of vision, and thanks solely to the advantageous 'surplus' which that field enjoys over every character, that is, thanks to that which the character cannot himself see or understand. This is the finalizing, monologic function of the author's 'surplus' field of vision" (*PDP*, 70). In Dostoyevsky's work, however, the hero "is not an objectified image but an autonomous discourse, *pure voice*; we do not *see* him, we hear him" (53; second emphasis added). Rather than an image, character is discourse (see 63), and the voice of the hero is "constructed exactly like the voice of the author himself in a novel of the usual type. A character's word about himself and his world is just as fully weighted as the author's word usually is; it is not subordinated to the character's objectified image as merely one of his characteristics, nor does it serve as a mouthpiece for the author's voice" (7). Voice, then, is that which exceeds and boils over the framing image.

I have already suggested that what Bakhtin celebrates here is certainly not merely a stroke of individual literary genius: it has its roots in the historical context of secularization, with its gains and its losses, and should thus be read against a broader cultural background. Dostoyevsky's work no longer fits in with the conception of aesthetics as articulated in "Author and Hero"; his "small-scale Copernican revolution" (*PDP*, 49) ushers in a new cultural paradigm, which ranges far beyond the realm of aesthetics; and his abdication of authorial transgredience is concomitant with the collapse of the metaphysical outlook that underlies the aesthetic relationship. The revolt of the [Dostoyevskian] hero, his refusal to be "finalized" (or "consummated") by an authorial other is not only an artistic transition. It entails—as we have already seen—a deeper ethical meaning. Human agency cannot be posited without the potential of this revolt, the sense that the "ultimate word" is yet to be uttered.

Clearly, then, the Dostoyevskian revolution is Copernican in magnitude in that, rather than a mere shift of artistic paradigms, it is the inscription of a different conception of subjectivity, ethical rather than aesthetic, wherein the subject's ability to "live and act" is founded on the impossibility of "consummation" from without; on the fact that it is always yet-to-be; on the certainty that it can never coincide with itself (see *PDP*, 51). In place of the scopic-monologic paradigm of the author's transgredience, Dostoyevsky posits an auditory and polyphonic ethical paradigm in recognition of the mutually constitutive relations between human beings. The aestheticized subject who was the object of the other's transgredient vision now gives way to a more porous mode of being in the world, a subject that does not coincide with itself, or, rather, with its reified image. The author's work, no longer grounded in a surplus of vision, thus becomes "excruciatingly ethical" (AH, 205).

THE LURE OF THE MIRROR

The seductiveness of the itinerary I have just outlined and the overlap of the rhetorical and the conceptual transition from a visual to the auditory frame of reference are compounded by the neat conflation of this move with the modern-postmodern divide—an open invitation, as it were, to see this paradigm shift in Bakhtin's work as a moment of entry into the canon of postmodernity. It has become something of a cliché to identify the cultural phase known as modernity—beginning with the Cartesian Enlightenment and ending at the turn of the twentieth century—with an ocular regime, a privileging of a specular epistemology that dichotomizes subject-object relations, and a vision-centered interpretation of knowledge, truth, and reality. Indeed, the convergence of theoretical discussions on the topic of "visuality," the identification of "seeing" with the exercise of mastery and the reification or downright annihilation of "otherness," and the consensus regarding the "scopic regime" of modernity spilled over the disciplinary boundaries of aesthetics into the discourse of culture studies, postmodernist philosophy, and literary theory.[1] The "gaze," as Caryl Emerson wryly notes, has received bad press ("The Next Hundred Years," 15). Were we to follow this "ocularphobic" cultural periodization, it would have been possible, compelling indeed, to argue that Bakhtin, who has made the transition from the ocular to the auditory, from image to voice, and—by extension—from the aesthetic to the ethical relationship between author and hero, is a postmodernist *avant la lettre*.

But the seductions of analogy are often misleading, and this is particularly true of Bakhtin, whose entire work can be read as a rejection of such neat theoretical articulations. And so, having followed the temptation for a while, let us now pull back and examine the complications that interfere with this construction.[2] In the first place, we should bear in mind Bakhtin's distinctive tendency to synesthetic rhetoric. As noted by Caryl Emerson in her translator's preface to *Problems of Dostoevsky's Poetics*, Bakhtin is distinctly partial to "spatial markers and metaphors: situation, positioning, orientation [*ustanovka*], point of view, field of vision. How a voice sounds is a function of where it is and what it can 'see'; its orientation is measured by the field of responses it evokes" (xxxvi).[3] However, as I suggest in this and in the following chapter, we may just as rightly turn this astute observation around: Bakhtin does "visualize voice," or spatialize time, as Emerson notes, but he also—to no lesser degree—temporalizes space, and the truly radical nature of his work may lie precisely in the rejection of such neat categorical binaries.

More significantly, however, what complicates or even invalidates the assumption of a rhetorical-conceptual shift is the motif of the mirror, which comes up again and again throughout the various phases of Bakhtin's work, and always, invariably, with pejorative overtones. Nowhere is the need for "consummation" by an authorial other more powerfully evident than in the encounter with one's image in the mirror. As a quasi-prosthetic device that compensates for the inability of the subject to see itself whole, the mirror ostensibly offers an enabling condition for the subject to see its own reflection, its own boundary lines, as it were. Mirroring is the ultimate instance of the subject's being identical to itself. Given the scopic-metaphysical framework of "Author and Hero," it may therefore seem surprising that Bakhtin should relate to mirroring in this text with more than a touch of suspicion:

> We evaluate our exterior not for ourselves, but *for* others *through* others. . . . We almost invariably attitudinize a bit before a mirror, giving ourselves one expression or another that we deem to be essential or desirable. . . . I am not alone when I look at myself in the mirror: I am possessed by someone else's soul. (AH 33)

Far from self-identity, what the mirror offers is a form of estrangement from oneself, as the reflected image is only that "possible other who is with us when we look at ourselves in the mirror, when we dream of glory, when we make plans for our life; the possible other who has permeated our consciousness and who often guides our acts, our value judgments, and our vision of ourselves side by side with our own *I-for-myself*" (152). As we can see, even in this early "metaphysical treatise," where Bakhtin seems to fully endorse an "aestheticized" scopic and metaphysical conception of the subject, where being framed and contained under the authorial gaze of the other is conceived of as a state of "grace," the mirror-reflected self is presented by Bakhtin as an *alien, inauthentic version of subjectivity*.

The striking and by no means anecdotal similarity of Bakhtin's conception of mirroring and the Lacanian conception of the "stage of the mirror" has been noted and discussed by several readers.[4] Both thinkers relate to literal and figurative mirroring as a fulfillment of the need for a reflective consciousness, a need generated by the subject's constitutional inability to see itself whole. Bakhtin writes of the "dark chaos of my inner sensation of myself"; of the "boundless, 'darkly stirring chaos' of needs and dissatisfactions, wherein the future dyad of the child's personality and the outside world confronting it is still submerged and dissolved" (50); of the fact that "for self-consciousness, this integral image [of the self] is dispersed in life and enters the field of seeing the external world only in the form of fortuitous fragments" (35); and of the consequent dependence on the gaze of the other that enables the subject to subsume itself "as a constituent in the unitary pictorial-plastic external world" (35). The "outwardly finished personality" of the subject, he says, is the creation of the other (36).

Lacan, too, writes of the "insufficiency" of self-experience in his description of psychic development (suggestively calling the infant an *hommelette*—a little man, but also the shapeless, liquid mass of an egg). This fragmented, unbounded sense of selfhood accounts for the gratification of seeing oneself in a mirror (literal or figurative) for the first time. The mirror creates the "lure of spatial identification," a total image of the self, offering an illusory sense of wholeness, which serves as a palliative for the infant's sense of fragmentation and incoherence.[5] It is important to note that the mirror stage is not only a developmental phase to be subsequently outgrown, but also a structure of psychic operation, which remains operative in its various guises throughout the life of the subject (Lacan, "The Mirror Stage," 4).[6]

But the affinity of Bakhtin and Lacan ends at this point. For Lacan, the reflexive-dyadic relation between the infant and the mirroring other (who, more often than not, is the mother) belongs in the Imaginary order, and is disrupted by the entry of the name-of-the-Father, the Oedipal crisis, which coincides with the acquisition of language and the initiation into the Symbolic order. Speech, as conceived of by Lacan, is a never-ending and foredoomed attempt to fill the void left gaping at the core of subjectivity after the expulsion from the imaginary plenitude of the dyadic relation.[7] For Bakhtin, however, language is there from the very beginning: it enables both a mode of ideological interpellation, that is, the kind of mirroring that reflects the subject back to itself as a fabricated whole, and at least a potential mode of liberation, a "loophole" out of the "rhythm," out of the pattern imposed by internalized oppressive ideological structure or narrative frames by an authorial other within or without. If we needed any further caveat against the incorporation of Bakhtin into the postmodernist canon, we may find it in this divergence: taking the Lacanian endorsement of the "centrifugal" function of language as paradigmatic of postmodernist thought, it is important to note Bakhtin's sustained paradoxical stance in this context. Language may be both an instrument of ideological containment or interpellation and a means of escape from the lure of the mirror.

Bakhtin's hostility to mirrors and mirroring comes up again and again in the course of his later work as well. In the fragment titled "The Person at the Mirror" (probably written in 1943),[8] Bakhtin writes of

> Falsehood and lies, inevitably showing through in relations with one's own self. The external image of a thought, the feeling, the external image of the soul. I do not look from within outward on the world with my own eyes, but rather look at myself with the eyes of the world, with someone else's eyes; I am possessed by the other. Here there is no naive wholeness of external and internal. To spy on one's own second-hand image. The naivety of fusing oneself and the other in the mirror image. The other's surplus. I do not have a point of view on myself from without. I have no approach to my own inner image. Someone else's eyes gaze out of my eyes.[9]

Once more, rather than a reflection of one's being, self-mirroring appears to be connected with falseness and lies, with "possession" by a stranger, an other whose eyes take over the subject's vision of itself. This is, perhaps, the most notable symptom of the tug-of-war between the centrifugal and the centripetal, the profound ambivalence of Bakhtin's texts.

On closer reflection, however, Bakhtin's hostility to mirroring, even in the ostensibly "scopic" phase of his work, is less of a contradiction than it seems. If mirroring is the ultimate case where the subject appears to coincide with itself, this self-identity, Bakhtin insists, is no more than a construct, as a human being, by virtue of its being human, never truly coincides with itself. It is only in a state of naïveté, of complete trust in a benign, transgredient divine Providence, that one can identify and rejoice in one's image in the mirror. This naïveté, however, is no longer given to the citizens of the post-Nietzschean world, and has never perhaps quite genuinely been possessed since the "question of the subject" first came up.

REFRACTION

As we can see, what emerges from the issue of mirroring in Bakhtin's texts is a conceptual itinerary that does not quite fit in with the visual-to-auditory construction. There is, however, another rhetorical modality—"refraction"—which cuts across the categorical opposition of space and time, the eye and the ear. This third dimension, as it were, already appears in the early works, but is most forcefully operative in "Discourse in the Novel," where Bakhtin translates some of the concepts developed for Dostoyevsky's poetics into a general poetics of the novel. This essay, ostensibly concerned with literature, is in fact significantly related to what we have called the "poetics of subjectivity." Though derived from the rhetoric of space and vision, the concept of refraction that features so prominently in this essay does not indicate a return to the specular sensibility of "Author and Hero." It is, in fact, used interchangeably with the concept of "re-accentuation," a different title (now borrowed from the rhetoric of voice) for the novelistic process of semantic dispersion.[10]

"Refraction" or "re-accentuation" introduces the dynamics of motion into the all-too-solid category of space and breaks the ruthless linearity of time through the parameters of angle and perspective. Much like a living body, a ray of light, or a sound wave, the "word" or the "utterance" has to make its way through the resistance of the medium. The word enters, as it were, a

> complex play of light and shadow . . . becomes saturated with this play, and must determine within it the boundaries of its own semantic and stylistic contours. . . . If we imagine the *intention* of such a word, that is, its *directionality toward the object*, in the form of a ray of light, then the living and unrepeatable play of colors and light on the facets of the image that it constructs can be explained as the spectral dispersion of the ray-word . . . in an atmosphere filled with

alien words, value judgments and accents through which the ray passes on its way toward the object; the social atmosphere of the word, the atmosphere that surrounds the object, makes the facets of the image sparkle. (DN, 277)[11]

To take just a few additional samples of this ubiquitous theme:

> Certain aspects of language directly and unmediatedly express (as in poetry) the semantic and expressive intentions of the author, others refract these intentions; the writer of prose does not meld completely with any of these words, but rather accents each of them in a particular way—humorously, ironically, parodically and so forth. . . . Yet another group may stand even further from the author's ultimate semantic instantiation, still more thoroughly refracting his intentions; and there are, finally, those words that are completely denied any authorial intentions. (299)

> The intentions of the prose writer are *refracted*, and refracted *at different angles*, depending on the degree to which the refracted, heteroglot languages he deals with are socio-ideologically alien, already embodied and already objectivized. (300)

> What conditions this re-accentuation of images and languages in the novel? It is change in the background animating dialogue, that is, changes in the composition of heteroglossia. In an era when the dialogue of languages has experienced great change, the language of an image begins to sound in a different way, or is bathed in a different light, or is perceived against a different dialogizing background. (420)

There is more, much more of the same, and it is important to note that the medium through which authorial intentions and words are refracted is not consistently sociological, psychological, or cultural; the discourse of the author or a character may be refracted through that of another character, through public discourse, or through the particular discourse of the literary genre (324). It may be any and all of those media of human interaction, and is invariably multidirectional (see also 295, 311, 313, 315, 326, 419).

From "Discourse in the Novel," the concept of refraction is extrapolated to discourse in general, most notably in "The Problem of Speech

Genres," where Bakhtin describes the utterance as "what radiates its expression (rather, our expression) to the word we have selected, which is to say, invests the word with the expression of the whole" (PSG, 86). "Our speech, that is, all our utterances (including creative works), is filled with others' words, [in] varying degrees of otherness or varying degrees of 'our-own-ness,' varying degrees of awareness and detachment. These words of others carry with them their own expression, their own evaluative tone, which we assimilate, rework, and re-accentuate" (89). Utterances are never indifferent to each other: they invariably respond to or anticipate other utterances; they may echo, affirm, refute, parody, or supplement these other explicit or implicit utterances, and these relations range indefinitely from immediately preceding or following utterances in a given context to the most distant and apparently unrelated utterances. This re-accentuation is an auditory rendering of what Bakhtin calls refraction in a visual context.

The ubiquity of refraction and its derivatives in these essays turns them from rhetorical tropes into working concepts. The origins of this concept can be traced back to *Problems of Dostoevsky's Poetics*, where Bakhtin posits the "orientation of one person to another person's discourse and consciousness" as "the basic theme of all of Dostoevsky's works" (*PDP*, 207). Tellingly, the concept of refraction is used in this text to describe the *internal dynamics* of both discourse and consciousness: "The other's rejoinder wedges its way, as it were into [the character's] speech, and although this rejoinder is in fact absent, its influence brings about a radical accentual and syntactic restructuring of that speech" (208); the character's self-awareness is "penetrated by someone else's consciousness of him" and his "own self-utterance [is] injected with someone else's words about him" (209). Whether visual or auditory, "the utterly incompatible elements comprising Dostoevsky's material are . . . presented not within a single field of vision but within several fields of vision" (16), and ideas and themes are *"passed through several unmerged voices, sounding differently in each"* (265).

Writing of the "internal dialogization" of the monologues of Dostoyevsky's characters, whose utterances are filled, or rather "inundated" with other people's words (237–38); whose voices are "reciprocally permeable [and] . . . partially intersect one another" (239), Bakhtin insists that this dialogic quality of discourse is not bilateral: the discourse of the Underground Man, for instance, "is entirely a discourse-address. To speak, for him, means to address someone; to speak about himself means to address his own self with his own discourse; to speak about another person means to address that other person; to speak about the world means to address the world. But while speaking with himself, with another, with the world, he simultaneously addresses a third party as well: he squints his eyes to the side, toward the listener, the witness, the judge" (236–37). The character's discourse is not addressed to his interlocutor alone; it is refracted through the virtual medium of a potential third party.[12] We shall come back to this triangulation of dialogue via the figure of the "superaddressee" in the last chapter of this study.

Most significantly for the issue at hand, Bakhtin describes the confessional discourse of the Underground Man as not only "a word with a sideward glance," but "a word with a loophole" (232–33), denoting, in this context, "the retention for oneself of the possibility for altering the ultimate, final meaning of one's own words" (233): "The loophole makes the hero ambiguous and elusive even for himself. . . . The loophole profoundly distorts his attitude toward himself. The hero does not know whose opinion, whose statement is ultimately the final statement on him" (234). It is not only the discourse of the Underground Man that has a "sideward glance"; it is also his face, refracted in the mirror, which "has its sideward glance, its loophole":

> It is as if interference, voices interrupting one another, penetrate his entire body, depriving him of self-sufficiency and unambiguousness. The Underground man hates his own face, because in it he senses the power of another person over him, the power of that other's evaluations and opinions. He himself looks on his own face [in the mirror] with another's eyes, with the eyes of the other. And this alien glance interruptedly merges with his own glance and creates in him a peculiar hatred toward his own face. (235)[13]

Refraction and loophole are both means of escape from containment ("finalization") under the eyes of an authorial other, as the "word with a loophole" is always "only the penultimate word and places after itself only a conditional, not a final period" (233). Looking at his reflected image, either literally or metaphysically (through others' judgments), the Underground Man says "No" to the mirror.

This conjunction of tropes suggests that, rather than a straightforward shift from a phenomenology of the gaze to a phenomenology of the voice, what Bakhtin offers is a transition from a predominantly *reflective* to a *refractive* paradigm.[14] And this more-than-rhetorical swerve may suggest not only a subtler understanding of Bakhtin's cultural position, but also a much needed corrective to an all-too-neat cultural periodization of modernity and postmodernity. Modernity, the story goes, is founded on the Cartesian legacy of the "optics" of consciousness, the conflation of reflexivity and reflection, of the visual and the mental:

> Descartes's equation of the self-identity of human reason with sunlight is based on a tradition which brings together scholastic and neoplatonic sources. . . . Descartes's definition of intuition posits an identity between the light of reason and divine reason, since reason remains identical to itself regardless of the objects that it reflects . . . [this equation postulates] an absolute resemblance between human and divine reason, so that divine reason is no longer necessary to mediate the perfect transparency of intuition. (Judovitz, *Subjectivity and Representation*, 62–63)

On this account, the metaphoric vehicle of visual reflection is essential both to the conception of modernity—metaphysically founded on the enabling axioms of subjectivity, presence, and sameness—and to the conception of the subject as autonomous and identical to itself. If modernity is essentially, as Rodolphe Gasché writes in *The Tain of the Mirror*, "the attempt to domesticate Otherness" (101), reflexivity is not merely an optional trope for the metaphysics of subjectivity, but the very principle of its constitution, "the method and substance, the very origin of philosophy itself as a discourse of radical autonomy" (15). The Cartesian *cogito* embodies the "founding reflexive act," the "first epoch-making achievement of the concept of reflection (17):

> Through self-reflection, the self—the ego, the subject, is put on its own feet, set free from all unmediated relation to being. In giving priority to the human being's determination as a thinking being, self-reflection marks the human being's rise to the rank of a subject. It makes the human being a subjectivity that has its center in itself, a self-consciousness certain of itself. (13–14)

Deconstruction, as Gasché sees it, is an anti-reflexive philosophical stance, "a critique of the Cartesian dream of self-foundation" (176), and it is thus arguable that Bakhtin's work, evolving from a reflexive (metaphysical, Cartesian) to a refractive philosophical discourse, looks ahead to Derrida's heterological project, "philosophy's thinking of Otherness" (88), which challenges the "'pre-suppositions' of Western philosophy" (101).

Far from a blandly benign endorsement of pluralism, Bakhtin's work constitutes a radical philosophical move, entailing a new and uncomfortable conception of subjectivity and ethics. The discursive alterity that Bakhtin calls "refraction" or "re-accentuation" is not mere negativity or contradiction, and does not ultimately resolve itself into a homogeneous whole. It may be read as a proto-Derridean principle, resisting the specular logic of modernity, anticipating the operation of difference (both temporal deferral and spatial differentiation); the displacement of constitution by inscription; the recognition of an otherness that inhabits or contaminates any naïve thesis of pure presence; and the disruptive power of the trace, as the indelible mark of otherness within every utterance. For Derrida, too, "Subjectivity . . . is an effect of *différánce,* an effect inscribed in a system of *différánce*" (*Positions*, 29). The Derridean mode of writing, its resistance to totalizing containment, its citational play, its transgression of textual boundaries, and its uninhibited grafting of others' texts can be viewed as the next step in the same heterological process inaugurated in the work of Bakhtin, and, as we shall see in the second part of this study, in that of his fellow exiles.[15]

BAKHTIN AS A MODERNIST

I cannot rest my case at this point. As ever, the story is more complicated than that. The Cartesian project is the launching pad of modernity, not only in that it gave birth to the Enlightenment subject, but also as the beginning of the secularization process that concluded with Nietzsche's diagnosis of the death of God. These two processes are, of course, closely related: in a culture undergoing a process of secularization, the "question of the subject" can no longer be referred to an Augustinian divine Providence. As noted earlier, the secularizing impulse is embedded from the outset in the Cartesian project, which uses its metaphysical scaffolding only to kick it away when the *cogito* appears to be firmly in place. It is, therefore, no coincidence that the novel began its meteoric rise as a literary genre in parallel with this ideological decentering. In the essay "Epic and Novel," Bakhtin extends the Dostoyevskian spirit backward, as it were, celebrating the genre of the novel as a subversion of cultural hegemony and monolithic ideological systems. "The novel," he elsewhere writes, "begins by presuming a verbal and semantic decentering of the ideological world, a certain linguistic homelessness of literary consciousness, which no longer possesses a sacrosanct and unitary linguistic medium for containing ideological thought" (DN, 367). Note, however, that even in this celebratory passage, Bakhtin—much like the nostalgic early Lukács, who sees the novel as "the epic of a world that has been abandoned by God" (*The Theory of the Novel*, 88)—diagnoses the process of secularization as a kind of "homelessness," a term that, as we have seen, is highly symptomatic and must be taken on board if we are to understand the constitutive ambivalence in Bakhtin's work and do justice to his architectonics of subjectivity.[16]

That said, an important caveat should be introduced at this point regarding the all-too-common tendency to speak of modernity and modernism as one and the same. The modern era, inaugurated at the Cartesian moment, came to a point of crisis, heralded by Nietzsche's philosophical hammer, at the turn of the twentieth century, but the tsunami of postmodernism did not rise until the 1960s, following two world wars and the cataclysmic effect of the Holocaust. What happened in between? The first cultural diagnosis of and response to the crisis of modernity at the turn of the twentieth century was that of the modernists—writers, painters, composers—whose work during the first three decades of the century shows them to have been profoundly aware of the fact that modernity was a dead end. The underlying coherence of the modernist movement, its determined and self-conscious break with artistic traditions and its search for an idiom appropriate to its time, ranging across the entire spectrum of the arts, and manifesting itself in diverse, eclectic, and often contradictory ways, is rooted in its awareness of change rather than continuity. This is true of the visual arts, of music, of the theater, of literature in general, and of the novel in particular.

To highlight the relevance of the modernist revolution, consider for a moment the transitional position of Henry James, a great master straddling both centuries, not only chronologically, but also in terms of his cultural and artistic sensibilities. In his magnificent study *The Subject in Question*, David Carroll offers a view of James as deeply divided between his insistence on the privilege of the point of view of the authorial *I*, the "founding consciousness of the author," standing firm behind the window in the notional "house of fiction" (58), and his reluctant awareness of the alterity that creeps into this construct, the recognition that "an other seems to be speaking (writing) in the voice of every 'eye'" (62). Point-of-view, Carroll writes, is "the origin and center of form, the product of a unified consciousness," but it only works when "the subject is assumed to be a unified presence," a presence that serves as a guarantee for "the unity and integrity of form as a visible, spatial, or linguistic entity." According to Carroll, James does not resolve the question of the subject as the origin of point of view in fiction, or at least not in the way he intended, since the authorial subject is ultimately displaced, leaving "the 'house of fiction' without a unique proprietor behind each window" (66).

To take this a step further, literary modernism, as represented by Conrad, Proust, Woolf, Joyce, and Faulkner, to name just a few of its figureheads, is marked by its aesthetics of uncertainty, epistemological skepticism, a problematization of the authorial viewpoint, or—translated into the terms of the present discussion—a problematization of the specular relation between author and character, subject and object, language and reality. Their singularities notwithstanding, all of these authors focus on subjective inner perception rather than commonly shared knowledge (which has become suspect). Through various forms of experimentation with multi-perspectivism, extreme perceptual subjectivism (which sometimes, it is argued, borders on solipsism), temporal shifts, and narrative techniques like the "stream-of-consciousness," they attempt to inscribe the actual workings of the human psyche: permeable, heteronomous, and ineluctably messy.

Needless to say, Bakhtin does not consciously engage with the modernists, and, in fact, seems to be suspicious at times of what he sees as their search for newness for its own sake.[17] And yet, as noted by many in the 1980s, when Bakhtin featured so prominently in studies of literary texts, his celebration of the Dostoyevskian revolution revolves on the introduction of an artistic outlook that anticipates literary modernism in many ways: one may well cite the polyphonic quality, that *"plurality of independent and unmerged voices and consciousnesses"* (*PDP*, 6) to describe Joyce's narrative technique in *Ulysses* or Faulkner's in *The Sound and the Fury*; Dostoyevsky's "stubborn urge to see everything as coexisting, to perceive and show all things side by side and simultaneous, as if they existed in space and not in time" (28) may be just as aptly related to Woolf's technique in *Mrs Dalloway*; and his keen ear for multi-voicedness, his ability to hear "in every expression a crack" (30) is not unlike the Conradian predilection for multiple and often contradictory narrative positions in *Heart of Darkness* and *Lord Jim*. One could, of course, go on and on.

Perhaps the most salient aspect of the modernist novel is its resistance to "the sense of an ending" as Frank Kermode astutely dubbed it, a resistance to narrative closure that translates into a self-conscious preoccupation with narrative framing in general and is evidenced in the notorious open-endedness of modernist texts. This seems to go against the very grain of storytelling: reading involves a process of "retrospective patterning," to use Paul Ricœur's term, being a configurative act that operates from the end backward. The very definition of plot—the rudimentary concept of narrative—is inextricably bound up with a sequential segmentation of events, with beginnings, middles, and ends, with causes and their effects, with a retroactive sense of coherence. The abdication of narrative closure—a resolution that enables the retrospective patterning of the whole—is tantamount to an abdication of the first principle of storytelling and narrative significance. But this is precisely what the modernists have done. To paraphrase Ortega y Gasset, the theme of the modernist narrative seems to be the collapse of narrativity.

Of course, like most such neat critical formulations, this proposition needs to be qualified. As Bakhtin recognized, the novel has never really had an unproblematic relationship with social structure or language, and the tension between the inherent messiness of "real life" and the patterning of narrative is embedded in the genre from its earliest beginnings. But that granted, it is still arguable that the post-Nietzschean phase of modernity, from which modernism emerged, has given birth to a deeper and more troubled awareness of this tension. Whatever stance one takes on the relation between nineteenth-century fiction and the novels written during the first three decades of the twentieth century, it is hard to overlook the profound shift of orientation with regard to "the sense of an ending": the modernist novel has lost the teleological orientation of the previous century, and its forms of closure are never as neat or gratifying. In giving up the structuring power of endings and their promise of a retrospective coherence, it has lost, in a nutshell, the (fictional) "consolations of form, order and concord" (Kermode, *The Sense of an Ending*, 144).

The modernist abdication of the sense of an ending takes us to the issue of death, or rather its absence, in Dostoyevsky's work. In "Author and Hero," Bakhtin writes of death as a "terminal point" in life, which is not available to the experiencing subject (I-for-myself), and thus cannot have a "plot-determining significance" (AH, 105) from the perspective of the subject itself:

> My own life, within its own context, lacks any aesthetic weight with respect to plot or storylines . . . and its value and meaning are located on a completely different axiological plane. I am in myself the condition of possibility for my own life, but I am not its valuable hero. I am not capable of experiencing the emotionally consolidated time that encompasses me, just as I am not capable of experiencing the space that encompasses me. (106)

It is only within the temporal enclosure to be found between birth and death that the meaning and value of a life can be aesthetically formulated, and it is the end of the narrative that determines the "rhythm" or the "plot-determining significance" of the interim period. But it is only through the viewpoint of the authorial other, the perspective that encompasses the totality of the temporal, spatial, and axiological enclosure, that this consummation can be granted (59).[18] As we have already seen, the transgredient position of the omniscient human author-other, a position outside and above the hero-self, which allows for an excess of vision, is modeled on a quasi-theological conception of the position of God in relation to his creatures; the aesthetic relationship is a projection of the divine otherness of God, and the human act of authoring is a delegation of transcendental authority.

No wonder, then, that within the "aesthetic" paradigm, Dostoyevsky's work is perceived as symptomatic of a "crisis of authorship" and explicitly related to the process of secularization. If the development of the genre begins with a "certain linguistic homelessness of literary consciousness, which no longer possesses a sacrosanct and unitary linguistic medium for containing ideological thought" (DN, 367), Dostoyevsky's work marks the watershed wherein the process of secularization is apparently all but concluded.[19] Bakhtin reiterates this diagnosis in his fragmented notes for the revision of the Dostoyevsky book (TRDB) and later on in his notes from the 1960s and 1970s (N70–71, 150–51). The "crisis of authorship," which gave birth to the Dostoyevskian novel, is bound up with the crisis of divine authority, and the absence of death in Dostoyevsky's work is conceived of by Bakhtin as evidence of the full extent of the author's abdication of transgredience:

> What matters here is not simply that one cannot spy upon death from within, cannot see it, just as one cannot see the back of one's own head without resorting to a mirror. The back of one's head exists objectively and can be seen by others. But death from within, that is, one's own death consciously perceived, does not exist for anyone: not for the dying person, nor for others; it does not exist at all. Precisely this consciousness for its own sake, which neither knows nor has the ultimate word, is the object of depiction in Dostoevsky's world. That is why death-from-within cannot enter this world; such death is alien to its internal logic. . . . In Dostoevsky's world death finalizes nothing, because death does not affect the most important thing in this world—consciousness for its own sake. (TRDB, 290)

But Dostoyevsky's avoidance of death is not necessarily a cause for celebration. What we have here is, not the death-defying spirit of the carnivalesque, the Rabelaisian conjunction of death and rebirth, but an absence of closure that is as terrifying as it is liberating. To get a sense of that ambiguity, we should turn to a similar conjunction of the decline of narrative with the changing conception of literary death offered by Walter Benjamin (who is very close to Lukács at some points and often invokes him). It is impossible, Benjamin writes, to accomplish meaning unless it is framed by narrative, and the meaning of a life can be finally consolidated and transmitted only as a memory of that life. The traditional "wisdom" imparted by the storyteller can be gathered only from the full trajectory, which includes an ending, whether metaphoric or literal:

> not only a man's knowledge or wisdom, but above all his real life—and this is the stuff that stories are made of—first assumes transmissible form at the moment of his death. . . . [Death] . . . imparts to everything that concerned him that authority which even the poorest wretch in dying possesses for the living around him. This authority is at the very source of the story.
>
> Death is the sanction of everything that the storyteller can tell. He has borrowed his authority from death. (Benjamin, "The Storyteller," 94)
>
> the reader of a novel . . . [looks] for human beings from whom he derives the "meaning of life." . . .
>
> The novel is significant, therefore, not because it presents someone else's fate to us, perhaps didactically, but because this stranger's fate by virtue of the flame which consumes it yields us the warmth which we never draw from our own fate. What draws the reader to the novel is the hope of warming his shivering life with a death he reads about. (101)

Going back to Bakhtin, we can trace a similarly elegiac note even in his most enthusiastic celebration of Dostoyevsky's "new artistic model of the world, one in which many basic aspects of old artistic form were subjected to a radical restructuring" (*PDP*, 2nd ed., Preface, 3). The abdication of authorial transgredience, triggered by the withdrawal (or the "immanentization") of the Auctor Mundi, entails a loss of the promise of wholeness that can only be accomplished at the end of one's life story. It is a loss of blissful naïveté, as keenly felt by Bakhtin as it was by Benjamin:

> I must become naive in order to rejoice. From within myself, in my own self-activity, I cannot become naive, and, hence, I cannot rejoice. Only being, and not my self-activity, can be naive and joyful; my self-activity is inescapably and irresolvably serious. . . . Joy is

> possible for me only in God or in the world, that is only where I partake in being in a justified manner *through* the other and *for* the other, where I am passive and receive a bestowed gift. It is my otherness that rejoices in me not I for myself. Celebration, too, is possible only for the naive and passive force of being; jubilant celebration is always elemental; I can celebrate and jubilate in the world and in God but not within myself. I can only reflect the joy of the affirmed being of others. The spirit's smile is a *reflected* smile. (AH, 136–37; see also 145)

The specular tropes used in the last sentence speak for themselves. Mirroring, reflection, complete identity with oneself are not necessarily illusory or false in a state of metaphysical naïveté. The same elegiac note, as we have observed, sounds in Bakhtin's late notes, where he looks back to that lost "earthly paradise" from which Dostoyevsky's heroes were expelled, and the "privilege" of naïveté that was denied them (N70–71, 139). There is a deep sense of nostalgia here, but it is not nostalgia for the "good old days," which Bakhtin is too wise to hark back to; it is a metaphysical nostalgia for a master narrative and a master author, as old as the Cartesian desire for grounding. And it fully recognizes its own impossibility.

Subjectivity, as it evolves through Bakhtin's work, is neither a foundation nor a fixed locus of certainty; it is neither a singular focused viewpoint nor a reflected whole object either under the (consummating or finalizing) gaze of the authorial other or in the mirror of its own objectifying gaze. Rather than the cozy, narcissistic, dyadic conception of subjectivity as an image reflected in its own mirror, Bakhtin recognizes the "eventness" of being, the invasion of sameness by alterity, the refraction of the image in a resistant medium. Unlike the reflected image, the refracted subject is never quite securely grounded, as its contours—volatile, scintillating, fluid—emerge out of a process of interlocution. As we have seen, however, even in its "refractive mode," the nostalgic overtones of Bakhtin's work do not allow for an easy assimilation of it into the canon of postmodernisms. It is much closer, in fact, to the work of literary modernists, who were there long before Derrida (as he would have been the first to acknowledge), and whose writing practices laid the ground for his philosophical insights. With the shift from a reflective to a refractive conceptualization of subjectivity, Bakhtin resists this amnesia of the mirror, its repression of time, the illusion of sameness, and the dream of self-grounding, which are all symptoms of our metaphysical homesickness. The Bakhtinian subject who looks at himself in the shattered mirror of modernity can no longer hope for the consolations of metaphysics. It has no home to go back to.

PART TWO

THE EXILIC CONSTELLATION

INTRODUCTION

THE TASK OF PHILOSOPHY is to make civilization explicit to itself, Leszek Kołakowski says. Great philosophers, however, not only provide that sense of coherence, but also "create points of discontinuity, ... push the 'spirit of the age' into a new direction," and, drawing on both the unspoken and perhaps unconscious anxieties of their culture and their own personal resources, "create, or co-create or perhaps actuate new languages" (Kołakowski, *Metaphysical Horror*, 100, 107). There is no better description of what Bakhtin, Bergson, Lévinas, and Merleau-Ponty—the four philosophers grouped together here as the "exilic constellation"—were trying to do.

The historical context of Bakhtin's life and work—brutal ideological censorship, exile, poverty, and bodily illness—did not allow for any philosophical interactions with his contemporaries in the West. His own project was fed exclusively by whatever reading he had done in his youth (including the work of Bergson, directly or indirectly), or could still do in his places of exile, and by an ongoing conversation with his ever-diminishing "circle." The almost uncanny affinities between Bakhtin's project and those of his continental contemporaries should thus give us pause. Some of these commonalities can probably be accounted for by tracking down common antecedents and influences—neo-Kantian philosophy (most notably represented by Herman Cohen), the philosophical work of Franz Rosenzweig, Søren

Kierkegaard, Franz Brentano, Edmund Husserl, and (somewhat embarrassingly) Max Scheler and Ernst Cassirer, neither of them fully acknowledged but both undoubtedly represented in the work of Bakhtin and his circle.[1] Indeed, issues of philosophical genealogy have been explored and discussed by some of Bakhtin's most astute readers, and there is undoubtedly scope for more work to be done along these lines.[2]

Part Two of this study pursues a different, somewhat riskier approach. Rather than a *retrospective* reading concerned with questions of paternity and filiation, influence and indebtedness, it offers a *prospective or, rather, proleptic* mode of reading in an attempt to carry over the respective insights of these philosophers, probe the intersections of their itineraries, and spin both their convergences and divergences into a dialogic exchange. To judge by these thinkers' keen awareness of the need to extend and draw out the implicit potential of others' thought and of the generative energy of such dialogic encounters, we may be justified in thinking that they would have approved of this mode of reading.

The conceptual framework for this part of the work has borrowed and adapted, in a rather loose way, Adorno's concept of "constellations" (which he had similarly borrowed from Benjamin). What is offered by Adorno in this philosophical construct is an interpretative approach that respects the specificity and individuality of phenomena, but, by clustering them as constellations around certain nuclei, illuminates "their participation in a typicality that is hidden from the participants themselves" (Adorno, *Negative Dialectics*, 162). What is required of philosophical thinking, Adorno writes, is a "circling" of its constellated objects, which can only be opened up to interpretation through a combination of numbers rather than a single key (163). Significantly, Adorno explains his preference for this term by claiming that "constellations [may] take the place of systematics," enabling a "third possibility beyond the alternative of positivism and idealism" (166). When read as a constellation, it becomes clear that the affinities between Bakhtin, Bergson, Merleau-Ponty, and Lévinas go far beyond questions of influence or familiarity, or even the commonality of their philosophical antecedents. They emerge, I argue, from the acute sense of philosophical and spiritual distress that they shared, and a common quest for an alternative ethical paradigm at the point of a momentous cultural shift.

What I attempt here follows from Bakhtin's proposed methodology of the human sciences, and the kind of creative license he recommends in the drawing of "dotted lines" as a working principle for the reading of texts. Ideas, he says, get a new lease on life only by transgressing their own temporal and cultural contexts and coming into contact with other, even remote contexts. Only this contact, or friction, as the case may be, creates the conditions in which "a light will flash" (*PDP*, 91; TMHS, 161–62). The philosophical conversations staged in this part of the book are meant to create that generative contact, but the fact that the connecting lines are dotted or, indeed, broken at times, should serve as a caution against the temptation to smooth out their singularities in quest of sameness, against the reduction and conflation of the voices of Bakhtin, Bergson, Lévinas, and Merleau-Ponty into a single one.

A smooth translation of one voice into another would be a betrayal of what each of them stands for. Their grouping as a "constellation" precludes both the question of who got there first and the presumption of a monolithic collective project: alongside the echoes and commonalities within this group, the convergence of common concerns born out of temperamental similarities and similar philosophical positions, which lead at times to uncannily parallel conceptual itineraries and intersections, there are also various junctions in which the philosophical itineraries of its members diverge and part ways. These mutual interrogations are no less valuable for our purposes: what is staged in this attempt to read these philosophers with and "through" one another is an ongoing conversation, where such interventions are often helpful in breaking through dead ends and opening new routes.

What binds these four thinkers into a constellation is the exilic sensibility that marks them in more than one sense. Their common philosophical point of departure is a profound disenchantment with the Cartesian conception of the subject and with the mode of philosophizing it sanctions. This sense of disillusionment, or philosophical exile, marks the beginning of what is now broadly recognized as "continental" philosophy, the counter-philosophical tradition whose origins lie, as we have noted, in the route leading from Montaigne through and against the Cartesian tradition of modernity, via Pascal, Kierkegaard, and other dissenters. It came into its own at the turn of the twentieth century, heralded by Nietzsche's philosophical hammer and his diagnosis of the deaths of both God and grammar, and became a force to be reckoned with in the work of Rosenzweig, Bergson, Husserl, and their philosophical descendants. The most consistent feature in the many variations of this line of philosophizing is "a commitment to the questioning of foundations," a conception of meaning as produced by intersubjective and intertextual relations, a renunciation of metaphysical, absolute grounding (see Kearney, *Continental Philosophy*, 2). Impelled by this philosophical distress, the members of the exilic constellation are all working their way toward an alternative "first philosophy," a genuine engagement with concrete human experience and the dynamics of ethical choice. It is an ambitious, risky project, a challenge to both the substance and the method of received philosophy, and an attempt to "think the unthought."

One of the earliest manifestos of this project is Franz Rosenzweig's "The New Thinking" (1925), conceived of as a supplement to *The Star of Redemption* (1921), which announces itself as a "system of philosophy that does not just want to bring about a mere 'Copernican turn' of thinking, after which he who has carried it out sees all things turned around—yet still only the same thing that he has seen before. But, rather, thinking's complete renewal" (69). To replace the reductive philosophy of "essence" with its "is-sentences," onion-like in that they invariably yield more of the same, translating and reducing different concepts into each other, Rosenzweig offers what he calls "experiential philosophy" (75), an approach that would attain maturity in the phenomenological project of his continental followers.[3] As early as 1917, in the "'Germ Cell' of the Star of Redemption" (a letter written to Rudolf Ehrenberg on 18 November 1917), Rosenzweig insists on the irreducibility of subjectivity and its resistance to philosophical "digestion":

> After it has taken everything into itself and proclaimed its exclusive existence, the human being suddenly discovers that he, who has after all long been digested philosophically, is still there . . . as "I who am after all dust and ashes." I, the quite ordinary private subject, I first and last name, I dust and ashes, I am still there. And I philosophize, that is: I have the gall to philosophize the sovereign ruler Philosophy. . . . *Individuum ineffable triumphans.* ("Germ Cell," 48)

The human subject, on this account, is that which "even within the system, still rattles the system's cage-bars," both free and unique in that it cannot be totally "absorbed into a system of relationships" (52). This singularity, most clearly evidenced in that the individual subject, the only one who can say *I*, exceeds any and all intersystemic relationships (social, political, ideological) that would objectify the individual as a "third person" (53), that is, a generalized, abstracted being. As we shall see in this part of the study, the immensity of this challenge to all philosophical digestive systems generates a peculiarly liminal sensibility, which entails a questioning of traditional boundary lines and categorical distinctions. Significantly, Rosenzweig's *Understanding the Sick and the Healthy* begins with a mock "preface to the expert" (complemented by a sardonic epilogue addressed to this reader, who, apparently, stands in for all professional philosophers), with the following lines: "Here, Sir, standing on the threshold, I bid you goodbye. / Remaining *a limine* in everything, / Respectfully, / *Your Author*" (36). A second mock preface, much warmer than the first, is addressed to "the [lay] reader" and concludes with a greeting from "Your Author, who now, on the threshold, bids you a friendly welcome" (38). What we seem to have here is the inauguration of a "threshold philosophy," a refusal to recognize both inter- and intradisciplinary boundary lines. As we shall see, this liminal sensibility also entails a shift to a temporal rather than a spatial philosophical outlook; an awareness of the constitutive dynamics of discourse; and an engagement (conscious or unconscious) with art and with literature.

But whereas this sense of philosophical disenchantment and its concomitant liminal stance are the hallmark of continental philosophy as a whole, the exilic sensibility of this particular constellation is also embedded in another context: these thinkers, I suggest, are also metaphysically disinherited, torn between a recognition of the secularization of culture and their profound, incurable metaphysical homesickness. This spiritual sense of exile—a phrase that cannot be easily written at the time when spirit and mind are rigorously separated, and "spirit" sounds oddly anachronistic, if not downright obsolete—is much harder to pinpoint. Except for Lévinas, the most philosophically self-conscious member of the group, this aspect of exile is often not fully acknowledged by the exiles themselves. In the case of Bakhtin, who may have been more fully aware of his own homesickness than his fellow exiles, the issue is even more complex, given the very real impossibility of an open engagement with metaphysics in his time and place. But the evidence of his anguish at this impossibility is not to be taken lightly.

As I have suggested in Part One of the study, the persistence of metaphysical desire, the incurable homesickness of the exiles and their nostalgia for grounding, aligns them with the modernist rather than the postmodernist response to the crisis of modernity, and—as in the case of the modernists—their need for some point of metaphysical anchorage, paradoxically recognized as both illusory and indispensable, is most poignant when it comes to the questions of ethics. Their diverse emphases notwithstanding, all four thinkers move away from a Cartesian conception of subjectivity to a phenomenological conception of intersubjectivity as primal and foundational for ethics. Unable to lay their interrogation to rest within Kantian, formal, universal ethics, they are concerned with the individual act in all its specificity, historicity, and uniqueness, with the lived, concrete event of ethical choice and action. Rather than normative formal and abstract systems, propositions and universal laws, they aim to address the unique, the private, and the concrete. What they offer as a viable first philosophy is "a phenomenology" (*TPA*, 32) of ethical subjectivity; a description of "the actual, concrete architectonic of value-governed experiencing of the world" (61)—of the position or, rather, the deposition, of subjectivity in the encounter with the other.

THE DEAD END OF OMNISCIENCE

READING BAKHTIN WITH BERGSON

> Man contends with God for an eye.
>
> Edmund Jabès, *The Book of Questions: Yaël*

THE FIRST DOTTED LINES toward a plotting of the exilic constellation lead to the truly stellar figure of Bergson, aptly dubbed the "philosopher of change" (H. W. Carr, *Henri Bergson*, 14), both with regard to the substance of his thought and his conception of what philosophy should be. Ranging across several disciplines, his work offered a philosophical breakthrough when the received Cartesian tradition seemed to have come to a dead end: its placing of the concrete, experiential body as a center of perception and action; its emphasis on the interpenetration of perception and memory; and—most of all—its anti-deterministic insistence, had turned him into one of the most influential intellectuals at the threshold of the twentieth century, the recognized voice of the zeitgeist. By the early 1920s, Bergson's major works had been widely translated into other European languages, including Russian, and he was awarded the Nobel Prize for literature (a category conceived rather more broadly than today) in 1928. Formidable as these accomplishments are, perhaps the most significant indication of his stature and the extent of his influence among his contemporaries is the fact that in 1914 his works were put on the Roman Catholic Church's Index of Prohibited Books. Indeed, one must credit the censorial readers of the Holy See for the astuteness of their perception, for despite the fact that Bergson was not explicitly concerned with theological dogma, he was actually more truly and radically subversive than many of his more outspoken predecessors, and his philosophical legacy—though often downplayed or completely disregarded today—laid the foundations for the philosophical work of an entire generation, including Bakhtin and the members of his circle.[1]

Bergson's relevance for our exilic constellation stems from his call to "get back to the real and concrete self and give up its symbolical substitute" (*Time and Free Will*, 139). To claim that this amounts to a conflation of the subject of philosophy and that of psychology may well border on anachronism: at the time of the writing, the latter was still a budding offshoot of the former, and the boundary lines between these disciplines were porous and fluid, as evidenced by the deeply sympathetic correspondence between Bergson and William James. But we should note that the direction taken by Bergson was, in fact, an inversion of the disciplinary hierarchy, moving from psychology to philosophy, from the experiential, concrete, situated subject to the philosophical question of the subject. In contradistinction to the received notion (shared by some members of the Bakhtin circle, and perhaps also by Bakhtin himself) of psychology as an essentially deterministic endeavor, Bergson's psychological point of departure lends considerable support to his philosophical stance with regard to the inalienable freedom of subjectivity.

A deterministic, purely causal view, modeled on the workings of mechanical systems, would maintain that given the same conditions, the same phenomena would follow in organic and human beings. But, Bergson says, such an account of human behavior (or even of complex living organisms in general) cannot but fail: the irreducibly singular position of the subject at any point in time, the workings of memory, where the past is an ever-changing, ever-growing aggregate, makes it impossible to relate to any specific situation as identical with another, and hence unthinkable that ethical or any other choices and modes of behavior can be predicted or determined in advance. We cannot, as Heraclitus observed, step twice into the same river.

This foundational insight would serve as a template for Bergson's lifelong project, whose difficulties are built in, since the very tools of philosophical thinking, generalizations and abstractions, are premised on the validity of what he actually seeks to discredit. These tools, Bergson says, are inadequate for our conception of our selfhood, of "inner states as living things, constantly *becoming*, as states not amenable to measure, which permeate one another and of which the succession in duration has nothing in common with juxtaposition in homogeneous space" (*Time and Free Will*, 231). Can this "real self," accessible only by "deep introspection," be philosophically conceptualized? Can we speak or write about it in any intelligible manner with any degree of certainty? These difficulties are real enough, but they are not insurmountable, and much of the work done by Bakhtin, Merleau-Ponty, and Lévinas can be seen as a response to the Bergsonian rallying call.

"CONTEMPORARY VITALISM"

Apart from the direct and often-polemical references to Bergson in Bakhtin's *Towards a Philosophy of the Act*, the most obvious (though, I would argue, least significant) piece of evidence for the latter's engagement with him is the essay "Contemporary Vitalism," attributed to Bakhtin, which was published in 1926 under the name of the biologist I. I. Kanaev (see Clark and Holquist, *Mikhail Bakhtin*, 99–102, 171–85).[2] This attribution appears to be less problematic than in the case of the other disputed texts, due to several independent testimonials to Kanaev's own confirmation of Bakhtin's authorship.[3] But it is clear that even if Bakhtin was the author of the article, he would also have had to draw heavily on the work of biologists, with Kanaev as the most likely source, for the minute and technical details of the experiments described in this text, which is almost exclusively focused on the work of the German biologist and philosopher Hans Driesch (1867–1941) and makes only a passing reference to Bergson as another "vitalist."

The first point of relevance for our concern with subjectivity is the "biological thinking" that, as Holquist has persuasively argued on more than one occasion, permeates Bakhtin's work.[4] More specifically, as pointed out by Ben Taylor, some of the organizing metaphors and tropes deployed in this essay on vitalism suggest an analogy between organic and cultural processes, and the grotesque carnivalesque body, center-staged in Bakhtin's work on Rabelais—amorphous, protean, and incomplete—is endowed with the same capacity for transformation and self-regeneration that characterize a biological organism like the hydra ("Kanaev, Vitalism and the Bakhtin Circle," 165). The astuteness of this analogy speaks for itself, but one should bear in mind that this is only one vector in Bakhtin's architectonics of subjectivity: the grotesque body has no interiority, and the celebration of its constant state of becoming and flux must be counterbalanced by a centripetal vector of inner cohesion and continuity.

Still more relevant to the present discussion is the quarrel of this essay with the implicit determinism of Driesch, who aims to offer an alternative to the naïve physical-mechanistic approach to biological process, but whose account still entails a deterministic conceptualization of self-regulation. Driesch, the essay claims, saw life as "characterized by autonomy, that is . . . governed by laws of its own . . . systematic, consistent and harmonious" (83). Unlike inorganic matter, machines, and mechanisms, the living organism, the hydra in this case, "can repair and restore itself on its own, in accordance with the amazing exactness of its complex constitutional plan" (83). Herein lies the bone of contention, as the very concept of a "constitutional plan" (the Aristotelian "entelechy" or unfolding of essence) entails a form of determinism, which does not allow for any degree of alternative potential development. Driesch's tautological reasoning is rejected in the essay as "a typical metaphysical argument, which crowns itself accordingly outside of time and space with the concept of entelechy," conceiving the outcome as "completely predetermined and pre-defined by the prospective potentials" (96).

Here is precisely the point where one would have expected Bergson to be invoked by the author, for in spite of the common identification of the Bergsonian concept of "élan vital" as one of the sources of contemporary vitalistic thought and the casual association of his name with the biological approach tagged by this term, nothing would have been further from his approach to life, evolution, or subjectivity than the kind of deterministic and tautological reasoning that the essay diagnoses in Driesch's work. In fact, Bergson's entire oeuvre was devoted to the opposition of any kind of determinism, causal or teleological, and the theses of *Creative Evolution* are entirely compatible with the critical commentary of "Contemporary Vitalism": the evolution of life, Bergson writes, is "something other than [either] a series of adaptations to accidental circumstances" or "the realization of a plan." It is "a creation unceasingly renewed" and "its future overflows its present" (*Creative Evolution*, 103). Oddly, though, Bergson does not make a grand entry at this point, and the Bergsonian reference remains tenuous and remote.

THE DEAD END OF OMNISCIENCE

Bakhtin, in any case, is more concerned with ethics than with biology, and his relationship with Bergson, whether direct or mediated, revolves first and foremost around questions of ethical subjectivity and free will, the same concerns that underlie not only Bergson's *Time and Free Will*, but the entire spectrum of his subsequent work on time, evolution, and culture. Bergson's point of departure, as succinctly put by Kołakowski, is the opposition to the Cartesian-Kantian abstract, spatialized, and homogenized conception of time as "a set of homogeneous segments placed next to each other and together composing an indefinitely long line." Against this conception he posits the notion of *durée*, neither homogeneous nor divisible, which cannot be abstracted from movement, but is, to use Kołakowski's formulation, "what each of us is: we know it intuitively, from direct experience." If Bergson's philosophy could be summed up in a single idea, Kołakowski argues, it would be formulated as "time is real." Bergson's position is profoundly anti-deterministic, founded as it is on the view "that the future does not exist in any sense" and that "the life of the universe is a creative process, whereby something new and thus unpredictable appears at every moment" (Kołakowski, *Bergson*, 2–3).

What is at stake in this alternative conception of time is a response to an ancient and persistent dilemma, which I would call the "dead end of omniscience." It is, at source, a fundamentally theological conception, an axiom rather, of a timeless, all-knowing metaphysical being, towering over and above the apparent open-endedness of human life as perceived by human beings, and encompassing past, present, and future in its vision. Divine knowledge, Boethius says, "transcends all movement in time. It abides in the simplicity of its present, embraces the boundless extent of past and future, and by virtue of its simple comprehension, it ponders all things as if they were being enacted in the present. . . . For this reason it is better to term it *providentia* ('looking forward spatially') rather than *praevidantia* ('looking ahead in time')" (*The Consolation of Philosophy*, 111–12). In stark contrast to this Christian theological view, it seems, Jewish thinkers have always been deeply troubled by the premise of omniscience. Perhaps the most ancient and certainly the most concise formulation of this issue, nearly two thousand years old, is expressed in an adage attributed to the Jewish sage

Rabbi Akiva: "Everything is foreseen and free will is granted [*Ha'kol tzafui ve'ha'reshut netuna*]" (*The Ethics of the Fathers* [*Pirkei Avot*], 3, 15).[5] This adage generated mountains of exegesis in the course of the following centuries, but the central paradox of religion-based ethics remains unresolved: if every act is foreseen and predetermined by the omniscient and all-powerful being we call God, how can there be any valid conception of free will? How can human beings be said to have any real ethical choice and be held accountable for what they do? Is the experience of free will a mere illusion arising out of our own shortsightedness?

This dilemma, however, is not confined to theological thought. It is just as acutely pressing in all forms of philosophical and scientific determinism—any and all systems of thought that are based on unilinear causality. In *Creative Evolution*, Bergson quotes Pierre-Simon Laplace as the Enlightenment spokesperson for this deterministic scientific paradigm: "'An intellect which at a given instant knew all the forces with which nature is animated, and the respective situation of the beings that compose nature—supposing the said intellect were vast enough to subject these data to analysis—would embrace in the same formula the motions of the greatest bodies in the universe and those of the slightest atom: nothing would be uncertain for it, and the future, like the past, would be present to its eyes'" (*Creative Evolution*, 37–38). There is more than a touch of irony in that quotation, in view of Laplace's famous dismissal of the "hypothesis of God" as redundant to his theory of the cosmos. For Bergson, neither the "impulsion of the past" (i.e., the mechanistic account) nor the teleological destination or the "attraction" of the future (i.e., neo-Lamarckian "finalism") are acceptable accounts of evolution, since they are equally deterministic mirror images of each other (39).

A conception of time that "regard[s] the future and the past as calculable functions of the present" and thus claims that "'*all is given*'" (37) holds true for artificial mechanical systems, Bergson says, but not for living ones. And then, in what sounds like a direct response to the formulation of Boethius, Bergson makes it clear that Enlightenment version of scientific determinism is no different from medieval theological determinism: "On this hypothesis, past, present and future would be open at a glance to a superhuman intellect capable of making the calculations" (43). Against the deterministic view—religious, scientific, or philosophical—of human beings as inextricably caught up in and subjected to the rhythm of spatialized and homogenized time, Bergson posits a radically different conception, not only of time, but also of subjectivity, "an attentive consciousness, a living self, whose [psychic] states, at once undistinguished and unstable," "permeate one another" in a "heterogeneous duration," and are characterized by "interpenetration" and a "qualitative multiplicity" (*Time and Free Will*, 236–37). Bergson's next step is to turn this conception into the very definition of subjectivity as a "center [or "zone"] of indetermination" (*Matter and Memory*, 32, 36, 104), which is the precondition for any position of agential choice and action. To return to the initial point, freedom is inherent in consciousness, which accumulates the past and produces the future, for "our self is at every moment, as it were, in a state of being born, absorbing its past and creating its future.... We are free by being conscious, by producing time" (Kołakowski, *Bergson*, 21).

Rosenzweig attributes what he calls the *apoplexia philosophica*, or sickness of philosophy, to the desire to remain "out of time," a desire that is generated by the fear of death, but ultimately leads to death-in-life (*Understanding the Sick and the Healthy*, 59). His "new thinking" is well aware that it cannot extricate itself either from its own temporality or from the language in which it is inscribed ("The New Thinking," 83). We must not, he cautions, confuse our sense of continuity, of self-sameness and self-presentness, provided by our name, with a conception of a timeless "essence":

> If the moment were essence, human freedom would suffer irreparable damage. It would be eternally swallowed up in the concatenation of cause and effect which is the law of the world.... To escape the power of the past, to transcend the law which constitutes causation, the moment must, at each instant, be reborn. This continuous renewal and resumption of the present is a contribution of the future. The future is the inexhaustible well from which moments are drawn; every instant new-born moments rise and replace the moments disappearing into the past. At each moment the future presents to man the gift of being present to himself. And so man may use his moments freely and then deposit them in the vast receptacle of the past. In the enduring process of receiving and using

his moments he is man, master of the present, of his present—for it is truly his, if it is present. It is indeed born anew each instant, and each instant it dies. (Rosenzweig, *Understanding the Sick and the Healthy*, 81–82)

Bergson is certainly one, if not the first, of Rosenzweig's "new thinkers." As noted in the previous chapter, the cultural phase that began with the Enlightenment and ended at the turn of the twentieth century has often been identified with an ocular, and ipso facto spatial, regime: a privileging of a specular epistemology that dichotomizes subject-object relations, a vision-centered interpretation of knowledge, truth, and reality. The de-Cartesianization of Western thinking has, at least on the received account, been accompanied by a correlative shift from an ocular-spatial to an auditory-temporal sensibility. It is thus not surprising that Bergson has been hailed as one of the standard-bearers of the end of the *"ancien* Scopic regime" (Jay, *Downcast Eyes*, 149–211), and the reading of his work as symptomatic of the broader paradigm shifts discussed in the previous chapter undoubtedly accounts for the revival of Bergsonianism in the late 1960s. The Bergsonian transition of sensibility from space to time is closely related, on this account, to a recognition of the mutually constitutive link between subject and object, and to a changing conception of subjectivity: the *I* who relates to the other as the object of its gaze and to itself as reflected and enframed in the other's eye, gives way to a more porous mode of being in the world, which unfolds as it generates real time and is always in the process of becoming.

Even if one feels a little uncomfortable with the sweeping breadth of this cultural diagnosis, it is still arguable that point-of-view no longer serves as an absolute organizing category for modernist authors responding in their work to the crisis of modernity. Thus Georges Poulet, a supremely astute reader, credits Bergson with having set the philosophical paradigm of twentieth-century literature: "to apprehend the present as the generative act of time in its concrete reality is . . . the tendency of our epoch" (*Human Time*, 36). Poulet may be overstating the case, but there can be little doubt that Bergson's philosophy of change did indeed inspire the modernist "aesthetics of uncertainty," its multi-perspectivism, its insistence on the fluidity of human consciousness, and its concern with subjective *durée*, as well as the narrative techniques associated with high modernism (e.g., stream-of-consciousness or the nonlinear treatment of time).

Both Lévinas and Merleau-Ponty are profoundly indebted to Bergson. Lévinas explicitly relates to Bergson's work as the "first contemporary influence" on his work, and to Bergson's theory of time as concrete duration as "one of the most significant, if largely ignored, contributions to *contemporary* philosophy" (in Cohen, ed., *Face to Face with Lévinas*, 13). Lévinas's move away from the ocular toward a temporalized conception of epistemology and ethics is undoubtedly an offshoot of the Bergsonian paradigm shift. Merleau-Ponty does not make a similar acknowledgment, but the interrelation of futurity and freedom in his *Phenomenology of Perception* is telling. "The very notion of freedom," he writes, "demands that our decision should plunge into the future . . . each instance, therefore, must not be a closed world" (437). "We are led to conceive freedom as a choice continually remade as long as we do not bring in the notion of a generalized or natural time" (453). In the case of Bakhtin, however, the indebtedness to Bergson is both more complex and, I believe, more productive.

BERGSON AND THE FORMALISTS

To understand this philosophical relationship, we should make a detour and examine it through the formalist lens. To recall the discussion in the previous chapter, Bakhtin's juxtaposition of "rhythm" and "loophole" and his privileging of the former in the experience of subjectivity can be read as closely related to the principle of "estrangement" in the workings of literature as Victor Shklovsky conceives it. Giving birth to itself through the transgression of regularities and the de-automatization of habitual perceptions, the "literary" is modeled on ethical subjectivity, which is never fully identical with itself and must constantly break free of any and all external or internalized "givenness."

Bergson's relation to the formalists is founded on the same principle. As James Curtis has persuasively suggested, there is a "Bergsonian paradigm"—focused on a fundamental heterogeneity, and informed by a passionate opposition to mechanical, habitual, and automatic perception—at the very core of formalist theorizing. This paradigm is not only evident in the formalists' direct borrowings and allusions; it is just as powerful in the essays that make no direct reference to Bergson, most obviously in the case of Shklovsky's "Art as Technique," with its abundance of Bergsonian tropes and concepts (Curtis, "Bergson and Russian Formalism," 113–15).

Neither a libertarian, nor an advocate of irrationality, Bergson is fully aware of the centripetal forces that shape human lives: social life requires commonality, stability, and fixity; processes are transformed into objects through social consensus, so that we can have some common ground to share for practical social ends. This fundamental fact of sociality is true of sensations, of emotions, and of states of mind, Bergson says, which need to be translated into and fixed in "the common element, the impersonal residue, of the impression felt in a given case by the whole of society. And this is why we reason about these states and apply our simple logic to them: having set them up as general by the mere fact of having isolated them from one another, we have prepared them for use in some future deduction" (*Time and Free Will*, 133). But as far as subjectivity goes—or the "states of consciousness," to use Bergson's terms—our social survival comes with a price tag. The solidification of process into object that enables us to "objectify" these states and to "throw them out into the current of social life" is an illusion when applied to consciousness and sensations, since these aspects of selfhood are inherently processual: fleeting, changeable, qualitatively multiple, and indivisible.

Notably, while the unavoidable social representation or the external projection of the self for practical purposes is conceived of in spatial terms as "a homogeneous space in which objects are sharply distinguished from one another" (*Time and Free Will*, 137), the process of deep introspection that takes us back into "the fundamental self" is related to the concept of *durée*. We are led

> to grasp our inner states as living things, constantly *becoming*, as states not amenable to measure, which permeate one another and of which the succession in duration has nothing in common with juxtaposition in homogeneous space. But the moments at which we thus grasp ourselves are rare, and that is just why we are rarely free. The greater part of the time we live outside ourselves, hardly perceiving anything of ourselves but our own ghost, a colourless shadow which pure duration projects into homogeneous space. Hence our life un-

folds in space rather than in time; we live for the external world rather than for ourselves; we speak rather than think; we "are acted" rather than act ourselves. To act freely is to recover possession of oneself, and to get back into pure duration. (231–32)

This is quite close to the formalist distinction between ordinary, practical communication and artistic perception, the definition of "literariness" as generated by the practice of "estrangement," and the formalist vision of art as aimed at an immediate accession of reality through the transgression of conventions, generalities, and habitual modes of perception and discourse. As I have already suggested, the formalist quest for "an epistemologically based aesthetics," as Boris Eichenbaum called it (quoted in Curtis, "Bergson and Russian Formalism," 109), is supremely relevant to ethics as well, since the practice of estrangement might restore what has been eroded by habituation and automatization: works, clothes, furniture, the love of one's wife, and the fear of war (Shklovsky, "Art as Technique," in *Russian Formalist Poetics*, 12).

Bergson, too, seems to glimpse the possibility—entirely hypothetical for him—of redemption through literature. He, too, concedes that the "veil" of practical language that lies between "us and our consciousness" is "thick for ordinary men, but thin, almost transparent, for the artist and the poet," and he turns to literature as a potentially redemptive sphere of human action:

> Now if some bold novelist, tearing aside the cleverly woven curtain of our conventional ego, shows us under this appearance of logic a fundamental absurdity, under this juxtaposition of simple states an infinite permeation of a thousand different impressions which have already ceased to exist the instant they are named, we commend him for having known us better than we knew ourselves. (*Time and Free Will*, 133)

This notional novelist, though having to use the homogenizing instrument of language, might succeed in evoking suspicion of the "extraordinary and illogical nature" of what lies behind the conventional shadow-self, by suggesting "something of that contradiction, that interpenetration, which is the very essence of the elements expressed," and help us, the readers, "put aside for an instant the veil which we interposed between our consciousness and ourselves. [This novelist would thus] have brought us back into our own presence" (134). The truly gifted novelist is known by "the power with which he lifts out of the common domain, to which language had thus brought them down, feelings and ideas to which he strives to restore, by adding detail to detail, their original and living individuality" (164). For a reader at the beginning of the twenty-first century, this is more history than wishful conjecture, as not long after these words were written, a whole generation of modernists, most notably Proust, Woolf, Joyce, and Faulkner, rose to the Bergsonian challenge and created new modes of writing all aimed at bringing us "back to our own presence." For Bakhtin, as we shall see, it was Dostoyevsky who had been there first.

THE DIVERGENCE ON LANGUAGE

Bergson does not develop his insight on literature beyond these comments on the potential contribution of literature in bringing us back to our own presence. What holds him back may be the distinction he makes between the "fundamental" private self and the social self, and his concomitant conception of language exclusively as an instrument of social survival. On both these issues, Bergson and Bakhtin part ways. On Bergson's account, language is the homogenizing medium that enables practical communication and accomplishes the erosion or leveling of the fundamental, protean, and singular self. It is the force that "solidifies," synchronizes, and immobilizes duration, converting process into object, and turning the protean and singular subject into a "shadow self" (*Time and Free Will*, 128)—fixed in place, but not quite real. As the instrument that carves out and stabilizes social reality, language "cannot get hold of [this fundamental self] without arresting its mobility or fit it into its common-place forms without making it into public property" (129):

> This influence of language on sensation is deeper than is usually thought. Not only does language make us believe in the unchangeableness of our sensations, but it will sometimes deceive us as to the nature of the sensation felt.... The word with well-defined outlines, the rough and ready word, which stores up the stable, common, and consequently impersonal element in the impressions of mankind, overwhelms or at least covers over the delicate and fugitive impressions of our individual consciousness. (131–32)

The leveling effect of language, generated by social needs and created at the cost of homogenizing individual subjectivity, masks the true nature of states of consciousness, which are "processes and not things," covers up their infinite diversity and singularity, and arrests their endless mutability (164, 196).

For Bakhtin, however, the irreducible liminality of the subject is analogous to that of discourse, which also "lives, as it were, on the boundary between its own context and another, alien, context" (TRDB, 284). It is only in and through language that the inherent diversity and mobility of the subject are inscribed. Rather than synchronize, immobilize, and spatialize duration, discourse is actually the best medium for the inscription of singularity, heteronomy, and fluidity—freedom-enabling aspects of subjectivity that Bergson sought to recover. We shall deal with this "borderline sensibility" at greater length in the next chapter, but note here that Bakhtin's conception of discourse has enabled him to take Bergson's temporalized subjectivity much further than Bergson himself did.

Leaving aside for the moment the fundamental divergence of these two thinkers on the subject of language, let us get back to the points of convergence, the echoes of the Bergsonian paradigm in Bakhtin's antideterminism and his conjunction of temporality and ethics.

THE CHRONOTOPE

Bakhtin's only work that is mostly concerned with time and space, "Forms of Time and the Chronotope in the Novel" (1937–38), offers a historical analysis of genre evolution. Like geological formations, or the rings of ancient tree trunks, literary genres are historical inscriptions, not only in terms of ideas and themes, but in their underlying matrices of time and space, or "chronotopes," as Bakhtin calls them. The spatiotemporal matrix is part of what we might call the cultural unconscious of the text, or, as Holquist sees it, "a set of unspoken assumptions about the coordinates of our experience" that "condition the very language people speak" (*Dialogism*, 141–42). A text may be constituted by more than a single chronotope, and it is often the relation of the conflicting modes of perception and the tension between them in a single text that render it valuable for the study of culture, since these interactions cross the lines of demarcation between authors, characters, performers, listeners, and readers. "All the novel's abstract elements—philosophical and social generalizations, ideas, analyses of cause and effect—gravitate toward the chronotope and through it take on flesh and blood" (Bakhtin, "Forms of Time and the Chronotope in the Novel," 250).

Less interesting for its specific literary insights, which are often rather fuzzy, the essay is noteworthy for its underlying philosophical premises and their implications for a theory of subjectivity. In "The Role of Chronotope in Dialog," Michael Holquist argues that for Bakhtin, time and space are not a priori transcendental categories, as they are for Kant, but rather "forms of the most immediate reality" that are constantly achieved and transformed in the negotiation between mind and world, as Bakhtin himself makes clear (FTC, 85). The implications of this insight need to be further elaborated, but in the meantime note that Bakhtin's position in this essay, though not fully articulated in philosophical terms, is indeed anti-Kantian, in that it does not allow for universality: if we accept the definition of chronotopes as the inscriptions of historical ideological formations, we ought to recognize the inescapable historicity of aesthetic time-space coordinates; the fact that narrative temporality is grounded in and symptomatic of contemporary perceptions; and the close relationship between time-space perception in the novel and its range of generic possibilities. If the underlying chronotope of a literary genre is produced by culture, history, and ideology, the time-space matrix is no longer a Kantian universal, at least insofar as this constitutive structure of the mind is subject to historical mutations. Briefly put, what Bakhtin is trying to articulate in "Forms of Time and the Chronotope in the Novel" is not only the evolution of literary genres, but the timeliness of time itself.

Literature, however, is more than a mere inscription of ideological forces. As the Soviet regime understood all too well, it exerts a formative power of its own, and it may ultimately generate cultural and ideological changes of seismic magnitude. With this in mind, we should turn to what may be called the "Dostoyevskian chronotope." From the rather general and sometimes fuzzy discussion of chronotopes and literary genres, Bakhtin zooms in for a moment on the organization of space in Dostoyevsky's novels, making a brief reference to the ubiquity of the threshold, the staircase, the front hall, and the corridor in these texts (FTC, 248). This is echoed and amplified in a section added to the revised edition of *Problems of Dostoevsky's Poetics*:

> The threshold, the foyer, the corridor, the landing, the stairway, its steps, doors opening onto the stairway, gates to front and back yards, and beyond these, the city: squares, streets, facades, taverns, dens, bridges, gutters. This is the space of the novel. And in fact absolutely nothing here ever loses touch with the threshold, there is no interior of drawing rooms, dining rooms, halls, studios, bedrooms. (*PDP*, 170; see also AH, 108)

Going back to the question of space in Dostoyevsky's work in his draft notebooks of the early 1940s, Bakhtin once more insists that it

> is not the ordinary terrestrial space of fiction, wherein the person is firmly localized and surrounded.... This is the narrow space of the threshold, the boundary, where one cannot settle down, find peace, establish oneself; where one can only step through, cross over.... The entire action, from the very beginning to the end, takes place at a point of crisis, at a breaking point. ("On the Questions of Self-Consciousness and Self-Evaluation, 74)[6]

Only in the late fragmented notes "Toward a Reworking of the Dostoevsky Book" are the implications of this liminal sensibility fully articulated. Subjectivity, according to Bakhtin, is neither autonomous nor sovereign; it is always liminal, always "on the boundary" (TRDB, 287). Uncharacteristically, Bakhtin alludes to his own work on Rabelais in the revised version of the Dostoyevsky book, recasting the conception of the carnivalesque in terms of liminality:

> Carnivalization is.... a peculiar sort of heuristic principle making possible the discovery of new and as yet unseen things. By *relativizing* all that was externally stable, set and ready-made, carnivalization with its pathos of change and renewal permitted Dostoevsky to penetrate into the deepest layers of man and human relationships....
>
> ... Everything is shown in a moment of unfinalized transition.
>
> It is characteristic that the very setting for the action of the novel—*Petersburg* (its role in the novel is enormous)—is on the borderline between existence and nonexistence, reality and phantasmagoria ... it, too, is on the threshold. (*PDP*, 166–67)

Arguably the most controversial concept in Bakhtin's work, the carnivalesque has been glorified by some readers as the culmination of the Bakhtinian spirit and seriously questioned by others as problematic, troubling, and unproductive. The reservations of Gary Saul Morson and Caryl Emerson are particularly cogent and instructive in the present context: the carnivalesque subject, they write, dissolves into the rhythms of collective communality (*Mikhail Bakhtin: Creation of a Prosaics*, 195). It is a "self that has no regrets because it has no past, a self that is not just open but pure loophole" (225). Whereas the emphasis in Bakhtin's "Author and Hero in Aesthetic Activity" is on the "body's boundedness, its location in a given space and time, and its unique point of view on other bodies and on the world" (Morson and Emerson, 225)—all of the factors that make up human responsibility, mortality, and vulnerability—the emphasis in Rabelais is on the body's orifices and the violation of boundaries between the individual self and the world (226), and this "'utopian' sense of the self produced by a carnival vision is one in which all the consequences of mortality for selfhood disappear" (226). Most important, to my mind, Morson and Emerson note that the carnivalistic self is no longer described in terms of the voice or of words, and thus loses the singularity that turns it into a responsive and responsible being: "Under carnival conditions, the self expands, rejoices, devours—and disappears" (229).

I believe that it is in this section on the carnivalesque quality in the revised *Problems of Dostoevsky's Poetics*—initially added to Bakhtin's notes of the 1940s, but added to the published version when the grip of ideological state terror had loosened to a considerable extent and Bakhtin could safely incorporate the concept into his thinking about subjectivity—that we may try to resolve the apparent incommensurability of the carnivalesque with the rest of Bakhtin's work. Perhaps it can be read, as suggested in the Introduction, as an invocation of Montaigne's ghost through the Rabelaisian body. Liminality, ambivalence, paradox, relativization, internal incompleteness—all the hallmarks of Montaigne's autobiographical project are there in the "non-Euclidian" (*PDP*, 176, attributed to Dostoyevsky and put in quotation marks in Bakhtin's own text) conception of time, space, genre, and, above all, of subjectivity in Dostoyevsky's work. This is the principle of freedom that enables the "creation of the *open* structure of the great dialogue" (177) and positions Dostoyevsky firmly within the counter-Cartesian tradition.

Using the same trope of the threshold, Bakhtin's notes are even more explicit on this point: following a reference to non-self-sufficiency (TRDB, 287), he relates to self-consciousness as "not that which takes place within, but that which takes place on the *boundary* between one's own and someone else's consciousness, on the *threshold*. And everything internal gravitates not toward itself, but is turned to the outside and dialogized, every internal experience ends up on the boundary, encounters another, and in this tension-filled encounter lies its entire essence" (287; see also *PDP*, 62). A few pages later, there is yet another brief note on "the threshold, the door, and the stairway. Their chronotopic significance" (TRDB, 299). But the liminality characteristic of both the Dostoyevskian space and the space of human subjectivity itself is not confined to space alone. Time, too, as suggested in "Forms of Time and the Chronotope in the Novel," can be spatially conceptualized. The chronotope is actually a "form of time." And so, it is to the rather more complex question of temporality and its relation to ethics that we should now turn. What, to take up the Bakhtinian metaphor, is the temporal equivalent of the staircase, the corridor, the threshold?

One aspect of this question, extensively discussed and highlighted by Gary Saul Morson in a number of essays, is Dostoyevsky's breach with the chronotope of "closed time," the prototype of realistic novelistic prose. Morson cogently argues that the conception of narrative perfection as a closed, spatialized structure where every occurrence is seen as the inevitable outcome of previous events, and is often foreshadowed by them, is "fatal to ethics, which is predicated on human freedom and depends on "the reality of real choice and genuine alternatives" ("Strange Synchronies," 478).[7] This, I believe, is very close to what I have called the "dead end of omniscience," but Morson pursues this issue in a different direction. Dostoyevsky's work, he argues, has overcome novel-writing's predisposition to "closed views of time" (483), and is informed by a different dynamics of creativity: its polyphony—that is, the unmerged, unsynthesized, unresolved plurality of voices and positions—is isomorphic with a conception of time where the future is truly open. It is, in Morson's view, the structural indeterminacy of Dostoyevsky's work that enables his novels to capture "the throb of presentness": the messiness of loose ends, the visibility of the "scaffolding," the false starts, and the clues that are never taken up (and are often perceived, quite understandably perhaps, as sloppy writing) are all informed by a resistance to narrative determinism. The endings of Dostoyevsky's novels are not immanent in their beginnings: rather than "foreshadowing," they offer "sideshadows," possible directions of the action that are often left suspended, which may or may not have developed into actualities. "Properly perceived," Morson writes, "time is the form of plurality; and freedom can only exist if time is so understood" (484). Further philosophical elaboration of these points is offered by Morson in his book *Narrative and Freedom: The Shadows of Time*, with William James's essay "The Dilemma of Determinism" as a point of departure.[8] The advantage of literature, Morson argues, is that through its representation of human action (rather than by explicit assertion), it can offer a model of "a pluralistic, restless universe, in which no single point of view can ever take in the whole scene" (87).

But Morson's account, thought-provoking though it is, focuses exclusively on the opposition of necessity and contingency in the unfolding of the plot, that is, on the *ontological* aspect of freedom, and Bakhtin's phenomenological quest is concerned, I believe, with the subject's mode of being rather than with ontological questions. There is still more to be learned of the philosophical challenge presented by Bakhtin's work, if we shift the focus from the temporality of plot to another aspect of temporality, articulated in the discursive dynamics of Dostoyevsky's work and the conception of borderline subjectivity that emerges from it. Furthermore, on Morson's account, Bakhtin's thinking evolves through three distinct phases (respectively evidenced in "Author and Hero in Aesthetic Activity," *Problems of Dostoevsky's Poetics*, and "Forms of Time and the Chronotope in the Novel"), whereas I would suggest that the resistance to determinism inherent in his ethical thinking already leads to the conception of the subject as noncoincident with itself in the early fragment *Toward a Philosophy of the Act* (1921–22).

FROM SPACE TO TIME

To get to the temporal equivalent of Dostoyevsky's "staircase chronotope," we should review the relation of "Author and Hero in Aesthetic

Activity" to *Problems of Dostoevsky's Poetics*, which, more than any of Bakhtin's explicit references, testifies to the profound relevance of the Bergsonian paradigm to Bakhtin's conception of subjectivity. To recall, the point of departure in "Author and Hero" is the phenomenological invisibility of the subject to itself, that is, the structural asymmetry between I-for-myself and I-for-the-other. Bakhtin approaches the relation of the subject to the other, and by extension, the issue of authorial omniscience, through the rather trivial observation that the limited subjective perspective does not allow the perceiver to see him/herself as a whole either in space (I cannot see my back or the top of my head) or in time (I cannot witness my own death). The other is "totally *in* time, just as he is altogether in space," but I-for-myself can never "coincide with me myself" as I always "exceed the bounds of this act's [i.e., the act of self-consciousness's] content" (AH, 109; see also 43 for reference to Bergson).

The most concise articulation of this constitutive asymmetry of the subject and the other is in the fragment "On the Questions of Self-Consciousness and Self-Evaluation":

> From the "objective" point of view there is a man, a person, etc., but the difference between the I and the other is relative: everybody and anybody is an I, everybody and anybody is an other. An analogy with the irrational distinction between the right and the left glove, between an object and its mirror image. Nevertheless, the I feels itself to be an exception, the only I in the world (all the others are others) and lives this opposition. This creates the ethical sphere of my absolute inequality to all others, of the eternal and absolute exclusion of the I (a justified exclusion). So, which phenomena of life [and] of artistic creation lie precisely in this sphere, are determined by the specific laws of this exclusion? Everything may be connected with this sphere, the lie, knowledge and ignorance (deliberate ignorance), illusions about oneself and self-deception. The construction of one's own image in the other and for others. (SC, 73)

As we have seen, the incontestable physical fact of the subject's inability to represent him/herself fully in space and in time are extrapolated by Bakhtin to the axiological level as well: the subject who cannot produce an autonomous axiological representation of itself needs to be reflected in the (hopefully benevolent) authorial other in order to have a full sense of selfhood and a coherent identity.

The structuring paradigm in "Author and Hero" is synchronic and ocular. The omniscient author, as a "principle of seeing," is the sum total of "the transgredient moments of seeing that are actively referred to the hero and his world" (AH, 208). Being able to see beyond the vision of the hero, the author can enframe, contain, and grant the hero the kind of wholeness that the latter cannot attain from his own necessarily partial viewpoint. The author's transgredient position is rendered in terms of a "surplus of knowledge" that, though couched in exclusively spatial-visual terms (103; see also 104–6), is nonetheless both spatial and temporal, inasmuch as it encompasses both the hero's beginning and his end—moments "not given" to the hero's self-consciousness. This "excess of knowledge" allows the author to partake of divinity. "Everything is foreseen" by the omniscient author, as it is by Boethius's divine Providence, and any sense of agency on the part of the hero is mere illusion, stemming as it does from the partiality of his own vision. What we have here is precisely the spatialization of time that, according to Bergson, hollows out the notion of freedom and ethical choice.

If aestheticized subjectivity is firmly positioned in a quasi-spatial enclosure by the authorial view, the ethical subject is forever positioned on borderlines. The Dostoyevskian "small-scale Copernican revolution"—the polyphonic mode of creativity—consists in his having turned "what had been a firm and finalizing authorial definition" into "an aspect of the hero's self-definition" (*PDP*, 49). His abdication of the authorial prerogative enables his characters "to outgrow, as it were, from within," to defy any and all externally imposed definitions. This, says Bakhtin, is the very condition of life and—it bears repeating—of all ethical agency and action, for "as long as a person is alive he lives by the fact that he is not yet finalized, that he has not yet uttered his ultimate word" (59). The Bergsonian echo is loud and clear at this point: "[O]ur personality shoots, grows and ripens without ceasing. Each of its moments is something new added to what was before. We may go further: it is not only something new, but something unforeseeable," and "we are creating ourselves continually" (*Creative Evolution*, 8, 9). Whatever their ideological positions may be, Dostoyevsky's characters can always refuse to be aesthetically contained and closed off. They can always say "no" to their author, who does not insist on having the last word.

Although the significance of the Dostoyevskian era—for it is indeed a new cultural phase, as far as Bakhtin is concerned—appears to be symptomatically marked by a shift from an ocular-spatial to an auditory-temporal frame of reference, this is far from a neat break, as we have already noted. But the shift of structuring metaphors between these two texts is still significant enough to note at this junction. Dostoyevsky has relinquished the viewpoint of authorial eye and turned himself into yet another voice among the equally authoritative living voices of his characters. The Dostoyevskian hero, no longer "consummated" or "finalized" under the authorial gaze, having become a voice or discourse in his own right, has been "de-reified" (*PDP*, 63).

Clearly inspired by the Bergsonian paradigm, Bakhtin's references to freedom of the character, the refusal of the character to be enframed or "consummated" by the authorial gaze, are invariably couched in diachronic terms of intentionality, temporality, and projection of the self into the future. For Bergson, too, freedom is a resistance to all forms of external enframing and containment that aim to turn the process and the project of becoming into a finished object. Freedom cannot be "observed and established as a fact 'from outside'. Having no means of living another person's conscious life, I cannot grasp his freedom as an empirical fact and thus, when inspecting another personality, I naturally convert it into a thing . . . and impose on it the conceptual method I employ when dealing with objects: homogeneous time, separable events, relations of cause and effect" (Kołakowski, *Bergson*, 22).

We should note, however, that the Bergsonian relation of ethics and diachronicity does not make its first appearance in the Dostoyevsky book: it is, as we have seen, already a foundational premise of Bakhtin's thought in "Author and Hero," where the opening into an unknown future—the yet-to-be—is a precondition of ethical freedom (AH, 13). The ethical subject, we should recall, is never adequate to itself; it is "in principle nonunitary" (83), "present to itself as a task," "incapable of being given, of being present-on-hand, of being contemplated" (100), and this non-coincidence with oneself, the self-projection of the subject ahead of itself in time, is translated in Bakhtin's work into the concept of the "loophole" (109). What this means, then, is that the invisibility (in the broadest sense) of the subject to itself that generates the need for the enframing gaze of the authorial other is *at the same time* the loophole that is the enabling condition of freedom.

This conception of ethics is already in place in *Toward a Philosophy of the Act*: "In its answerability the act sets before itself its own truth [*pravda*] as something-to-be-achieved" (*TPA*, 29). Ethics cannot be construed through abstractions, propositions, and laws; it "can only be a description, a phenomenology of that world. An event can be described only participatively. . . . When I experience an object actually, I thereby carry out something in relation to it: the object enters into relation with that which is to-be-achieved, grows in it—within my relationship to that object. Pure givenness cannot be experienced actually" (32).

Bergson, too, relates to freedom as "the relation of the concrete self to the act which it performs," but claims that "this relation is indefinable, just because we are free" (*Time and Free Will*, 210). Translating the tension between the universal and the singular into the relation of space and time, Bergson's critique of Kantianism is founded on its failure to draw a distinction between these two modes of consciousness, and his insistence that the question of ethics is premised on the real indeterminacy of the future and the singularity of our choices. It is impossible to analyze the ethical act in abstraction from its concrete and singular context, for

> we can analyze a thing, but not a process; we can break up extensity, but not duration. Or, if we persist in analysing it, we unconsciously transform the process into a thing and duration into extensity. By the very fact of breaking up concrete time we set out its moments in homogeneous space; in place of the doing we put the already done; and, as we have begun by, so to speak, stereotyping the activity of the self, we spontaneously settle down into inertia and freedom into necessity. (220)

Nothing is simpler to understand than this impossibility, he says. All we have to do is "carry ourselves back in thought to those moments of our life when we made some serious decision, moments unique of their kind, which will never be repeated," and then

> We should see that, if our action was pronounced by us to be free, it is because the relation of this action to the state from which it issued

could not be expressed by a law, this psychic state being unique of its kind and unable ever to occur again. We should see, finally, that the very idea of necessary determination here loses every shred of meaning, that there cannot be any question either of foreseeing the act before it is performed or of reasoning about the possibility of the contrary action once the deed is done, for to have all the conditions given is, in concrete duration, to place oneself at the very moment of the act and not to foresee it. (238–39)

This is very close to Bakhtin's critique in *Toward a Philosophy of the Act*, his rejection of the universalism of Kantian formal ethics, and the shift from content ethics to the ethical act. The singularity and unrepeatability of every human act—situated in a particular time and place, and being the action of a particular embodied individual—cannot be abstracted or translated into a system of laws. It is, he says, our very concrete historicity, the very particularity of our circumstances, that makes us fully accountable for every choice. This singularity is precisely why "that which can be done by me can never be done by anyone else." This is why we have no "alibi in Being" (*TPA*, 42). Being positioned at a singular point in time and space, we cannot be "elsewhere" (which is the literal translation of *alibi*), but it is this very same experiential concreteness that makes the future truly open-ended and allows us to assume both agency and responsibility for our acts.

To get back to Dostoyevsky, the refusal of the character to be enframed or "consummated" by the authorial gaze is analogous to the dynamics of any living discourse: both these phenomena are couched in diachronic terms as a projection of subjectivity into the future, and it is this diachronicity that Bakhtin sees, even in the earliest essays, as a precondition *of ethical freedom and agency*. It is in *duration* rather than *time* that the subject of the act experiences its freedom of choice. Living on its own borderlines, the subject's mode of being is always diachronic, projected ahead of itself. The principle of polyphony that informs Dostoyevsky's work—a multiplicity of irreducibly different voices, which cannot be harmonized into a chorus or subsumed under the authorial word—is not just a shift from the ocular to the auditory, or from synchrony to diachrony. It is, first and foremost, a transition from aesthetics (as narrowly conceived in "Author and Hero" and in some of Bakhtin's unpublished fragments) to ethics, or a broader understanding of aesthetics as inclusive of and constituted by the disruptive, ethical function. Dostoyevsky's characters, set as they are within a polyphonic text that offers them loopholes of escape from "aesthetic necessity," are also perceived as free to break away from the dead end of omniscience, inasmuch as for Bakhtin, "ethical freedom ('freedom of the will') is not only freedom from cognitive necessity (causal necessity), but also freedom from aesthetic necessity" (AH, 119). The inspiration of Bergson is clearly there.

This, I believe, is where the relation of polyphony and dialogicity may be articulated. Both these terms appear in *Problems of Dostoevsky's Poetics*, and they are at least genetically related—to the chagrin of the Bakhtinian establishment, they are in fact all too often conflated in academic discussions. "The new artistic position of the author with regard to the hero in Dostoyevsky's polyphonic novel is a *fully realized and thoroughly consistent dialogic position*, one that affirms the independence, internal freedom, unfinalizability, and indeterminacy of the hero" (*PDP*, 63). Taking issue with the view of polyphony as chronologically and ontologically prior to dialogics in Bakhtin's thinking, I would argue that it is rather, as the quoted passage indicates, the other way around. If we relate to Bakhtin's earlier references to the liminality of the ethical subject (as a being that lives on its borderlines) as articulations of dialogicity, we would have to conclude that this concept is, in fact, ontologically and chronologically constitutive of polyphony. What marks the Dostoyevskian (or, rather, Bakhtinian revolution) is the extrapolation of the early phenomenological insights to the dynamics of literature.

The next step, to be discussed later at greater length, is yet another extension of the same principles to discourse as such:

> The dialogic orientation of discourse is . . . the natural orientation of any living discourse. . . . The word in living conversation is directly, blatantly, oriented toward a future answer-word. (DN, 279)

> Forming itself in an atmosphere of the already spoken, the word is at the same time determined by that which has not yet been said but which is needed and in fact anticipated by the answering word. Such is the situation in any living dialogue. (280)[9]

The polyphonic paradigm of Dostoyevsky's work is a translation and an offshoot of the same rejection of containment, a rejection of the spatial conception of wholeness, and self-identity. Bakhtin makes it clear that this rejection is not only intersubjective, that is, addressed to the authorial other—it is also, primarily perhaps, intrasubjective: the non-coincidence of the Dostoyevskian hero with himself, or with any finalizing authorial vision, is analogous to the position of the subject of ethics, the position of I-for-myself. As we should remind ourselves, the analogy is explicitly reiterated in *Problems of Dostoevsky's Poetics*:

> A man never coincides with himself. One cannot apply to him the formula of identity A≡A. In Dostoevsky's artistic thinking, the genuine life of the personality takes place at the point of non-coincidence between a man and himself, at this point of departure beyond the limits of all that he is as a material being, a being that can be spied on, defined, predicted apart from its own will, "at second hand." (*PDP*, 59)

Once again, the profound significance of this paradigm shift is highlighted and encapsulated in a little-known fragment from Bakhtin's notebooks of the early 1940s, which is worth quoting at some length:

> Putting the subject [the object of knowledge] to death is a prerequisite for knowledge; the subordination of the world (turning it into an object of devouring) is its aim. Wherein lies the deadening power of the artistic image: to circumvent the object through his future, to show him as already exhausted, thus depriving him of an open future, to present him with all his boundary lines, both external and internal, leaving no way out of all this framedness—here he is, all here, and nowhere else; if he is all here completely, then he is dead and can be devoured, he is removed from unfinalized [*nezavershennaia*] life and becomes a possible object of consumption; he ceases to be an independent participant in the event of life, walking on alongside us; he has already uttered his last word, no open inner nucleus, no inner infinitude, has been left in him. He has been denied *freedom*. The act of cognition seeks to surround him from all sides, to cut him off from open-endedness [*nezavershennost'*], and hence from freedom, from his future in time and in meaning, from his unresolvedness and from his inner truth. ("Rhetoric," 65)[10]

In this passage Bakhtin conflates the act of cognition and aesthetic form-giving: both, he says, are subtle forms of violence, objectifying the subject by enframing it, denying its freedom to outgrow its own boundary lines, insensitive to its "internal infinitude" and real openness to the future. In Dostoyevsky's work, "*the ultimate word of the world and about the world has not yet been spoken, the world is open and free, everything is still in the future and will always be in the future*" (PDP, 166).[11] When the subject is "resolved," given once and for all, fully known and encompassed within the gaze of an authorial or authorizing other, it is no longer free to choose or act. Ethical agency is conditioned on freedom, which, for both Bergson and Bakhtin, is synonymous with the unresolved and incomplete perspective, the "internal infinitude" that is the "inner truth" of the subject and the precondition of the ethical act ("Rhetoric," 65). The conception of the subject, diachronic rather than synchronic, shared by Bergson and Bakhtin, is that of a being that constantly transcends its own borderlines and projects itself into the "temporal and semantic future." This self-projection and the diachronic unraveling of subjectivity are the preconditions of ethical freedom. In enabling his characters to outgrow any external definition, in his abdication of authorial omniscience, Dostoyevsky has shifted his ground from aesthetics to ethics.

The distinction between the ontological and phenomenological is crucial here: even if the actual unfolding events were indeed inexorably preordained, the subjective ethical position of human beings must still be premised on the validity of choices between various real alternatives. Even in circumstances where the subject is granted very little real autonomy, where he or she is named by others, as Bakhtin would say, there is the I-for-myself mode of being that still remains open to the future, which exceeds and transcends any and all external definitions and names; which breaks every set rhythm and offers a loophole through every enclosure. Given the historical and biographical circumstances of Bakhtin's own work, we may safely assume that he would have embraced this distinction.

To conclude this chapter, let us go back to Holquist's view of the chronotope as a "master key" to Bakhtin's theory of dialogue. Following the Kantian connection, Holquist suggests that Bakhtin models his I-for-myself and I-for-the-other on Kant's distinction between the empirical and the transcendental I, and that for both these philosophers, the desire for unity is no more than a "deeply held desire" (Holquist,

"The Role of Chronotope," 14), or, in terms of the present study, an incurable homesickness. Bakhtin does not try to suppress or mend the Kantian rift—on the contrary, he "exploits the potential estrangement of such a world as a key to a revitalized understanding of synthesis (*Verbindung*) that has the reverse effect of alienation: indeed, it becomes the foundational element in a new dream of community" (15). Holquist maintains that unlike Kant, Bakhtin recognizes the role of language in the interaction of mind and world and argues that "chronotopes have their natural—their only—home in language. In our daily use of chronotopes the abstractness of time/space is domesticated when we deploy them in speech" (16). Significantly, Holquist cites the linguistic observations of Émile Benveniste at this point, noting that when a person utters the word *I*, he/she provides "the central point needed to calibrate all further time and space discriminations: 'I' is the invisible ground of all other indices in language, the benchmark to which all its spatial operations are referred, and the Greenwich mean time by which all its temporal distinctions are calibrated. 'I' marks the point between 'now' and 'then' as well as between 'here' and 'there'" (16).

As I suggest in my own references to Benveniste in the next chapter, the conception of subjectivity that emerges from his observations on shifters and deictics is "performative" in more than one sense. But the question of ethics, as suggested in the previous chapters, cannot be simply equated with discourse, for while it is true that intersubjectivity—as inscribed in language—is constitutive of subjectivity, it is unfortunately not the case that all language users are moral beings. We need, therefore, to narrow down the general discursive conception of subjectivity and supplement it with the practice of "estrangement" in literary discourse (which, it must be said at the outset, is not confined to that which is found between the covers of a book): it is only when we recognize the constitutional strangeness within ourselves that the performativity of discourse takes on its ethical significance. Only when we can read ourselves in quotations marks.

Looking back to our point of departure, the dead end of omniscience, should we give up the idea of God in order to preserve our conception of free will? Not necessarily. It is only the idea of God as an omniscient being that can encompass and comprehend the universe, past, present, and future in its vision that we need to give up. This emerges from the only reference to God in *Creative Evolution*: "God has nothing of the ready-made, he is uninterrupted life, action, freedom, and the creation, so conceived, is not a mystery; we experience it in ourselves when we act freely" (249). We may conclude, then, that if we are to retain a sense of the sacred after the death of God, it must be a relation with a divinity that, like Bakhtin's Dostoyevsky, has abdicated the authorial prerogative of omniscience, the "surplus of knowledge" that would homogenize the past and the future. Unlike the omniscient author who partakes of divinity in his excess of vision, Dostoyevsky "never drowns out the other's voice, never finishes it off 'from himself.'" His divinity is modeled on a completely different relation of God to man, "a relation allowing man to reveal himself utterly (in his immanent development), to judge himself, to refute himself" (TRDB, 285). The post-Nietzschean subject has no metaphysical home to go back to, no safe enclosure of time and space under the benevolent gaze of an all-knowing Auctor Mundi. But, as Bakhtin might have said, if he had been free to speak out, it is precisely this state of metaphysical exile that enables our ethical mode of being, our living on borderlines, always yet-to-be.

IN THE BEGINNING WAS THE BODY
READING BAKHTIN WITH MERLEAU-PONTY

> "I" is always a nay become audible. "I" always involves a contradiction, it is always underlined, always emphasized, always an "I, however." . . . "I" is simple [sic] always willy-nilly subject in all sentences in which it occurs. It can never be passive, never object.
>
> **Franz Rosenzweig,** *The Star of Redemption*

BAKHTIN'S REFUSAL to grant the existence of a sovereign and autonomous internal territory, his insistence that subjectivity is wholly and always on the boundary, and his acknowledgment that self-nomination is an impossibility or a lie bring him very close to Merleau-Ponty's recognition: "I borrow myself from others; I create others from my own thoughts" ("The Philosopher and His Shadow," in *Signs*, 159). This dignified assertion of non-self-sufficiency is the foundation of a position on ethics the two thinkers share. Their profoundly liminal vision begins in the living, perceiving body, the medium of the subject's consciousness and relationship with the world, moves on to the workings of discourse, and evolves into a conception of subjectivity that is not predicated on either body, discourse, or a "turn" from the former to the latter: its truly radical potential lies in the isomorphism of the somatic and the semiotic. The profound affinities between the respective post-Cartesian projects of Bakhtin and Merleau-Ponty have been discussed in depth by Michael Gardiner and noted in passing by other readers as well.[1] The aim of this chapter is to take the discussion one step further and draw out the implications of their commonalities in order to trace some missing links in Bakhtin's work and highlight its underlying coherence.

DISENCHANTMENT WITH PHILOSOPHY

Merleau-Ponty's work was cut short upon his untimely death in 1961, and his last work, *The Visible and the Invisible*, remained incomplete and was published posthumously along with his "Working Notes." Like Bakhtin about forty years earlier, Merleau-Ponty introduces this last work on a note of philosophical disenchantment, expressing an acute sense of the bankruptcy and failure of the Cartesian paradigm. Rejecting the mode of theorizing that identifies true knowledge with abstraction, generalization, and systematization and strives to assimilate the other to the same, he boldly claims that the aim of his own project is to start anew from the "ruin of philosophy"; to "take up again the whole philosophical movement in a 'fundamental thought'"; and to work toward a "complete reconstruction of philosophy" ("Working Notes for *The Visible and the Invisible*," 183, 193). This is a huge undertaking, but I believe it is amply substantiated if we read this unfinished and sometimes enigmatic work, not as a new departure, but as the final articulation of Merleau-Ponty's entire life's work, which is also, albeit implicitly, driven by the same disillusionment.[2]

Having invoked Montaigne's ghost to counter the Cartesian divide, let us turn for a moment to Merleau-Ponty's fond reading of this writer, whom he perceives as entirely preoccupied with the "ambiguous self," "self-consciousness," the "paradox of a conscious being" ("Reading Montaigne," in *Signs*, 198–99), and "all that is fortuitous and unfinished in man" (202)—the very themes of his own work centuries later, at a point when the Cartesian imperatives had relaxed their hold on philosophy. Interspersing his reading of Montaigne's *Essays* with his own commentary in a nearly seamless manner, Merleau-Ponty is explicit in his proleptic conception of Montaigne against Descartes: "Montaigne's consciousness," he writes,

> is not [the Cartesian] mind from the outset; it is tied down at the same time that it is free, and in one sole ambiguous act it opens to external objects and experiences itself as alien to them. Montaigne does not know that resting place, the self-possession, which Cartesian understanding is to be. The world is not for him a system of objects the idea of which he has in his possession; the self is not for him the purity of an intellectual consciousness. (199)

What is offered instead of the Cartesian pure intellectual consciousness is a constant sense of wonder, which, for Merleau-Ponty, is not a problem to be overcome, but the very condition of the quest: "There cannot in all conscience be any question of solving the human problem; there can only be a question of describing man as problematic. Hence this idea of an inquiry without discovery, a hunt without a kill, which is not the vice of a dilettante but the only appropriate method for describing man" (202). Against the Cartesian link of subjectivity and true knowledge, Merleau-Ponty evokes Montaigne's loving acceptance of paradox, ambiguity, mutability, and the recognition that "truth contradicts itself" (198). The origin of that paradoxical epistemology is the question of the "ambiguous self," a question Montaigne knew better than to try to resolve. Rather than doctrine, Montaigne proposes "a questioning addressed to the opaque being that he is," as "every doctrine, when it is separated from what we do, threatens to be mendacious" (199).

Clearly inspired by Montaigne's interrogation, Merleau-Ponty's critique of the Cartesian vantage point of philosophy, to which he wittily refers as *pensée de survol* ("high-altitude thinking"), though often taken as related to epistemology, applies to any ethical system founded on universal abstractions and divorced from the concreteness, temporality, and particularity of human existence (*The Visible and the Invisible*, 13). The conception of subjectivity, whether epistemological or ethical, cannot be premised on any doctrine or system, but must take our "terrestrial inherence," the here-and-now of our embodiment and historical situatedness, as its point of departure ("Reading Montaigne," 203). The Cartesian "philosophy of reflection," he says, is predicated on its distortion of the ethical subject, its "rendering unthinkable its relations with other 'subjects' in the world that is common to them" (*The Visible and the Invisible*, 43; see also 45). In a little note scribbled at the margin of the text, he adds: "show that reflection suppresses intersubjectivity" (8).[3]

Bakhtin, too, we should recall, begins his lifelong philosophical project with a diagnosis of the "peculiar state of sterility" (*TPA*, 19) produced by what he calls "fatal theoreticism" in contemporary philosophical thinking (27). He, too, sets out in search of an alternative "first philosophy" that proceeds, not by "constructing universal concepts, propositions, and laws," but by offering "a description, a phenomenology of that world" (31–32). And he, too, objects to the abstraction and universalization of the subject: "Man-in-general," he writes, "does not exist; *I* exist and a particular concrete *other* exists—my intimate, my contemporary (social mankind), the past and future of actual human beings (of actual historical mankind)" (47). Rather than a system of values or laws, Bakhtin proposes to study the "ought" as "a certain attitude of consciousness, the structure of which we intend to disclose phenomenologically" (6). The approach to ethics begins, not with norms, but with the "moral *subiectum*" (6). As we can see, the common point of departure for both Bakhtin and Merleau-Ponty in this quest for an alternative conception of ethics is an attempt to reclaim the first casualty of the Cartesian divide—the perceiving, living, singular human body.

IN THE BEGINNING WAS THE BODY

Merleau-Ponty's work is both an extension of and a departure from the phenomenology of Husserl, beginning with an attempt to capture the "facticity" of human existence, the singularity and situatedness of the experiential subject. His first major work, *Phenomenology of Perception*, is an attempt to offer a "descriptive psychology," an account of "space, time and the world as we 'live' them" (vii), and of the subject's relatedness to and inherence in the world, which is first and foremost corporeal: our consciousness of the world is that "being-towards-the-thing," for which the body is the medium (82, 138–39). It is, then, impossible to detach the somatic from the semiotic, and the "psycho-physical event can no longer be conceived after the model of Cartesian physiology" (88). From this foundational claim, Merleau-Ponty launches a rigorous analysis of bodily intentionality, spatiality, motility, and temporality and then moves on to "The World as Perceived," articulating his conception of the body in terms of sense experience and relations with the world outside itself.

But while it is obvious that these relations are somatic and perceptual long before they can be verbalized, it is crucial to understand that Merleau-Ponty is not interested in either the self-evident temporal primacy of sense perceptions or some idealized return to a more "authentic" mode of being: the body, for him, is "essentially an expressive space" (146), a "meaningful core" (147), which is just as semiotically constituted and charged as language itself. The phenomenological subject cannot transcend its own inherence in the world: it is a "network of relationships" (xx) that begins with the perception and the neediness of the body and continues with language, significations, and all forms of human interaction.

Like Bakhtin, Merleau-Ponty insists on the asymmetry of self-experience from within and the reflection of the self as a whole, through the eyes of the other. Already in *The Phenomenology of Perception*, he concedes, in a remarkably Bakhtinian idiom, the interactions of the two categories of consciousness, "for Others" and "for Oneself," and the experience of an "alter ego" that "presupposes that already my view of myself is halfway to having the quality of a possible 'other'" (448). The subject, on this account, is not a mere compromise formation between these two modes of consciousness, but always a temporary and conditional point of arrest in the struggle between them: "I am a general refusal to be anything, accompanied surreptitiously by a continual acceptance of such and such a qualified form of being. *For even this general refusal is still one manner of being and has its place in the world*" (452).

The crucial distinction between the self-perception of subjectivity and that of the objectified subject is further amplified in *The Visible and the Invisible*: living one's perception "from within," Merleau-Ponty says, means that it is impossible for the subject to "coincide" with the other, to live the other's life as the other lives it. The knowledge that the other, too, "has a private landscape" is derived from, but not identical to, the perceptual experience and the singular perspective of I-for-myself: there cannot be a relation of full reciprocity between me and the other, "since I am alone to be myself, since I am for myself the sole original of humanity" (*The Visible and the Invisible*, 58, 78–79). Against the Cartesian "philosophy of vision" that postulates a symmetry of the I-other relation, Merleau-Ponty insists, like Bakhtin, on their absolute asymmetry: "If there is an other, by definition I cannot install myself in him, coincide with him, live his very life: I live only my own. If there is an other, he is never in my eyes a For Itself, in the precise and given sense that I am, for myself" (78; see also 80).

The "network of relationships," somatic and semiotic, between the singular subject and the other is very close to the Bakhtinian architectonics of subjectivity. Bakhtin, we should recall, also focuses in "Author and Hero" on the concrete perceiving body, and he, too, relates to the asymmetry, predicated on the physical impossibility of self-perception from within, of I-for-myself and I-for-the-other. This point of departure serves to highlight the radical singularity and irreplaceability of the subject, the "fact that each of us occupies a singular place at a given time as a figure for (and a consequence of) our radical singularity in many other respects. Physical and temporal specificity is a sort of synecdoche of our larger irreplaceability," Morson and Emerson note (*Mikhail Bakhtin: Creation of a Prosaics*, 185).

As we have already seen, the experiential-perceptual impossibility of self-representation in space is extended by Bakhtin to the inaugural and terminal points of one's life (the moment of birth and the moment of death, which cannot be subsumed by one's consciousness), and concludes with the subject's axiological need for "consummation" by the authorial, presumably benevolent, other, whose position outside the subject guarantees a "surplus" of vision. Hence, the nonrepresentability of *I-for-myself* generates the need for the aestheticizing authorial gaze of the other, the external vantage point from which the subject would be perceived as whole. For Merleau-Ponty, too, this partial perspective is at the origin of the need for the other: "at the very moment when I experience my existence . . . I fall short of the ultimate density which would place me outside time . . . I discover in myself a kind of internal weakness standing in the way of my being totally individualized: a weakness which exposes me to the gaze of others as a man among men" (*The Visible and the Invisible*, xii; see also 106).

The striking convergence of these thinkers foregrounds their crucial divergences as well. Merleau-Ponty's work on the corporeal perceiving subject and its inability to represent or thematize itself to itself focuses on the vulnerability of the exposed body, the "bite of the world," as he calls it earlier (*The Prose of the World*, 137), and introduces an element of reversibility (not to be identified with symmetry) into the relation between self and other. This may be read as a needed corrective to the Bakhtinian account in "Author and Hero" with its overly benevolent construction of the authorial gaze. For Merleau-Ponty, the other exerts a decentering, rather than an "authorial" or "consummating" force. Rather than a subject-object relationship, of "pure gaze upon pure being," he postulates in his (still ocular-centric) account a relational system that allows for a mutual decentering of equal agents, an intersection of witnessing by two subjects. The self-other perceptual relationship is a "system of partial perspectives, referred to one same world in which we coexist and where our views intersect"; "for the other to be truly the other . . . it is necessary and it suffices that he have the power to decenter me, to oppose his centering to my own" (*The Visible and the Invisible*, 81–82). For readers who can no longer trust to a benign authorial being above and beyond the human, Merleau-Ponty's inscription of the relation in terms of a mutual decentering between equals, which leaves some room for reversibility and mutuality, is undoubtedly easier to accept.

Be that as it may, the initial focus on the perceiving body opens up an approach to ethics that may well set up an alternative to the Cartesian-Kantian doctrine and addresses the apparent paradox of a *universal singularity*. When Merleau-Ponty writes of the "radical originality of the for-itself of another," he explicitly alludes to the universalist approach as that which "under the pretext of placing us, [the other] and myself, in the same universe of thought, ruins the alterity of the other and hence marks the triumph of a disguised solipsism" (79). It is, then, precisely this irreducible alterity, the experience of the singular, embodied subject facing the prohibited experience of the other, that underwrites the ethical commitment. What renders us "wholly implicated," as Merleau-Ponty puts it (72–73), what makes it impossible for the individual to claim an "alibi," as Bakhtin puts it, is the uniqueness and unrepeatability of our context, our bodily being in time and space. This embodied singularity—the "generalization of my corporeal relation to the world (*The Prose of the World*, 136)—becomes, in effect, an ethical imperative more powerful than any formal categorical and abstract law: it both isolates and connects the subject and the other, and ensures their mutual decentering and mutual responsibility to and for each other. It is, in other words, this universal singularity that turns our solitude into a commonality. The same asymmetry of self and other, Merleau-Ponty insists, is not only immanent in the structure of perception, but also the precondition of any epistemology (and, I would add, ethics) that is not solipsistic.

Notably, a similar argument is advanced by Michael Holquist in his essay on Bakhtin's "biological thinking," which he puts forward as a response to the problem of cultural relativism: the logic of embodied perception, Holquist writes, may serve as the kind of "relative universal" that would mediate between the uniqueness of the human body and its difference and separateness from all other bodies—a singularity that is common to all humans. This "paradox of a shared uniqueness" may offer a way out of the impossible position between the Scylla of relativism and the Charybdis of authoritarian universalism, since "the very separateness of our bodies is the one thing we all have together. What we share is uniqueness" (Holquist, "Bakhtin and Beautiful Science," 225).

But this can be taken a step further if we bear in mind that the liminality that is the hallmark of the perceiving and speaking body is—for both these thinkers—not only *intersubjective* but *intrasubjective* as well. The most explicit formulation of this isomorphism is to be found in Merleau-Ponty's most "Bakhtinian" text, *The Prose of the World*, where dialogue serves as a key word for the "power of speech" (133), and the dialogic relationship with an irreducible alterity is extrapolated to intrasubjectivity as well:

> The problem . . . is to understand how I can make myself into two, how I can decenter myself. The experience of the other is always that of a replica of myself, of a response to myself . . . it is in the very depths of myself that this strange articulation with the other is fashioned. The mystery of the other is nothing but the mystery of myself. . . . It is because I am a totality that I am capable of giving birth to another and of seeing myself limited by him. For the miracle of the perception of another lies first of all in that everything which qualifies as a being to my eyes does so only by coming, whether directly or not, within my range, by reckoning in my experience, entering my world. (135)

This isomorphic relation between the architectonics of subjectivity and the relation of the subject to its other offers a possible resolution of the paradox of universal singularity:

> Speaking is not just my own initiative, listening is not submitting to the initiative of the other, because as speaking subjects we are continuing, we are resuming a common effort more ancient than we, upon which we are grafted to one another and which is the manifestation, the growth of truth. We say that the true has always been true, but . . . the foundation of truth is not outside of time; it is the

opening of each moment of knowledge to those who will resume it and change its sense. (143–44)

In his notes "Toward a Reworking of the Dostoevsky Book," which is, in fact, the product of his own "Copernican revolution," Bakhtin, too, concludes that

> I achieve self-consciousness, I become myself only by revealing myself to the other, through another and with another's help. . . . It turns out that every internal experience occurs on the border, it comes across another, and this essence resides in this intense encounter. . . . The very being of man (internal and external) is a profound communication. To be means to communicate. To be means to be for the other, and through him, for oneself. (Translated in Todorov, *The Dialogical Principle*, 96)[4]

Constitutionally unable to remain cocooned and insulated, the subject must constantly engage in the perception of the other (the world, other subjects) and in subsequent self-modification. The embodied, situated subject is indeed singular, but by no means monadic, self-sufficient, or identical with itself, for there is an alterity, a split at the very core of subjectivity itself. What saves us from solipsistic enclosure within our perceptual field is what Merleau-Ponty calls our "constitutive transcendence" (*The Visible and the Invisible*, 233), the "refusal to be anything at all" (*Phenomenology of Perception*, 452). It is, as he earlier calls it, a paradox: "that which makes me unique, my fundamental capacity for self-feeling, tends paradoxically to diffuse itself" (*The Prose of the World*, 135).[5] Briefly put, the human subject lives on the borderlines, constituted by a reversibility of touch, vision, and language in relation to the other. It is hardly surprising, then, that the underlying principle of Bakhtin's dialogism is a similarly liminal conception of subjectivity. If intersubjectivity is prior to subjectivity, we can no longer relate to the self as a territorial enclosure. Living on borderlines is what we should all do.

FROM BODY TO LANGUAGE

The body is indeed "in the beginning" for both Bakhtin and Merleau-Ponty, but the dynamics of embodied perception and interaction with the world serve as a template for the dynamics of discourse. Merleau-

Ponty insists on this non-Cartesian conception at the very outset: "our body," he writes, "is not an object for an 'I think,' it is a grouping of lived-through meanings which moves toward its equilibrium" (*Phenomenology of Perception*, 153). As W. J. Froman astutely notes, "just as it was necessary to conclude that the actual motion of the body follows from a prior dynamic situation or orientation of the body, so it is necessary to acknowledge that speech follows from a prior dynamic orientation of the body in the speaker's world of meaning. In the case of speech the phenomena toward which and away from which the body is already oriented are words, and these words are inhabited by meaning" (*Merleau-Ponty*, 65). Bodily intentionality is thus a paradigm for the operation of language as well. Perception, as described by Merleau-Ponty, is necessarily and invariably liminal and predicated on *differentiation*. Signification is always the articulation of separation, divergence, or gap (*écart*) between figure and ground ("Working Notes for *The Visible and the Invisible*," 187, 197), which is the enabling principle of the transition between the somatic and the semiotic, and it is in the dynamics of discourse that the foundational *écart*, or constitutive dissonance within subjectivity itself, is most powerfully evident.[6]

That Merleau-Ponty is aware of the need to move from body to language is already evident in *The Prose of the World* (139), where speech is conceived of as a sublimation of our bodily inherence in the world; as a gesture toward the other that "abolishes the limit between mine and not-mine, and ends the alternative between what has sense for me and what is non-sense for me, between me as subject and the other as object" (145). It is in discourse that the paradox of universal singularity may be resolved, for "speech is [on the one hand] peculiarly my own, my productivity, and yet speech is so only to make meaning out of my productivity and to communicate that meaning. The other who listens and understands joins with me in what is most singular in me" (141). Discourse, or rather dialogue, is born out of the commonality of language, which is a storehouse of "sedimented" significations, yet enables the expression of a singular subjectivity. It is the "ambiguous [bodily or spoken/written] gesture which makes the universal out of singulars and meaning out of our life" (146), and the dialogic dynamics of discourse that most clearly inscribe the inherence of the other in the self, the intercorporeal and intersubjective foundation of subjectivity.[7]

Merleau-Ponty's budding discursive orientation seems to mature a decade later in *The Visible and the Invisible*. In formulating his concept of the "Chiasm," this "strange adhesion of the seer and the visible" (139), and the asymmetrical reflexivity of the touching and the touched (142), he is impelled to move from the visible to the audible, and recognize the workings of phonation as a better instantiation of the chiasmic flesh. In a note at the margin of the text, he writes, "what are those adhesions compared with those of the voice and the hearing?" (143), and further on:

> I am a sonorous being, but I hear my own vibration from within; as [André] Malraux said, I hear myself with my throat. In this, as he also has said, I am incomparable; my voice is bound to the mass of my own life as is the voice of no one else. But if I am close enough to the other who speaks to hear his breath and feel his effervescence and his fatigue, I almost witness, in him as in myself, the awesome birth of vociferation. As there is a reflexivity of the touch, of sight, and of the touch-vision system, there is a reflexivity of the movements of phonation and of hearing; they have their sonorous inscription, their vociferations have in me their motor echo. This new reversibility and the emergence of the flesh as expression are the point of insertion of speaking and thinking in the world of silence. (144–45)

Wonderfully indifferent to the borderlines between philosophy and psychology, Merleau-Ponty follows this discursive orientation by defining individuality as style, "a certain manner of managing the domain of space and time over which it has competency, of pronouncing, of articulating that domain, of radiating about a wholly virtual center" (115). One need hardly point to the similarity of this poetic-philosophical definition and the psychological conception of Christopher Bollas, who derives similar insights from his own literary beginnings, and relates to selfhood as a "private idiom" (*Being a Character*, 51), a style of being. To be a character, as Bollas so beautifully puts it, is "to release one's idiom into lived experience" (54), and that idiom is inhabited and shaped by our internal objects, the idioms of others.

Merleau-Ponty's "discursive turn" may account for the enigmatic "invisible" in the title of the last work, where he writes of "our existence as sonorous beings for others and for ourselves," about language being everywhere; a landscape "overrun with words as with an invasion," and about voices belonging to no one and to everyone" (*The Visible and the Invisible*, 155; see also 175).[8] In the "Chiasm" section of *The Visible and the Invisible*, he announces his intention "to follow more closely this transition from the mute world to the speaking world" (154) and concludes "*if we were to make completely explicit the architectonics of the human body, its ontological framework, and how its sees itself and hears itself, we would see that the structure of its mute world is such that all the possibilities of language are already given in it*" (155; italics added). This last sentence, with its striking Bakhtinian resonance, is where I rest my case.

Merleau-Ponty did not live to pursue his discursive orientation, but his explicit analogy between the somatic and the semiotic as forms of signification, his insights as to the inherence and constitutive role of alterity within the subject, and his conception of universal singularity as enabled by the dynamics of language can highlight the underlying coherence of Bakhtin's work. The Bakhtinian tenor of Merleau-Ponty's architectonics of subjectivity takes us back, yet again, to the transition from "Author and Hero" with its attendant philosophical embarrassments to *Problems of Dostoevsky's Poetics*. This transition from phenomenological introspection to an intersubjective, sociological orientation is construed as a shift to a "Galilean linguistic consciousness" by Morson and Emerson (*Mikhail Bakhtin: Creation of a Prosaics*, 312, 328), and, from a different perspective, as "a linguistic turn" by Hirschkop ("Bakhtin's Linguistic Turn," passim).[9] "The early phenomenological works," Hirschkop writes, "are early in the usual sense, their insights blunted by a certain share of naiveté" (34). We have already seen that "naïveté," for Bakhtin, can be synonymous with faith in a transcendent authorial being, a "sense of faith," for which he is distinctly nostalgic. But, as Hirschkop reads Bakhtin, this line of work was discarded, inasmuch as the "linguistic turn" takes place in *Problems of Dostoevsky's Poetics*, where "Bakhtin's efforts are wholly bent on the analysis of *slovo*, the 'word' or 'discourse'. What he discovers or decides is that from here on afterwards, whatever his interests or concerns are, they will have to be articulated in the analysis of *language*" (Hirschkop, "Bakhtin's Linguistic Turn," 24).

I take issue with Hirschkop on this point: rather than a shift away from the phenomenology of the perceiving body, Bakhtin's focus on language in *Problems of Dostoevsky's Poetics* is, like Merleau-Ponty's late discursive turn, a direct carryover and amplification of his previous insights concerning the body. Bakhtin's own awareness of this continuity may be detected in the notes published under the title "Toward a Reworking of the Dostoevsky Book," where the analogy between body and discourse is explicit. Bakhtin writes there of the

> exceptionally keen sense of *one's own* and *the other* in the word, in style, in the most subtle nuances and twists of style, in intonation, in the speech gesture, in the body (mimic) gesture, in the expression of the eyes, the face, the hands, the entire external appearance, in the very way the body is carried.... In everything a person uses to express himself on the outside (and consequently, for *another*)—from the body to the word—an intense interaction takes place between *I* and *other*. (TRDB, 294–95)

He calls the Dostoyevskian revolution both "the birth of a new form of novel (a new form of visualization and a new human being-personality; overcoming materialization)" and "a new mode of wearing the clothing of the word, the clothing of language, a new mode for wearing one's own body, one's embodiment" (291).[10]

Undoubtedly, this analogy needs to be more fully articulated, and it is impossible to discard what is so glaringly obvious about *Problems of Dostoevsky's Poetics*, namely, its radical shift of conceptual and rhetorical modalities in relation to the earlier essay. As we have already seen, Dostoyevsky's abdication of the authorial prerogative (the constitutive *transgredience* and the "surplus of vision" that would have enabled him to enframe and to "consummate" his characters) is cited in "Author and Hero" as an example of aesthetic failure, a lack of "any unitary countenance" (AH, 20), and a preclusion of "aesthetic concord ... the concord intrinsic to prayer" (146). The very same abdication is celebrated in *Problems of Dostoevsky's Poetics* as a revolutionary move of a Copernican magnitude (PDP, 49). We have also noted that this apparent conceptual shift is accompanied by a different rhetorical modulation, inasmuch as Bakhtin seems to discard the ocular-centric approach of the earlier essay. The Dostoyevskian character is here "a carrier of a fully valid word and not the mute, voiceless object of the author's words," and "by the very construction of the novel, the author speaks not *about* a character, but *with* him" (63). The voice of the characters "is constructed exactly like the voice of the author himself" (7), and the privileged excess of vision has given way to "multi-voicedness" (16). The "firm and finalizing authorial definition" advocated in the aesthetic vision has turned in Dostoyevsky's work into just one "aspect of the hero's self-definition" (49; see also TRDB).

However, radical as this conceptual and rhetorical shift may seem, I would argue that the transition from the premises of "Author and Hero" to *Problems of Dostoevsky's Poetics* is not a departure from but an *enhancement* of Bakhtin's phenomenological orientation. The extrapolation from bodily-perceptual to discursive relations is an attempt—similar to that of Merleau-Ponty—to break through and away from the still-dualistic perspective of Husserl's phenomenological legacy by taking the concrete, embodied, experiential body as a point of departure and moving on to the dynamics of discourse as *entirely analogous to somatic relations*.

An explicit articulation of the analogy appears in "The Problem of the Text in Linguistics, Philology, and the Human Sciences," where Bakhtin relates to the human act as a "potential text" that can be understood "only in the dialogic context of its time (as a rejoinder, as a semantic position, as a system of motives)" (PT, 107). The ontological primacy of the body is deconstructed through the analogy of body and discourse: both are situated, relational, and diacritical. Both obtain their significance on the borderlines and in between the subject and the other.[11] In turning from the liminality of the body to the liminality of discourse, Bakhtin and Merleau-Ponty may have earned their membership in the "linguistic turn" that permeates the work of European intellectuals in the twentieth century, but though clearly indebted to the Saussurean conception of language as diacritical, they both turn away from the abstract, formalized, synchronic conception of *langue* that is, according to Saussure, the domain of linguistic research. Their own *terra incognita* is the living act of speech, or—to use Bakhtin's term—the utterance.

DISCOURSE AND SUBJECTIVITY

The earliest and most extensive exposition of this departure was provided by V. N. Voloshinov, who is distinctly echoed in Bakhtin's contemporaneous and subsequent work.[12] In *Marxism and the Philosophy of Language* (1929), Voloshinov opposes Saussure's "abstract objectivism," claiming that it has failed to account for the workings of language, because it excludes the utterance, the concrete speech act from its realm of inquiry (MPL, 58–82). Voloshinov sees his own task as the study of what he calls "inner speech," which "lies at the juncture between psychology and the concerns of the ideological sciences": "the units of which inner speech is constituted are certain *whole entities* somewhat resembling a passage of monologic speech or whole utterances. But, most of all, they resemble *the alternating lines of a dialogue.*" These units "are joined with one another and alternate with one another not according to the laws of grammar or logic but according to the laws of *evaluative* (emotive) *correspondence, dialogical deployment,* etc." (38).

Most significantly, though, consciousness, or subjectivity, for Voloshinov, is precisely what is constituted by "inner speech," inasmuch as the psyche is located at and formed by the semiotic encounter between the organism and the outside world. The "subjective psyche," he writes, is "to be localized somewhere between the organism and the outside world, on the *borderline* separating these two spheres of reality," whose point of contact is the sign. Psychic experience, he says, is "the semiotic expression of the contact between the organism and the outside environment," and *"the reality of the inner psyche is the same reality as that of the sign"* (26). "The semiotic material of the psyche is preeminently the word—*inner speech.* Inner speech, it is true, is intertwined with a mass of other motor reactions having semiotic value. But all the same it is the word that constitutes the foundation, the skeleton of inner life" (29).[13]

Echoes of Voloshinov's psycholinguistic theory (but *not* of its Marxist inflection) are clearly evident in *Problems in Dostoevsky's Poetics* and in "Discourse in the Novel," where Bakhtin explicitly relates to the constitutive liminality of both discourse and psyche, reinforcing the analogy through corporeal metaphors:

> Discourse lives, as it were, beyond itself, in a living impulse [*napravlennost'*] toward the object; if we detach ourselves completely from this impulse all we have left is the naked corpse of the word, from which we can learn nothing at all about the social situation or the fate of a given word in life. *To study the word as such, ignoring the impulse that reaches out beyond it, is just as senseless as to study psychological experience outside the context of that real life toward which it was directed and by which it was determined.* (DN, 292)

But Bakhtin's most extensive discussion of the utterance is to be found in "The Problem of Speech Genres," where the concept of the utterance is formulated as the basic unit of what Bakhtin would later call "metalinguistics," an alternative to the subject matter of Saussurean linguistics. In an uncharacteristically dismissive manner, Bakhtin relates to Saussure's diagrammatic depiction of the distinction between "speaker" (active party) and the "listener" (the passive party) and the "unified speech flow" between them as "fictions," which are still current in linguistics, and distort the complexity of the process of active speech communication and the active role of the other in this process (PSG, 68–69). As Michael Holquist notes in "Answering as Authoring," Bakhtin's metalinguistics does not simply turn to the *parole*, that is, the concrete instantiation of an abstract system (*langue*), but offers a study of language *as communication*. Unlike the sentence, the "utterance" cannot be studied in isolation from the specific instance of communication: the relationship and positions of listener and speaker, the extraverbal context of communication, the degree to which the utterance responds to or anticipates other utterances. The "speech experience" of the individual is a process of assimilation of and response to others' utterances, with "varying degrees of otherness or varying degrees of 'our-own-ness,' varying degrees of awareness and detachment. These words of others carry with them their own expression, their own evaluative tone, which we assimilate, rework, and re-accentuate" (PSG, 89). The "essential (constitutive) marker of the utterance is its quality of being directed to someone, its *addressivity*" (95), and in order to understand it, it should be studied within this context of "addressivity and the influence of the anticipated response, dialogical echoes from others' preceding utterances, faint traces of changes of speech subjects that have furrowed the utterance from within" (99).

Bakhtin's metalinguistic theory is by now sufficiently familiar, and further illustrations may be redundant, but we should note the same fusion of utterance and consciousness that we have seen in Voloshinov's work, mostly evident in Bakhtin's insistent anthropomorphizing of the utterance:

> Utterances are not indifferent to one another, and are not self-sufficient; they are aware of and mutually reflect one another. These

mutual reflections determine their character. Each utterance is filled with echoes and reverberations of other utterances to which it is related by the communality of the sphere of speech communication. (91)

Far from a theoretical abstraction or heuristic device, the utterance is not only formed by its singular and concrete context of addressivity; it is also endowed with full bodily and spatial presence: the utterance "finds" its object "enveloped in an obscuring mist" or in the "'light' of alien words that have already been spoken about it" (DN, 276); it makes its way like "a ray of light" through "an atmosphere filled with alien words, value judgments and accents" (277). "The other's rejoinder wedges its way, as it were, into [the character's] speech, and although this rejoinder is in fact absent . . . its shadow, its trace, falls on his speech, and that shadow, that trace is real" (PDP, 208). Discourse "lives, as it were, on the boundary between its own context and another, alien, context" (DN, 284). There is more, much more, of the same.

As we can see, then, both Bakhtin and Merleau-Ponty relate to discourse as necessarily intentional, dialogized, contextualized, and addressive. But this addressivity, or living-on-borderlines, is not only *intersubjective*; it is fundamentally and entirely *intrasubjective as well*. The most explicit articulation of this internal liminality can be read in Bakhtin's later notes, where his observations on the dialogicity of consciousness in Dostoyevsky's characters are extrapolated to subjectivity in general:

> A character's self-consciousness in Dostoevsky is thoroughly dialogized: in its every aspect it is turned outward, intensely addressing itself, another, a third person. Outside this living addressivity toward itself and toward the other it does not exist, even for itself. In this sense it could be said that the person in Dostoevsky is the *subject of an address*. (PDP, 251)

The dialogic nature of consciousness, the dialogic nature of human life itself. The single adequate form for *verbally expressing* authentic human life is the *open-ended dialogue*. Life by its very nature is dialogic. To live means to participate in dialogue: to ask questions, to heed, to respond, to agree, and so forth. In this dialogue a person participates wholly and throughout his whole life: with his eyes, lips, hands, soul, spirit, with his whole body and deeds. He invests his entire self in discourse, and this discourse enters into the dialogic fabric of human life, into the world symposium. (TRDB, 293)

Having followed some of the dotted lines leading from Bakhtin's breach of the boundary lines between body, discourse, and subjectivity to the work of Merleau-Ponty, it should now be easier to understand why the latter sounds so much like Bakhtin in his reflections on the ineluctable dialogism of embodied, discursive, human subjectivity:

> When I speak to another person and listen to him, what I understand begins to insert itself in the intervals between my saying things, my speech is intersected laterally by the other's speech, and I hear myself in him, while he speaks in me. (*The Prose of the World*, 142)

> I am not active only when speaking; rather, I precede my thought in the listener. I am not passive while I am listening; rather, I speak according to . . . what the other is saying. (143–44)

The trinitarian conception of body, discourse, and subjectivity is thus fully established: language, for Bakhtin, is never dissociated from the body, just as it cannot be dissociated from the concrete dynamics of subjectivity. Rather than being the mere conduit of consciousness, the utterance is its very embodiment, "coming into being" through a process that involves intentionality, retention, and anticipation of another word or utterance, actual or potential. It passes through a contextual background that "complicates the path of any word toward its object" (DN, 281) and sometimes finds its object "populated—overpopulated—with the intentions of others" (294).

Like Bakhtin, Merleau-Ponty discards the Saussurean systemic and abstract conception of language for a *phenomenology of living speech* ("On the Phenomenology of Language," in *Signs*, 86).[14] Language, as an "institution," a product of the "cultural sedimentation which bestows upon our words and gestures an accepted common background," is the centripetal vector, to use the Bakhtinian term, against which speech—the centrifugal power of subjectivity—can "transcend itself as a gesture" (*The Prose of the World*, 139, 141). Like Bakhtin, he begins with the perceiving body, our "carnal relation to the world and the other," which, he writes, is not "an accident intruding from outside upon a pure cognitive subject," but "our first insertion into the world and into truth" (139). Refusing to honor the dualism of body and language, Merleau-Ponty sees both as equally primary forms of engagement with the world. Any conception of subjectivity must therefore move back and forth between bodily perception and language: the insights derived from the experiential, perceptual, material body can be translated into the discursive domain, and the reversibility of the seeing and the visible is entirely analogous to that of speech. Most significantly, Merleau-Ponty, too, is ultimately concerned with in-betweenness, the bodily and discursive relation of self and other (to which he variously refers as the "chiasm" or the "flesh").

Having dubbed this philosophical affinity "uncanny," it should not surprise us to find Merleau-Ponty deploying some quasi-Bakhtinian tropes in relation to the nexus of body, discourse, and subjectivity: he, too, speaks of "a whole landscape . . . overrun with words as with an invasion," and of "the architectonics of the human body," its ontological framework, and "how its sees itself and hears itself." The mute world of the self-perceiving body, he says, already contains "all the possibilities of language," "everything required for there to be speech from one to another, speech about the world" (*The Visible and the Invisible*, 155). In another remarkably Bakhtinian passage, he says:

> *Words are behind me, like things behind my back, or like the city's horizon round my house,* I reckon with them or rely on them, but without having any "verbal image." . . . I do not need to visualize the word in order to know and pronounce it. It is enough that I possess its articulatory and acoustic style as one of the modulations, one of the possible uses of my body. *I reach back for the word as my hand reaches towards the part of my body which is being pricked;* the word has a certain location in my linguistic world, and is part of my equipment. I have only one means of representing it, which is uttering it. (*Phenomenology of Perception*, 180)

But these echoes are, in fact, anything but uncanny or accidental. It is not only the materiality of words, their spatial presence, tactile quality and visibility, which is significant here, but *the analogy between the process of articulation and the I-for-myself mode of perception.* In his essay

"On the Phenomenology of Language" (*Signs*, 84–97), Merleau-Ponty goes back to "the quasi-corporeality of the signifying" (88):

> [Discourse, or "speech," as he calls it] is comparable to a gesture because what it is charged with expressing will be in the same relation to it as the goal is to the gesture which intends it. . . . my corporeal intending of the objects of my surroundings is implicit and presupposes no thematization or "representation" of my body or milieu. . . . The significative intention (even if it is subsequently to fructify in "thoughts") is at the moment no more than a *determinate gap* to by filled by words—the excess of what I intend to say over what is being said or has already been said. (89)

What we ultimately encounter in Merleau-Ponty's work, then, is a full-fledged deconstruction of the dualism of body and language, a rejection of the primacy of body as that which is irreducible, self-evident, and axiomatic. The life of the human body, he writes in his working notes for *The Visible and the Invisible*, "cannot be described without it becoming a psycho-physical body" (168). This deconstructive move, implicit in Bakhtin's work, but not quite fully formulated, is articulated in Merleau-Ponty's philosophical interrogation: the focus on embodied perception is not, as it is often viewed, a return to a more primordial and "authentic" layer of subjectivity; it is the medium of subjectivity, insofar as it is analogous to discourse, and can therefore be described in the very same terms reserved for the study of language as "a diacritical, relative, oppositional system" ("Perception and Language," in *The Visible and the Invisible*, 214).[15] Vision itself, he says, in an echo of Lacan, is "structured like a language" (*The Visible and the Invisible*, 126). If speech can be conceived of as a sublimation of the body (a verbal gesture, as it were), the flesh, according to Merleau-Ponty, is just as conceivably an embodiment of speech.[16]

This is not a rhetorical exercise. If "the word and speech must somehow cease to be a way of designating things or thoughts, and become the presence of that thought in the phenomenal world, and moreover, not its clothing but its token or its body" (*Phenomenology of Perception*, 182), it is no longer possible to relate to language as representational. "The analysis of speech and expression," Merleau-Ponty writes, "brings home to us the enigmatic nature of our own body even more effectively than did our remarks on bodily space and unity" (197). Like the perceiving and moving body, language in use is intentional, directional, and—in a very particular sense of the word, to which we now turn—performative.

The concept of performative utterances, coined by J. L. Austin, refers to a particular class of speech acts. Unlike constative utterances, which describe or report a state of affairs, as in "he promised to pay me," performative utterances actually create a state of affairs through the process of enunciating it, as in "I promise to pay you" (Austin, *How to Do Things with Words*, 9–11). This paradigmatic case needs no further elaboration here, but what is noteworthy about this class of utterances is that it complicates the propositional relationship of language and truth. Constative utterances can be deemed true or false by virtue of their correspondence to a referent (an accurate description, report, or statement of reality), but performative utterances cannot be subjected to that test. They are speech acts (of promising, naming, cursing, etc.), which become valid only when and if they are uttered by the subject in the first person in a particular constellation of "conditions of felicity" (i.e., the speaker's position, intention, situational framework, etc.). The category of the performative, then, is *not referential but contextual*.

The implications of Austin's conception of performativity for discourse in general were articulated by Émile Benveniste, a fellow linguist, who, like Bakhtin, Voloshinov, and Merleau-Ponty, also conceives of language as the very medium, or "element" (rather than "instrument") of subjectivity.[17] Like them, Benveniste (who draws on the work of Yehoshua Bar-Hillel and Roman Jakobson) insists on "the profound difference between language as a system of signs and language assumed into use by the individual" ("The Nature of Pronouns," in *Problems in General Linguistics*, 220). What enables the conversion of the former to the latter is the performativity of "empty" signs, distinctive for being nonreferential with respect to 'reality.'" Personal pronouns, demonstratives (e.g., "here," "now") have no material reference in reality and only "become 'full' as soon as a speaker introduces them into each instance of his discourse." The role of these deictic signs is to convert language into discourse. They are not propositional and hence are not subject to "the condition of truth." They are purely performative in that, like Austin's special verbs, they derive their validity from the context, the relation, the position of the speaker (219–20).

It is through these "empty" discursive signs that subjectivity is constituted. The speaker who designates him/her self as "I" identifies him/herself as a unique person and sets him/herself up as a subject (219–20). But this can only be done through discourse, that is, in an interactional context (including, of course, purely internal dialogue):

> "Ego" is he who says "ego." That is where we see the foundation of "subjectivity," which is determined by the linguistic status of "person." Consciousness of self is only possible if it is experienced by contrast. I use *I* only when I am speaking to someone else who will be a *you* in my address. It is this condition of dialogue that is constitutive of person, for it implies that reciprocally I become you in the address of the one who in his turn designates himself as *I* . . . a polarity [which] does not mean either equality or symmetry . . . it is in a dialectic reality that will incorporate the two terms and define them by mutual relationship that the linguistic basis of subjectivity is discovered. (Benveniste, "Subjectivity in Language," in *Problems in General Linguistics*, 224–25)

The pronoun "I," Benveniste writes, "refers to the act of individual discourse in which it is pronounced, and by this it designates the speaker" (226). It thus has, like other deictics, only a here-and-now reference and the reality to which it refers is the reality of the "instance of discourse" that is "constitutive of all the coordinates that define the subject" (227).

Benveniste's performative conception of language goes a long way toward explaining why Bakhtin and Merleau-Ponty have felt the need to move from body to discourse: it is only the *relational* quality of language-turned-discourse that makes it possible for the speaker to become a subject by designating him/herself as such in and through a dialogic encounter. Intersubjectivity, experienced and enacted through discourse, precedes and enables the foundation of subjectivity. Insisting on the unfinished, incomplete quality of the world, Merleau-Ponty stipulates that the body, too, is "never completely constituted," and that there must be "an open and infinite unity of subjectivity," which is "invoked rather than experienced each time I perform an act of perception, each time I reach a self-evident truth, and the universal I is that background against which these effulgent forms stand out: it is through one present thought that I achieve the unity of all my thoughts.... I am a field, an experience" (*Phenomenology of Perception*, 406).

This is certainly not the "prison-house of language" posited by contemporary thinkers who conceive of subjectivity as an illusory structure, a fiction fabricated by the workings of language, interpellated by ideology and devoid of both sovereignty and agency. Discourse, to Benveniste again, is as primordial, irreducible, and foundational as the body, since "it is speaking man we find in the world" ("Subjectivity in Language," in *Problems in General Linguistics*, 224). It is the enabling condition of subjectivity because "it always contains the linguistic forms appropriate to the expression of subjectivity" (227). The same discursive conception of subjectivity as performative, singular, and relational informs the ethical vision of both Bakhtin and Merleau-Ponty. Their respective versions of "linguistic turn" in European philosophy are, in fact, very far from the more recent developments of this turn, which have replaced the notion of agential subjectivity with the relentless, ideological workings of discourse. For both of them, the power of discourse is precisely what opens up a loophole in the encounter of self and other, and offers a way out of the potentially petrifying gaze of the authorial/authoritative other.

When Merleau-Ponty describes the act of speech as "the subject's taking up of a position in the world and of his meanings" (*Phenomenology of Perception*, 193), when he insists on the distinction "between a *speaking word* and a *spoken word*" (to be echoed in Benveniste's *énonciation* and *énoncé* a few years later), he is working toward a conception of discourse as "the surplus of our existence over natural being ... [an] ever-recreated opening in the plenitude of being" (196–97). Like Bakhtin, Merleau-Ponty sees the human subject as living on borderlines, essentially tuned to the other, within and without. Dialogue, Merleau-Ponty says, is the "silent relationship with the other" that accounts for the "most essential power of speech" (*The Prose of the World*, 133):

> The others' words make me speak and think because they create within me an other than myself, a divergence (*écart*) by relation to ... what I see, and thus designate it to me myself. The other's words form a grillwork through which I see my thought. ("Working Notes for *The Visible and the Invisible*," 224)

Dialogism, then, is not only an intersubjective phenomenon but an intrasubjective articulation of non-self-coincidence. For Merleau-Ponty, the "coincidence of myself with myself" on which the *cogito* is premised is not real but merely "intentional and presumptive." In fact, he says, "between myself who have just thought this, and myself who am thinking that I have thought it, there is interposed already a thickness of duration" (*Phenomenology of Perception*, 344). There is a distinctly Bergsonian echo in the observation that "subjectivity is not motionless identity with itself; as with time, it is of its essence, in order to be genuine subjectivity, to open itself to an Other and to go forth from itself. . . . We must not treat the transcendent Ego as the true subject and the empirical self as its shadow or its wake" (426). We are, Merleau-Ponty concludes, "the upsurge of time" (428), ever-changing, ever-relativized, inevitably decentered. The recognition of the foundational *écart* within the self is, indeed, vertiginal and unsettling. But it does not do away with the ethical subject.

To recapitulate: both Bakhtin and Merleau-Ponty are working toward a recognition of the inescapable liminality of our embodiment, discourse, and subjectivity, but their respective itineraries do not lead to the disempowerment of agential subjectivity that has gained such currency in postmodernist thought. The dynamic of mutual decentering that emerges from the work of Bakhtin and Merleau-Ponty does the very opposite of this: it is precisely this living on borderlines—not *relative* but *relational*—that highlights the immense responsibility of being human and grants us the freedom of contraband.

BACK TO LITERATURE

This is by no means the end of the road. There would have been no need for an inquiry into ethics if it were not for the gap between "is" and "ought," if we were all ethical beings solely by virtue of our linguistic competence; and neither the analogy of the somatic and the semiotic nor the performative conception of discourse is sufficient in and of itself for the foundation of a non-Cartesian approach to ethics. This is the reason, as argued in the previous chapter, that Bakhtin turns from philosophy to poetics, to the language of art, which, he says, is "closer than any of the abstract cultural worlds taken in isolation to the unitary and unique world of the performed act" (*TPA*, 60). The significance of this claim may be highlighted, once again, through Merleau-Ponty's profound engagement with both literature and the visual arts.

In *The Prose of the World*, Merleau-Ponty offers a distinction between the "algorithmic" use of language and "speech." The "algorithm," which, he says, finds its best form in the language of the exact sciences, is a realm of "pure significations and pure signs," within which new meanings emerge from the old ones only through a procedure of internal transformation, and are thus always immanent to and presupposed by it (131). The "truth of the algorithm" is, therefore, "a truth of transparency, recovery, and recollection" (133), entirely consistent, in other words, with traditional epistemology, which conceives of truth as propositional or thetic. "Speech," however, has the power "to say as a whole more than it says word by word, to precede itself, whether in throwing the other toward what I know which he has not understood, or in carrying oneself toward what one is going to understand. It is speech which accomplishes those anticipations, encroachments, transgressions, those violent operations through which I build within the form and change its operation to make literature and philosophy turn into what they are" (131).

Before we pursue this turn to literature, however, we should note that, far from a crude or simple-minded distinction between the "humanities" and the "sciences," these two types of thinking about language cross the boundaries of disciplinary fields and their respective modes of inquiry:

> The living relation between speaking subjects is masked because one always adopts, as the model of speech, the statement or the indicative. One does so because one believes that, apart from statements, there remain only stammering and foolishness. Thus one overlooks how the tacit, unformulated, and nonthematized enters into science, contributing to the determination of science's meaning, and as such provide tomorrow's science with its field of investigation. One overlooks the whole of literary expression, where we must precisely mark out what may be called "oversignification" and distinguish it from non-sense. (144)

"Oversignification," which is the hallmark of literature, is precisely what allows creative thinking and discovery in the sciences as well. But the power of "speech," which finds its most powerful and authentic expression in the language of literature, has nothing to do with "what" it says (its propositional contents)—it is to be found in the "how," the peculiar dynamics of literary discourse: "It is the same thing to speak to and to be spoken to. *This is the irreducible fact that all militant speech harbors and which literary expression brings before us, if ever we were tempted to forget it*" (142; emphasis added).

Once again, we should turn to Shklovsky's concept of "estrangement," which so aptly encapsulates the very same principles.[18] As we have seen, Shklovsky's point of departure in his formalist manifesto "Art as Technique" (1917) is "the general laws of perception," the habituation, automatization, and routinization that blind us to our surroundings and to other people. This process of "learning to ignore" (11) applies not only to sense perceptions, but also to other modes of interaction with the world. It also applies—most powerfully perhaps—to the way we use language. Even more tellingly, Shklovsky refers to the language of "algebra"—just as Merleau-Ponty will refer to the "algorithm"—as the paradigm for this mode of language: "in this process, ideally realized in algebra, things are replaced by symbols. . . . By this 'algebraic' method of thought we apprehend objects only as shapes with imprecise extensions; we do not see them in their entirety but rather recognize them by their main characteristics. We see the object as though it were enveloped in a sack. We know what it is by its configuration, but we see only its silhouette" (11–12). "Estrangement" (or "defamiliarization," as it is sometimes translated) is thus the deliberate disruption of this algebraic mode of thought, a practice of wrenching things (words, images, concepts) out of their habitual contexts and thereby restoring them to life and to renewed perception.

A very similar conception of the dynamics of art emerges from Merleau-Ponty's description of style as a "coherent deformation" that makes the meaning of art perceptible ("On the Phenomenology of Language," in *Signs*, 90–91; "Indirect Language," ibid., 54–55), "an almost imperceptible inflection of ordinary usage," or a "consistency of a certain eccentricity" (*The Prose of the World*, 132), whose effect is precisely that which Shklovsky describes as "estrangement" as opposed to practical communication:

> What is hazardous in literary communication, or ambiguous and irreducible to a single theme in all the great works of art, is not a pro-

visional weakness of literature which we could hope to overcome. It is the price we must pay to have a conquering language which, instead of limiting itself to pronouncing what we already know, introduces us to new experiences and to perspectives that can never be ours, so that in the end language destroys our prejudices. (Merleau-Ponty, "On the Phenomenology of Language," 90)

The power of literature is most evident when it "manages to throw our *image* of the world out of focus, to distend the dimensions of our experience and pull them toward a new meaning" (91). This is in direct continuity with the conception of speech in *The Prose of the World*, where Merleau-Ponty writes of the "anticipations, encroachments, transgressions," "violent operations" of speech. We shall, he writes, be able to "understand this trespass of things upon their meaning, this discontinuity of knowledge which is at its highest point in speech, only when we understand it as the trespass of oneself upon the other and of the other upon me" (133). The alterity at the very core of subjectivity, the voice of the other within the self, is amplified in the literary, that is, "estranged," use of language.[19] For Merleau-Ponty, this is also true of painting, where the "upheaval" created by the violence of the disruption leads to "a new set of equivalences," "a truer relation between things," whose "ordinary ties are broken" ("Indirect Language," 56). The experience of reading, then, must entail some disruption of "well-worn available significations" in order to be productive (*The Prose of the World*, 11–12).[20]

For Merleau-Ponty, the fundamental performativity of discourse is amplified and enhanced in literary usage. Insisting on the inseparability of thought and language, he dispenses with traditional philosophical binaries of "inside" and "outside," dismisses metaphors like "screen" or "mask" that uphold the division of content and form, and refuses to entertain the concept of pure ideality, or a priori meaning. Ideas, he writes, are not given to us in any form except in their "carnal experience," that is, through their articulation in language (*The Visible and the Invisible*, 149–50). Language, like music, produces meaning in its "arrangement" (153). There is no separation between life and language, the somatic and the semiotic, because "what is lived is lived-spoken" (126). And literature, more than other uses of language, is a mode of discourse that cannot be emptied out of its verbal "container." The literary word is not a vehicle, not a conduit, but the very embodiment and flesh—the "lining" and "depth"—of the idea (149).[21]

Significantly, when Merleau-Ponty writes about language in general and the language of literature in particular, he proposes very similar distinctions. In *The Prose of the World*, he offers a distinction between *le langage parlé* and *le langage parlant*, translated (somewhat awkwardly but justifiably, I think) as "sedimented language" and "speech." The former is "language after the fact, or language as an institution, which effaces itself in order to yield the meaning which it conveys." The latter is "the language which creates itself in its expressive acts, which sweeps me on from the signs toward meaning" (10). For Merleau-Ponty, this distinction precisely marks off the literary from the instrumental use of language:

> Sedimented language is the language the reader brings with him, the stock of accepted relations between signs and familiar significations. . . . But speech is the book's call to the unprejudiced reader. Speech is the operation through which a certain arrangement of already available signs and significations alters and then transfigures each of them, so that in the end a new signification is secreted. (13)[22]

Like Bakhtin, who extends his literary insights first from Dostoyevsky's work to the novel in general, and then from the novel to discourse, what Merleau-Ponty aims at goes far beyond a theory of aesthetics. Prompted by the sense of philosophical disillusionment with which he introduces his work, it is, in fact, a theory of subjectivity designed to address the epistemological and the ethical need for a new philosophical idiom. Alongside what he calls "the analytic truth espoused by the algorithm," a truth of "transparency, recovery, and recollection," which is the product of "high-altitude thinking," abstraction, and generalization, he proposes another kind of truth, better known to poets and artists, "in which we participate, not insofar as we think *the same thing* but insofar as we are, each in his own way, moved and touched by it" (133). Philosophy, as traditionally conceived, and literature, are different in that the writer of fiction, when speaking "of the world and of things," does not make the claims of universality through abstraction and generalization, but transforms the "deepest partiality" of his audience into "a means of truth": "We shall completely understand this trespass of things upon their meaning, this discontinuity of knowledge which is at its highest point in speech, only when we understand it as the trespass of oneself upon the other and of the other upon me" (133).

The language of literature is, then, the language of contraband, which carries both speaker and addressee across the territory of what is already known. "Speaking language"—language as an event and a process rather than a sedimented, finished product—is the underlying performative principle in Merleau-Ponty's invocation of the Lacanian formula, when he writes that "the vision itself, the thought itself, are, as has been said, 'structured as a language'" (*The Visible and the Invisible*, 126).

This is a conception of truth that is not the truth of correspondence and adequation to a referent, but is predicated on the "authentic functioning" of language: it is "not a simple invitation to the listener or reader to discover in himself significations that were already there. It is rather the trick whereby the writer or orator, touching on these significations already present in us, makes them yield strange sounds" (*The Prose of the World*, 13). The notion of truth that emerges from this is, in fact, very close to that of psychoanalysis: "One can have no idea of the power of language until one has taken stock of that working or constitutive language which emerges when the constituted language, suddenly off center and out of equilibrium, reorganizes itself to teach the reader—and even the author—what he never knew how to think or say . . . [language] is the vehicle of truth" (14).

It is, then, the use of coherent deformation—a language that is "off center and out of equilibrium"—which allows for language to be used authentically, to become "speech." And "speech," we should remember, is very far from the Saussurean conception of *langue*—the sedimented, institutionalized, abstract system: speech is a singular act or a gesture that sets up "a milieu of communication, an intersubjective diacritical system" ("Working Notes for *The Visible and the Invisible*," 175).

Most important of all, the turn toward the language of literature, or the authentic act of speech, can offer a different conception of ethics. With Cleanth Brooks's "heresy of paraphrase" and the inherent performativity of language that works through estrangement in mind, we should realize that the ethical implications of reading are not to be found in any explicit theses or arguments that seem to emerge from the literary text, or in anything that a text has to "say *about* ethics," but in the way it *acts*, generating its truth in and through the encounter of self and other. The power of literature to subvert the reader's "imaginary sovereignty" (*The Prose of the World*, 12), to move the reader into a transcendence of self (14) and make her/him recognize an otherness within and without the self, is predicated on the disruption of habitual perceptions:

> My relation to a book begins with the easy familiarity of the words of our language, of ideas that are part of our makeup, in the same way that my perception of the other is at first sight perception of the gestures and behavior belonging to "the human species." But *if the book really teaches me something, if the other person is really another*, at a certain stage I must be surprised, disoriented. If *we are to meet not just through what we have in common but in what is different between us—which presupposes a transformation of myself and of the other as well*—then our differences can no longer be opaque qualities. . . . when I am reading, there must be a certain moment where the author's intention escapes me, where he withdraws himself. (142–43; emphases added)

It is, then, in the experience of reading, which "projects us beyond our own thoughts toward the other person's intention and meaning" (14), that we are made to recognize the asymmetrical reversibility of self and other; through the power of others' words, which do not merely vibrate "like chords" in our "machinery of acquired significations," but can "throw" us toward new and unknown truths that neither of us had known before (142).

The practice of reading, the performance of the text, which underscores the borderline position of the subject, is thus a thoroughly ethical mode of communication, in that it does not allow the subject to assimilate the other or to be assimilated by it. It generates a constant modification of one's self-definition—a reading of oneself in quotation marks, as it were—in the contact with the other. Engaging with the particular, the concrete, and the personal, the language of literature does not recognize any Kantian categorical imperative absolutes, but it does entail an absolute and primary orientation toward the other within and without the subject. This principle allowed Bakhtin to extrapolate his reading of Dostoyevsky to the novel in general and thence to the discursive-ethical as such. The language of literature—if and when we adopt it as our mode of interaction with others—cannot be anything but thoroughly relational.

Neither Merleau-Ponty nor Bakhtin is a formalist, after all. And at least in one important sense, their own engagement with art is, in fact, a reversal of the formalist position: if the formalists are after that elusive figure in the carpet, the exclusive property of art that they call "literariness" (*literaturnost*), for Merleau-Ponty and for Bakhtin, the distinction between the language of literature and the language of life is only a matter of degree, and the dynamics of literature—the adhesion of form and content, the performativity of language, and the effects of estrangement—are also potentially evident in the discourse of the subject and the other and that of the subject with itself. The language of literature is, to put it briefly, just like everyday language, only more so. And it is the literariness of everyday speech that can take the subject out of its anonymity and express his/her irreducible singularity (*The Prose of the World*, 113). To be better human beings, we need to learn how to use this language that is given to us; to speak it and make it speak for the otherness that is within us, even as we are spoken by it.

FROM DIALOGICS TO TRIALOGICS
READING BAKHTIN WITH LÉVINAS

> Who is the third who walks always beside you?
>
> When I count, there are only you and I together
>
> But when I look ahead up the white road
>
> There is always another one walking beside you . . .
>
> T. S. Eliot, The Waste Land, V,
"What the Thunder Said"

THE DOTTED LINES DRAWN IN THIS CHAPTER between Bakhtin and Lévinas are not designed to retrace the movements of earlier readers who have already highlighted and discussed the affinities of these two thinkers in depth.[1] The discussion will briefly follow their respective itineraries along several points of convergence, but then change course, beginning with the implications of Bakhtin's and Lévinas's different readings of Dostoyevsky, which, I believe, are symptomatic of a profound divergence of their philosophical positions. Working my way from this divergence, I propose that Bakhtin's discursive conception of subjectivity may offer a way out of a certain impasse at the core of Lévinas's work and point toward a more viable thinking of exilic ethics.

The most outspoken and self-conscious member of the exilic constellation, Emmanuel Lévinas offers an explicit articulation of the link between his metaphysical sensibility and his mode of philosophizing. Against the Odyssean prototype of homecoming, signifying the assimilation of alterity and return to the same, he posits the figure of Abraham, the Jewish patriarch, an exile, a stranger, and a wanderer who is never at home in the world (*Totality and Infinity*, 36–43). Profoundly religious as he is, it is no longer possible for him to return to the God of philosophers, "a god adequate to reason, a comprehended god who could not trouble the autonomy of consciousness, which finds itself again in all its adventures" ("The Trace of the Other," 346). In place of this adequation Lévinas posits a thinking of alterity that naturally aligns him with Derrida—another exilic Jew—on the one hand, and with Bakhtin on the other. But whereas Derrida, at least up to the latest phases of his work, did not explicitly articulate the relation of this homelessness to the ethical, Lévinas would insist on the connection at the very outset. Writing of "man's foreignness in the world," he calls for an extrapolation of this strangeness, an ungrounded state of being that becomes a precondition for ethics:

> The condition (or the uncondition) of being strangers and slaves in the land of Egypt brings man close to his neighbor. In their uncondition of being strangers men seek one another. No one is at home. The memory of this servitude assembles humanity. The difference that opens between the ego and itself, the non-coincidence of the identical, is a fundamental non-indifference with regard to men. ("Humanism and An-archy," 148–49)

Living on its own borderlines, facing the other, the exilic subject is not only irremediably vulnerable but infinitely responsible as well.[2] The exilic state of being—in both the cultural and the subjective senses—is not only recognized and acknowledged, but turns into an operative principle of ethics in Lévinas's work.

As with Bergson and Merleau-Ponty, the common point of departure for Bakhtin and Lévinas is a profound disenchantment with Western philosophy as a mode of theorizing that identifies true knowledge with abstraction, generalization, and systematization; that strives to assimilate the other to the same. Bakhtin introduces what was to be a lifelong philosophical project with a diagnosis of the sterility of contemporary philosophical thinking, the dissociation incurred as a product of theoreticism. His philosophical distress revolves on the failure of philosophical ethics, which he perceives as dissociated from the lived, concrete experience of ethical choice and action. The "theoretical world," Bakhtin writes, "is obtained through an essential and fundamental abstraction from the fact of my unique being and from the moral sense of that fact—'as if I did not exist'" (*TPA*, 9); it "loses the individual act or *deed*" in its specificity, historicity, and uniqueness (25).

Lévinas, too, rejects the "nostalgia for totality" (*Ethics and Infinity*, 76) characteristic of traditional Western philosophy, which, he writes, "can be interpreted as an attempt at universal synthesis, a reduction of all experience, of all that is reasonable, to a totality wherein consciousness embraces the world, leaves nothing other outside of itself, and thus becomes absolute thought" (75). Lévinas's entire work can be read as an ongoing struggle against a philosophical totalitarian theology that might take—as both Bakhtin and Lévinas knew all too well—the most dangerous and lethal secular ideological forms. The somewhat cumbersome neologisms coined by Lévinas—"otherwise than being" (*autrement qu'être*), "beyond essence" (*au-delà de l'essence*), "non-indifference"—are all generated in the attempt to capture that which is not recognized by the language of philosophical knowledge.

In response to this philosophical disenchantment, both thinkers are trying to articulate an alternative conception of a first philosophy that would address the questions of ethics and subjectivity. Rather than normative formal and abstract systems, propositions and universal laws derived from the Cartesian grammar of subjectivity, they relate to the unique, the private, and the concrete. What they offer is "a phenomenology" of ethical subjectivity (*TPA*, 32): a description of "the actual, concrete architectonic of value-governed experiencing of the world" (61), of the attitude and the position of the subject in the encounter with the other. Their respective rhetorical formulations of this phenomenological conception are strikingly similar.

For Bakhtin, "it is not the content of an obligation that obligates me, but my signature below it—the fact that at one time I acknowledged or undersigned the given acknowledgment" (38).[3] Against the universalizing ambition of formal ethics, the performance of the act of undersigning, the "answerable deed," can only be accomplished by the singular, concrete subject, in a specific and unrepeatable context of time, place, and circumstances. This is precisely why "the ought" cannot be conceived of as an abstract universal principle or a categorical imperative: "[it is] a certain attitude of consciousness, the structure of which we intend to disclose phenomenologically. There *are* no moral norms that are determinate and valid in themselves as *moral* norms, but there is a *subiectum* with a determinate structure . . . and it is upon him that we have to rely" (6).

The singularity of the subject, its unique position in time and space at any given moment, is translated ethically as "my non-alibi in Being," a sense of ineluctable responsibility, inasmuch as "[t]hat which can be done by me can never be done by anyone else" (40). The ethical, or "answerable" act, is "precisely that act which is performed on the basis of an acknowledgment of my obligative (ought-to-be) uniqueness" (42); it is the specific and concrete decision, the act performed, the choice made at a particular moment by a singular human being.[4]

Lévinas, too, contends that "the character of value . . . comes from a specific attitude of consciousness, of a non-theoretical intentionality . . . irreducible to knowledge. . . . The relationship with the Other can be sought as an irreducible intentionality" (*Ethics and Infinity*, 32). What is proposed here is the interpellation of the ethical subject by his or her concrete acknowledgment—or "testimony," as Lévinas calls it—of responsibility, which is "not a simple attribute of subjectivity, as if the latter already existed in itself, before the ethical relationship. Subjectivity is not for itself; it is, once again, initially for another. . . . I say: here I am! [*me voici*]" (96–97). It is, of course, significant that the response to the other echoes the biblical form of response to the summons of divinity (Gen. 22:1, 7, 11), but rather than in the higher authority of a supreme authorial being, the source of the ethical command is to be found in the constitution of the subject by this alterity and in its irreducible singularity. The recognition that "my responsibility is untransferrable" is derived from the recognition that "no one could replace me." No one else can occupy the same position in the same context, and herein lies the charge of responsibility that is the "supreme dignity of the unique" or—to use Bakhtin's forensic term—the impossibility of an alibi: "I am I in the sole measure that I am responsible, a noninterchangeable I. I can substitute myself for everyone, but no one can substitute himself for me. Such is my inalienable identity of subject." The authority cited by Lévinas at this point is—unsurprisingly—Dostoyevsky: "It is in this precise sense that Dostoyevsky said: '*We are all responsible for all men before all, and I am more than all the others*'" (*Ethics and Infinity*, 100–101).

Leaving the Dostoyevsky connection aside for a moment, we should first focus on the meaning of liminality in this context. The link between the subject's singularity and ethical responsibility is mediated through the "deposition of the sovereign I," a conception of subjectivity as preceded and constituted by intersubjectivity and living on its own borderlines: "I become a responsible or ethical 'I' to the extent that I agree to depose or dethrone myself—to abdicate my position of centrality—in favor of the vulnerable other" (Kearney, "Dialogue with Emmanuel Lévinas," in Cohen, ed., *Face to Face with Lévinas*, 27). Paradoxically, perhaps, the ethical moment is a "putting in question" of the knowing subject, a dismantling of his or her claims to autonomy and sovereignty. But rather than a loss of agency, this deposition entails a heavy burden of responsibility.

For Bakhtin, too, the ethical subject is always already displaced and deposed. "A passionate rejection of one's place in life becomes the premise on which one's life is based" ("Rhetoric," 64). As in the thought of Lévinas, this foundational a-topia of subjectivity is the central paradox of being that hollows out all claims to sovereignty and autonomy and at the same time lays the fullest measure of responsiveness and responsibility on the deposed subject who lives on his or her own borderlines. The lived, experienced relation to the other does not lend itself to the universal generalized conception of the subject of philosophy: it is invariably asymmetrical, inasmuch as that "I-for-myself" mode of being creates the ethical sphere of absolute incommensurability of I to all the others. What emerges from the work of Bakhtin and Lévinas is, then, a phenomenological conception of ethics predicated on the non-coincidence of the subject with itself and its radical openness to the other.

To be truly ethical, the encounter with the other must not be an assimilation of the other into the same; it must recognize alterity rather than attempt to domesticate it; above all, it must grant the other's innate ability to break through any and all forms of containment and closure from without. It is thus that the distinction between knowledge and love emerges, since it is the speaking face of the other, rather than his or her (cognitively or aesthetically) reified image, that elicits the ethical response and calls for the responsibility or, as it has been rendered in translation, the "answerability" (*otvetstvennost'*), of the subject. Only in love can the other—no longer an object of cognition or aesthetic framing—retain the mode of being that Bakhtin calls "I-for-myself," which allows for "inner infinitude" ("Rhetoric," 65), for alterity, and for change. "Knowledge has always been interpreted as assimilation," Lévinas writes. "Even the most surprising discoveries end by being absorbed, comprehended, with all that there is of 'prehending' in 'comprehending.' The most audacious and remote knowledge does not put us in communion with the truly other; it does not take the place of sociality; it is still and always a solitude" (*Ethics and Infinity*, 60). If knowledge amounts to a "suppression of alterity," love is that which does not reduce the other to the same. "Alterity and duality do not disappear in the loving relationship. The idea of a love that would be a confusion between two beings is a false romantic idea. The pathos of the erotic relationship is the fact of being two, and that the other is absolutely other" (66). Lévinas's inspiration for the juxtaposition of knowledge and love may well come from Rosenzweig's *Star of Redemption*, where the "Grammar of the Logos or the Language of Cognition" (124–31) is pitted against the "Grammar of Eros or the Language of Love" (173–85). The position of "dialogue" as the first entry in the glossary of the latter speaks for itself.

In the Lévinasian idiom, the correlate of unassimilated alterity is the face of the other. But rather than a visual phenomenon, an object of the gaze that would enframe, contain, and absorb it, Lévinas relates to the face in terms more appropriate for voice. The face of the other is that which makes the ethical demand, the demand for a response:

> One can say that the face is not "seen." It is what cannot become a content, which your thought would embrace; it is uncontainable, it leads you beyond. It is in this that the signification of the face makes it escape from being, as a correlate of a knowing. Vision, to the contrary, is a search for adequation; it is what par excellence absorbs being. But the relation to the face is straightaway ethical. . . . Face and discourse are tied. The face speaks. It speaks, it is in this that it renders possible and begins all discourse. I have just refused the notion of vision to describe the relationship with the Other. It is Discourse, and, more exactly, response or responsibility which is this authentic relationship. (*Ethics and Infinity*, 86–88)

Why, one may wonder, does Lévinas insist on a metaphor that, being primarily visual, requires such a degree of modification and qualification? The answer may have to do with the Hebrew root of the word *panim* (face), which is the same as the verbal root of "turning." Noting this relation, Susan Handleman reads the figure of the face as a "facing relation," a "turning toward the other," which calls into question the separate, narcissistic ego—facing, Handleman says, is therefore "a disruption" of the autonomous, sovereign self-identical Cartesian subject ("Facing the Other," 50, 61).[5] Indeed, Lévinas will repeatedly insist that rather than being an object of vision, the face is that which breaks through form, which speaks to and interpellates the other (*Totality and Infinity*, 39, 50, 66). Whether this justifies the diagnosis of a full-fledged Lévinasian "linguistic turn," as diagnosed by Simon Critchley and Edith Wyschogrod, remains moot, but the shifts from viewing to listening, and from the face to the voice—these analogous moves in the work of Bakhtin and Lévinas—are evident enough to require no further elaboration.[6]

What needs to be highlighted at this point is the concomitant shift from a spatial to a temporal orientation. For Lévinas, the ethical moment, implicitly equated with love, is a "putting in question" of the knowing subject, a dismantling of his or her claims to autonomy and sovereignty. The encounter with the other is not resolved through assimilation, containment, and comprehension. "*Eros* differs from possession and power. . . . It is neither a struggle, nor a fusion, nor a knowledge. . . . It is the relationship with alterity, with mystery, that is with *the future*, with what in the world where there is everything, is never there" (*Time and the Other*, 81; *Ethics and Infinity*, 68). Time, for Lévinas, is the subject's "very relationship with the Other" (77; see also *Ethics and Infinity*, 57). It is "not a simple experience of duration, but a dynamism which leads us elsewhere than toward the things we possess. It is as if in time there were a movement beyond what is equal to us. Time as a relationship to unattainable alterity and, thus, an interruption of rhythm and its returns" (*Ethics and Infinity*, 61).

This is very close to the Bakhtinian formulation: living on its own borderlines, the subject's mode of being is always diachronic, projected ahead of itself. It is always "yet-to-be." Lévinas is similarly concerned with the future orientation of subjectivity, with what is yet-to-come (*a-venir*), a reaching out toward an unknowable alterity that disrupts the presumed self-presence of the "sovereign I." The absolute alterity that defines the future is the mode of being that is always yet-to-be, never identical to itself, and always points beyond its presence to itself. "The other is the future," Lévinas says. It is unknowable and impossible to grasp and possess. It is not merely time but the openness into futurity that underwrites the subject's relationship with the other (*Time and the Other*, 77 and passim; *Ethics and Infinity*, 57). This equation of alterity with futurity is probably the most significant move for our present concerns, since it brings in the intrasubjective dimension of alterity, preempting the reductive and all-too-common understanding of dialogue as merely intersubjective.

Lévinas extrapolates this temporalized conception of alterity, an "untotalizable diachrony" (Kearney, "Dialogue with Emmanuel Lévinas," in Cohen, ed., *Face to Face with Lévinas*," 21–22), onto the relationship with God: "Time fashions man's relation to the other, and to the absolutely other or God, as a diachronic relation irreducible to correlation" (23). Like the human other, this nontheological conception of God is premised on a recognition of an absolute alterity "irreducible to the synchrony of the same" (21–22). What is most interesting about this analogy is the reversal of relations between the sacred and the profane: rather than deducing the interhuman or intrahuman relationship from the divine, Lévinas sets out from human alterity, which becomes a template for the radical alterity of God.

As we have already seen, Bakhtin also conceives of the projection of the self into the temporal and semantic future as a precondition of ethical freedom, and he, too, relates to the ethical moment as a diachronic unraveling of subjectivity: the need to be "open" to oneself; the "yet-to-be" mode of being; the conception of subjectivity from within as "non-unitary" by definition; the nongivenness of selfhood and its temporal projection ahead of itself (AH, 13, 83, 100) converge in the concept of the "loophole": "I myself as *subiectum* never coincide with me myself: I—the *subiectum* of the act of self-consciousness—exceed the bounds of this act's content . . . [a] *loophole* out of time, out of everything given, everything finitely present on hand. I do not, evidently, experience the *whole* of myself in time" (109). The most explicit connection is made in the fragment "Rhetoric, insofar as it is false . . . ," where the concept of freedom is synonymous with the unresolved and incomplete perspective of "the temporal and semantic future" and the "internal infinitude" that is the "inward truth" of the subject and the precondition of the ethical act (65).

Both Bakhtin and Lévinas conceive of the aesthetic relationship in terms of closure, temporal framing, and sameness. Art, as understood by Lévinas, is on the side of knowledge and of timelessness, and it hence becomes the target of an atypically scathing critique. Obviously, one might (and does, in the case of the present author) wish to contest Lévinas's understanding of art, or even the very lumping of various modes of artistic production into an overarching concept.[7] But, be that as it may, we should note that his vehement opposition to aesthetics does *not* have its source in the Platonic privileging of truth, but in the identification of the totalizing representational claims of both art and knowledge and their ostensible suppression of alterity.[8] The position he takes in relation to art is, in fact, profoundly anti-Platonic, inasmuch as it diagnoses the same totalizing desire in both aesthetics and philosophy. To redeem itself and get back to the city, art should move from aesthetics to ethics, from the image to the voice.

To unpack this argument, let us look at Lévinas's poignant indictment of art in "Reality and Its Shadow." "The most elementary procedure of art," he writes, "consists in substituting for the object its image," which "neutralizes" our real relationship with the object (3). Art, on this account, is that which freezes duration, suspends the future, and turns freedom into necessity. And while it is more readily understood in the case of the visual, plastic arts (Laocoön will forever remain caught up in the grip of the serpents), it is just as true, he argues, for forms of art like music and literature that only appear to introduce temporality into their form.

> [Characters in a novel] can be narrated because their being *resembles* itself, doubles itself and immobilizes. . . . The characters of a novel are beings that are shut up, prisoners. . . . A novel shuts beings up in a fate despite their freedom. . . . Something somehow completed arises in it, as though a whole set of facts were immobilized and formed a series. They are described between two well-determined moments, in the space of a time existence had traversed as though through a tunnel. The events related form a *situation*—akin to a plastic ideal. That is what myth is: the plasticity of a history. What we call the artist's choice is the natural selection of facts and traits which are fixed in a *rhythm*, and transform time into images. (Lévinas, "Reality and Its Shadow," 10, emphasis added; see also id., *Totality and Infinity*, 201–2)[9]

The convergence of terms is striking. Like Bakhtin's juxtaposition of "rhythm" and "loophole," the Lévinasian conception of rhythm designates imposition of a pattern, a denial of freedom, choice, or agency: "because the subject is caught up and carried away by it . . . in rhythm there is no longer a oneself, but rather a sort of passage from oneself to anonymity" ("Reality and Its Shadow," 4). This, says Lévinas, happens when the subject becomes part of its own representation—a concept that can only be understood as equivalent to Bakhtin's conception of I-for-the-other. Our capitulation to the "magic" of rhythm and the seductions of art is inherently immoral, the "devil's part," as it were:

> We find appeasement when, beyond the invitations to comprehend and act, we throw ourselves into the rhythm of a reality which solicits only its admission into a book or a painting. Myth takes the place of mystery. The world to be built is replaced by the essential completion of its shadow. This is not the disinterestedness of contemplation but of irresponsibility. The poet exiles himself from the city. From this point of view, the value of the beautiful is relative. There is something wicked and egoist and cowardly in artistic enjoyment. There are times when one can be ashamed of it, as of feasting during a plague. (12)

These are heavy guns, and one cannot help thinking that only a person highly susceptible to the magic of art would so passionately denounce it as the "devil's part" and feel so guilty about the indulgence of artistic enjoyment. Significantly for the present discussion, Lévinas does offer a redeeming clause toward the conclusion of his essay, where he turns to Dostoyevsky, who, like other "intellectual" authors,

> manifests a more and more clear awareness of this fundamental insufficiency of artistic idolatry. In this intellectualism the artist refuses to be only an artist, not because he wants to defend a thesis or cause, but because he needs to interpret his myths himself. Perhaps the doubts that, since the Renaissance, the alleged death of God has put in souls, have compromised for the artists the reality of the henceforth inconsistent models, have imposed on him the onus of finding his models anew in the heart of his production itself, and made him believe he had a mission to be creator and revealer. The

task of criticism remains essential, even if God were not dead, but only exiled. (13)

The connection made here between the death of God and the altered conception of the authorial position in Dostoyevsky's work is very close to Bakhtin's construction of the "small-scale Copernican revolution" inaugurated by Dostoyevsky, explicitly related to what is conceived as secularization of culture. As we shall soon see, however, the Dostoyevskian connection is not only a point where the conceptual itineraries of Bakhtin and Lévinas intersect and converge; it is also a point of significant divergence, which may well be far more interesting for our present concerns.

Bakhtin, too, links knowledge and aesthetics and draws the same distinction between these forms of totalization on the one hand and love on the other, when he writes of an "element of violence in knowledge and in the artistic form." The prerequisite for both knowledge and aesthetic form-giving is a "subordination" and "deadening" of the object, a representation of the object (i.e., the other) as "already exhausted," closed off from the openness of the future, bounded, resolved, determined, "consummated," and finalized—dead, in short ("Rhetoric," 65).

■ ■ ■ ■

This conflation of cognition and the act of aesthetic authoring under the banner of violence is a far cry from Bakhtin's benign "centripetal" view of authorial "consummation from without" in "Author and Hero." Its hostility to both aesthetic and cognitive finalization (a particular type of objectifying "knowledge") clearly echoes Dostoyevsky's abdication of authorial transgredience. "Consummation" from without by an authorial other who creates "the deadening image [of the hero] *in absentia* . . . is devoid of dialogicity and unfinalizability" ("Rhetoric," 69). In terms uncannily similar to those of Lévinas, Bakhtin sets love against the power of knowledge and aesthetics. Unlike these relations that define, "consummate," and "finalize" the subject from outside, love does not seek to contain and enframe its object; it recognizes its alterity and does not speak of it "in absentia," but addresses it face to face. Love can thus "see and depict the inner freedom of its object," allowing for its "inner infinitude" (66, 65), described in a Bergsonian spirit as real openness into the unknowable future. Unlike knowledge or aesthetic finalization, love is commensurate with the "inner axiological infinitude" of the subject, and it allows its object—the human subject—to transcend itself.

Returning to the early distinction between truth as *pravda* and truth as *istina*, Bakhtin takes a distinctly "centrifugal" position here with regard to any truth (aligned in this context both with knowledge and with the aesthetic relation) imposed on the subject from without, alienating it from its inner infinitude and silencing its inner voice. Even "grace," that gift of selfhood that, in the terms of "Author and Hero," is granted by the benevolent authorial enframing vision, is now conceived of as a false gift. Whether it descends as a blow (*udar*) or as a gift (*dar*), as long as it is superimposed from without and "makes full use of all the privileges of . . . outsideness," it always involves some element of "residual violence" ("Rhetoric," 67).

We have already noted that Bakhtin's apparent shift from a spatial-visual to a temporal-auditory frame of reference coincides with his dismissal of the authorial position of aesthetic transgredience in favor of Dostoyevsky's polyphonic poetics. Remarkably, Bakhtin also proposes a similar juxtaposition through a distinction of "image" and "face" in this passage. The image, for him, is a product of cognition, of aesthetic consummation and definition from without. It "closes off" the subject and denies it the gift of the future, "ignores the possibility that he would change, become different." It forces the subject to "coincide with himself," casting him into "the hopelessness of the consummated and the ready-made," making use of "the privilege of its outsideness" (67). Whether conceptual or aesthetic, there is an element of violence in the image that encloses the subject within boundaries imposed from without, turning it into an object of consummation and consumption. Conversely, the face, the unconsummated image, he says, in what sounds like a prefiguration of Lévinas, is that which *speaks* (68).

At the opposite pole of the aesthetic image, as Lévinas conceives of it, we find the upsurge of discourse, the enactment of the relation between the same and the other (*Totality and Infinity*, 39). Discourse, Lévinas says, "*implies transcendence, radical separation, the strangeness of interlocutors, the revelation of the other to me . . . the experience of something absolutely foreign*" (73). It is not a *representation* but a *performance* of the relation to the other, and is thus, in essence, ethical (216). Lévinas already describes ethics as a "kind of waking up from aesthetic existence, with its primacy on vision, and 'the visual experience to which Western civilization ultimately reduces all spiritual life'" in his 1949 essay "The Transcendence of Words" (147). Discourse interrupts the self-sufficiency and totality of the aesthetic outlook that Lévinas associates with visual representation. It is the medium of awakening from aesthetics to ethics, a relation to the other that cannot be reduced to the same, wherein the subject's living on its own borderlines is most clearly enacted and legislated.[10]

At this point, it is surely no longer necessary to rehearse the centrality of discourse in Bakhtin's work, but we should, perhaps, reiterate his insistence on the essential future-orientation, the temporal openness, and the rejection of containment or anticipation that aligns real conversation with the ethical yet-to-be modality, the orientation of the living word toward a "future answer word": "Forming itself in an atmosphere of the already spoken, the word is at the same time determined by that which has not yet been said but which is needed and in fact anticipated by the answering word. Such is the situation in any living dialogue" (DN, 280).

Here, again, we should look back to the groundbreaking work of Franz Rosenzweig, who sought to cure the sickness of philosophy by recourse to living discourses, "speech-thinking" (*Sprachdenken*), as he calls it.

> [In the "new thinking,"] speech takes the place of the method of thinking . . . [which] is timeless and wants to be timeless. . . . Speech is bound to time, nourished by time, and it neither can nor wants to abandon this ground of nourishment; it does not know beforehand where it will emerge; it lets itself be given its cues from others; it actually lives by another's life, whether that other is the one who listens to a story, or is the respondent in a dialogue, or the participant in a chorus; thinking, by contrast, is always solitary, even if it should happen in common, among several "symphilosophers": even then, the other is only raising the objections I should actually have made myself,—which accounts for the tediousness of most philosophic dialogue, even the overwhelming majority of Plato's. In actual conversation something really happens. I do not know beforehand what

the other will say to me, because I do not even know beforehand what I will say; perhaps not even whether I will say anything at all. ("The New Thinking," 86)

[The difference between these two modes of thinking] does not lie in sound and silence, but in the need of another and, what is the same thing, in the taking of time seriously. Here, "thinking" is taken to mean thinking for no one and speaking to no one (for which, you can substitute "everyone," the so-called "general public," if you think it sounds better). But speaking means to speak to someone and to think for someone; and this Someone is always a very definite Someone, and doesn't merely have ears like the general public, but also a mouth. (87)

Rosenzweig, we can safely assume, would happily have included Merleau-Ponty, Lévinas, and Bakhtin among the "speech-thinking philosophers."

But—as we have already noted with regard to Merleau-Ponty—to speak of a "linguistic turn" in the work of either Bakhtin or Lévinas is to risk missing the complexity of language in use, as the mere facticity of discourse is certainly not a guarantee of ethics. Lévinas is explicit about it: the distinction between the ontological and the ethical is translated in his work into a distinction between the propositional content of discourse, labeled "the said" (*le dit*), and the act of interlocution, the implicit relation to the other, labeled "the saying" (*le dire*). The latter is, to use Simon Critchley's succinct formulation,

my exposure—corporeal, sensible—to the Other, my inability to refuse the other's approach. It is the performative stating, proposing, or expressive position of myself facing the other. It is a verbal or non-verbal ethical performance, whose essence cannot be caught in constative propositions. . . . The content of my words, their identifiable meaning, is the Said, while the Saying consists in the fact that these words are being addressed to an interlocutor. The Saying is the sheer radicality of human speaking, of the event of being in relation with an Other; it is the non-thematizable ethical residue of language that escapes comprehension, interrupts philosophy, and is the very enactment of the ethical movement from the Same to the Other. (Critchley, *The Ethics of Deconstruction*, 7)

The distinction between these two modes of thinking about discourse, fundamental to the work of Lévinas through its various phases, is extrapolated to a distinction between the ontological and the ethical: language as the "pure exposure of the saying," which inscribes an "ethical openness to the other," is pitted against the "totalizing closure of the said," which is an "ontological closure to the other" (Kearney, "Dialogue with Emmanuel Lévinas," in Cohen, ed., *Face to Face with Lévinas*, 28–29). It is thus the addressivity of discourse, to use the Bakhtinian idiom, rather than its content, that makes for the significance of discourse.

Recall here that Merleau-Ponty, too, makes a similar distinction between what he has called "algorithmic" language, a language of "pure signs," which carries the "truth of transparency, recovery, and recollection" (*The Prose of the World*, 133), and another form of language use that he calls "speech," which can "say as a whole more than it says word by word, to precede itself, whether in throwing the other toward what I know which he has not understood, or in carrying oneself toward what one is going to understand," to perform "those anticipations, encroachments, transgressions, those violent operations through which I build within the form and change its operation to make literature and philosophy turn into what they are" (131). As we have seen, the very same distinction is synonymous in Merleau-Ponty's work with that between *le langage parlé* (sometimes also translated as "sedimented language"), which refers to "language after the fact," and *le langage parlant*, which is language in process, the language of literature, which has an unlimited power to "secret new significations" (*The Visible and the Invisible*, 10), enabling signs to "trespass upon their meaning" (*The Prose of the World*, 133). Once again we encounter the power of literature, which lies not in its *constative* utterances, in what it has to say *about* ethics, but in its *performative* ability to subvert and transcend the sedimented, algorithmic language of mechanized, habitual conceptions.

Unlike Merleau-Ponty, Lévinas does not extend his distinction between the saying and the said to art, which remains—at least at the level of explicit articulation—entirely in the realm of the "said," that is, of representation. In fact, he often relates to art as an example of "representation," "image," "pure theme," or "pure exposition" (*Otherwise than Being*, 39, 40). But it is interesting to note that whenever he tries to instantiate the concept of the "saying," he has recourse to particular kinds of literature, which are, apparently, exempted from his general critique of aesthetics. The claim that "the ethical Saying must proceed through an abuse of language" (188), takes us very close to the concept of literary estrangement discussed in the second chapter of this study, and the equation of this abuse of language with a disruption of the habitual economy of selfhood leads Lévinas to the conclusion that "man can give himself in saying to the point of poetry—or he can withdraw into the nonsaying of lies" (Kearney, "Dialogue with Emmanuel Lévinas," in Cohen, ed., *Face to Face with Lévinas*, 29).[11]

Arguably, this relation of the saying to the said, which may be described as "asymptotic," is not a new philosophical idea in and of itself. As noted in the first chapter of this study, it is already clearly evident in Montaigne's *Essays*, and it inevitably shadows any autobiographical text, be it a volume or a single sentence: the *I* who generates the text is not identical to the *I* who is its grammatical subject; it would always exceed and overrun its own framedness, as the saying would always exceed the said. What is new, however, is the conception of the ethical significance of this relation—a point of convergence for the exilic constellation. This, as we have seen, is the underlying principle of Bakhtin's architectonics of subjectivity. The human subject can remember itself or perceive itself from without, as it were, but in this act of "self-objectification," he/she would never coincide with him/herself. What is brought out in this formulation is the depth of distinction between the anonymous "subject," or—to use the anonymous grammatical person—"one," and *"I-for-myself,"* which exists only in the "*act* of this self-objectification, and not in its product": "I am incapable of fitting all of myself into an object, for I exceed any object as the active *subiectum* of it" (AH, 38).

Similarly to the constructions offered by Lévinas and Merleau-Ponty, Bakhtin's conception of the "loophole" is directly translatable into the transcendence of the saying over the said, the non-coincidence of the speaking subject with its objectified selfhood (see 109). Rather than an essential, ontologically prior essence, the human subject is constantly in the process of becoming; in the diachronic rather than the synchronic position of the "I"; in its future orientation rather than its presumed self-presence. However, unlike Lévinas, whose conception of ethics is premised on the encounter with and recognition of the alterity of the other person (a tautology that appears to be built into his thought),[12] Bakhtin is equally concerned with the encounter with the alterity that inheres in subjectivity itself. In Bakhtin's architectonics of subjectivity, the atopic principle is given full scope in the becoming of the ethical subject that is never adequate to itself, that is—to repeat the Bakhtinian formulae—"in principle nonunitary," "present to itself as a task," "incapable of being given, of being present-on-hand, of being contemplated" (83, 100). Subjectivity is generated in and through the process of interlocution.

THE DOSTOYEVSKY CONNECTION

Having followed the convergences of Bakhtin and Lévinas so far, let us now look at their profound divergences. Both enlist Dostoyevsky in their engagement with the ethical relationship of the subject and its other, but rather than yet another junction of convergence, it is precisely in this invocation that we can best see how far apart they are. In a study of Lévinas's relationship with literature, Jill Robbins quotes his reply to the question "What led you to philosophy?" as "I think it was first of all my reading in Russian, especially Pushkin, Lermontov, and Dostoyevsky, above all Dostoyevsky," and his assertion that "the Russian novel was my preparation for philosophy" (Robbins, *Altered Reading*, xix).[13] But while these answers, she says, seem to presuppose "a translatability or equivalence between literature and philosophy and, ultimately, a subsumption of literature by philosophy," or a certain "secondarization of literature in relation to philosophy," this presumption of translatability or subordination would depend on the conception of literature as "something that happens primarily on a denotative level" (xix–xx). Robbins argues that Lévinas's response, and his tendency to use literature to illustrate philosophical arguments, "in fact covers up the specificity of the literary and the real question of Lévinas and the literary. It perpetrates a domestication of literature at the hands of philosophy" (xx).

Lévinas's formulation of "I am responsible to all and for all, and I more than all the others," directly and explicitly borrowed from Dostoyevsky, recurs about a dozen times in his work, and becomes the credo of his ethical position.[14] What he offers in this Dostoyevskian allusion is a kenotic conception of subjectivity, modeled on the Russian spiritual tradition of the saints' lives, and premised on the subject's "radical humility," its "originary or preoriginay responsibility or guilt," on a relationship of radical asymmetry and nonreciprocity between self and other (147). It is no wonder, then, that Lévinas should focus on the hagiographical sections of Dostoyevsky's work. His reading of the texts, conventionally thematic in its assimilation of and convergence with their kenotic aspects, is entirely in keeping with his own postulates: the radical asymmetry of the subject and the other, the absolute primacy of the other, the nonreciprocity of the ethical relationship, the vocabulary of "summons" and "injunction." All of these postulates, I would argue, are not only deeply problematic, but also conflict with other aspects of Lévinas's own thinking, since they are clearly on the side of the "said," the categorically imperative. As Paul Ricœur has succinctly put it: "Lévinas's entire philosophy rests on the initiative of the other in the intersubjective relation. In reality, this initiative establishes no relation at all, to the extent that the other represents absolute exteriority with respect to an ego defined by the condition of separation. The other, in this sense, absolves himself of any relation" (Ricœur, *Oneself as Another*, 188–89).[15]

Regardless of his own theoretical insistence on the primacy of the "saying" over the "said" and his nonvisual conception of the face as that which "speaks," Lévinas retains the metaphysical absoluteness of the unconditional, nonreciprocal subjection to the other.[16] His perception of the ethical subject thus remains entirely within the realm of the "said," as his self-abdicating saintly subject takes its cue from the explicit imperative of a particular Dostoyevskian character and becomes "more responsible than everyone else." It is entirely in keeping with this perception, therefore, that when it comes to the encounter with the other, Lévinas consistently uses the third person rather than the far more appropriate second-person designation. Given the Dostoyevskian kenotic formula that serves as the credo of Lévinasian ethics, one would have to agree with Carrol Clarkson, who astutely reads his use of the third person as a symptom of his wish to avoid the association with Buber's "I-Thou" relation of reciprocity.

Bakhtin's reading of Dostoyevsky is entirely different. For him, as Robbins astutely notes, "the hagiographical sections of Dostoyevsky's work are the sole parts of it that are *not* constructed according to the polyphonic structure of unmerged voices that elsewhere prevails" and are, therefore, "monological" (Robbins, *Altered Reading*, 149–50). Indeed, the Dostoyevsky book is quite explicit about this: "'the hagiographic word is a word without a sideward glance, calmly adequate to itself and its referential object" (*PDP*, 248). Recall again that the "Copernican revolution" launched by Dostoyevsky has little to do with what any of the characters say, their ethical positions, personalities, or religious convictions. Rather than in any thematic formulation or thesis, the revolutionary potential of Dostoyevsky's work lies entirely in the "how," in the discursive relationship between author and character and among the characters themselves. Dostoyevsky's abdication of authorial transgredience—the "aesthetically productive" relation of the author to his characters that would have enabled him to enframe, contain, and "consummate" his characters—is a transition to lateral ethics. His characters are no longer finalized, "deadening" artistic images ("Rhetoric," 65), but living voices that will not be contained by or subsumed under the authorial word.

Much more than a literary innovation, the abdication of the deadly authorial prerogative is, in fact, a new cultural paradigm, which ranges far beyond the realm of aesthetics and entails a deeper ethical meaning, since "a living human being cannot be turned into the voiceless object of some secondhand, finalizing cognitive process" (*PDP*, 58). The very principle of non-coincidence with oneself, of a "yet-to-be" mode of subjectivity, which characterizes Bakhtin's ethical subject, is extended to Dostoyevsky's fictional characters, who can "outgrow," as it were, from within; who can challenge and void any external definition, including that of the author, of who they are; who are truly subjectified as ethical beings in that they always exceed their own boundary lines and do not coincide with any given selfhood (see 59). It is, then, in Bakhtin's reading, which focuses on the discursive dynamics of Dostoyevsky's novels rather than any thesis or profession of faith, that the radical move from the "said" to the "saying" is made, and it is this move that enables a conception of the ethical as predicated on the subject's discursive position in relation to the other. While Lévinas might say that "it is only because I acknowledge the other's claim on me that I subsequently 'speak' to the other" (Crowell, "Kantianism and Phenomenology," 29), Bakhtin would certainly put discourse first. This is not a question of rhetoric, but an entirely different conception of subjectivity and ethics. Bakhtin is not afraid of reciprocity. Neither does he advocate an unconditional surrender and martyrdom of the self confronted with the demand—any demand—of the other. Bakhtin's conception of ethics, fragmented as it is, can offer a corrective to Lévinas's because the distinction between the "saying" and the "said," or—to use Bakhtin's terms—the "utterance" and the "sentence," remains operative throughout it.

THE IMPASSE

Response and responsibility, answer and answerability (*otvetstvennost'*)—these etymological links seem to testify to the wisdom of language itself. But to become what we ought to be, we need to acknowledge our responsibility and take on the burden of singularity that puts us into an obligatory relationship with the rest of the world. Having recognized that subjectivity is constituted by intersubjectivity, that responsiveness is built into our very being, we should still account for the conversion, for which there are no guarantees, of this constitutional responsiveness into ethical responsibility, since the deposition of the sovereign, self-identical Cartesian subject still leaves us with some fundamental questions unanswered: how does the subject—needy and responsive as it may be—bridge the gap between the "is" and the "ought"? What is the power that guarantees or elicits an ethical response—the signature, the acknowledgment—in a given context? In the absence of the Kantian universals, what signposts point the way toward the good? On what grounds—given the subject's response to the call of the other—can one make a choice between multiple others?

Questions proliferate. As we saw in the previous chapter, the conversion of responsiveness to responsibility, of the factual into the axiological, is by no means trivial or assured.[17] To put it simply, perhaps somewhat crudely, if we were as constitutionally good as we are constitutionally embodied or language-using creatures, the question of goodness would never come up. The phenomenological description of subjectivity in terms of need and response, though taking a step beyond formal ethics, still falls short, it seems, of an alternative conception of ethics. The transition from the dialogic encounter, the private dyadic and intimate relationship, to an alternative conception of ethics is a difficult one, for it is precisely in the absence of this relationship, namely, in our dealings with the stranger, unloved but equally deserving of justice, that the need for signposts will arise most powerfully. It is precisely in the absence of a personal bond or subjective addressivity that we seem to need regulative ethics for our social togetherness.

Bakhtin's architectonic construction has to withstand heavy pressures on both sides. The "centripetal" mode of being, authorially framed and wholly "consummated," involves the danger of trying "to fit oneself into one's own *in absentia* image, to put out the infinitude of one's axiological self-consciousness in it, to die in it and to become an object of devouring and consumption" ("Rhetoric," 68), deprived of moral agency and freedom of choice. But the alternative "centrifugal" mode of being, premised on the contextual, specific, and singular, that mode of living purely from within, refusing any and all containment, may in turn lead to solipsism and to the madness of total relativism in which, as Calvin Schrag writes in a similar context, "all criteria for moral action are divested of obligatory force and every perspective, every interpretation, and every moral point of view is considered as good as and no worse than any other perspective, interpretation, and moral point of view. . . . [and] no claims, either of an epistemic or a moral sort, transcends the historically specific" (*The Self After Postmodernity*, 102).

Within the framework of his "ethics of the fitting response" Schrag elegantly resolves this dilemma by pointing to the basic theoretical fallacy of either/or: "Whereas the relativist embraces contextuality and contingency in the mistaken belief that no transcendence of the contextualized and contingent particular practices is possible, the absolutist harbors the same mistaken notion about contextuality and contingency and yearns for a foundationalist universality and necessity wherewith to ground a transcending critique that is wholly contextless" (108). "Transcendence" is the operative term here and it works both ways: just as human thought can break away from and transcend any and all given ideological frameworks and metanarratives, it can similarly transcend any and all immediate contexts, particular traditions, and local perspectives. Allowing for the existence of what Bakhtin would call "loopholes" in both the centripetal and the centrifugal modes of being offers an escape clause from the either/or of absolutism and relativism. The tensile relation of these forms of transcendence is a Bakhtinian architectonics under another name.

However, elegant as this both/and solution is, it is still not sufficiently compelling to exorcise the looming specter of relativism that persistently stalks any conception of ethics with no recourse to an order higher than the judgment of the human subject, as both Bakhtin and Lévinas knew. To whom should the "fitting response" be addressed? What degree of proximity is at stake here? How does one reconcile the "fitting response" to the intimately related, individual other with the "fitting response" to the communal other? How does one make a choice between, say, one's ethnic and universal affinities when they are in conflict? To whom does one owe the loyalty of allegiance? It is no wonder that these dilemmas have nurtured some of the best works of fiction. They are part and parcel of our real lives.

ENTER THE THIRD

The impasse of a purely dyadic conception of subjectivity, and the recognition of the danger of relativism that looms large over it, lead both Lévinas and Bakhtin toward a gesture of triangulation enabling the move from the phenomenology of a dialogic subjectivity to a responsible philosophical conception of ethics. In Lévinas's work, this move takes place with the introduction of "the third" (*le tiers*). In Bakhtin's work, it is signaled by the entry of an apparently new player, the superaddressee, who makes his appearance in the texts of the 1960s. However, this ostensible point of convergence, where we see both Bakhtin and Lévinas taking a step back from an unqualified endorsement of the dyadic, contextual, singular, and concrete ethical relationship by resorting to a form of triangulation, is also a junction of profound divergence.

In this last section of the chapter, I would argue that Bakhtin's superaddressee is a principle of transcendence in an entirely different sense, almost the opposite of Lévinas's *le tiers*. Whereas the latter offers recourse to vertical transcendence, addressing the necessity for social coherence and regulation, namely, the sedimentation or codification of the saying into the said, Bakhtin's superaddressee is firmly on the side of the saying. It is a principle of both vertical and lateral transcendence, in that it allows subjectivity to break out of the said, of any frame of reference posited as irrefutable and any context established as inescapable. In Lévinas, the paternal prophetic voice of *le tiers*, however benevolent, serves to contain particularity within the communal, to grant coherence and cohesion to human society, and is thus closer to the "consummating" authorial other in "Author and Hero." Bakhtin's superaddressee, on the other hand, an actor who may be described as a personified or animated loophole, enables the subject to break out of any imposed coherence or "finalization." As we shall see, the transition from a vertical to a lateral metaphysical orientation, whether sought or actually attained by either thinker, is still fraught with questions, and I would suggest that it is Bakhtin's work, fragmented though it is, that fully accomplishes this radical shift.

To unpack the argument, let us take a closer look at these two modes of triangulation. The Lévinasian "third" (*tiers*) is a concession that modifies the intimate dyadic relation between the subject and his/her intimate, particular other:

> How is it that there is justice? I answer that it is the fact of the multiplicity of men and the presence of someone else next to the Other, which condition the laws and establish justice. If I am alone with the Other, I owe him everything; but there is someone else. . . . The interpersonal relation I establish with the Other, I must also establish with other men; there is thus a necessity to moderate this privilege of the Other; from whence comes justice. (Lévinas, *Ethics and Infinity*, 89–90)[18]

Recognizing the insufficiency of the dyadic relation for the establishment of justice in the sociopolitical body that ensures human survival, Lévinas concedes that even though the ethical, as *prima philosophia*, entails extreme exposure and absolute responsibility of the subject to a particular other, ethics must, eventually, be translated into morality and legislated in order to regulate social interchanges among all the members of a society. As soon as we move beyond into the political world of the impersonal "third," the world of "government, institutions, tribunals, prisons, schools, committees, and so on," ethics needs to "harden its skin," to move, in other words, from the saying into the said (Kearney, "Dialogue with Emmanuel Lévinas," in Cohen, ed., *Face to Face with Lévinas*, 29–30).

In his discussion of this transition from ethics to morality, or to politics, as it evolves from *Totality and Infinity* to *Otherwise than Being*, Simon Critchley relates to Lévinas's introduction of the theme of *le tiers* as a constructive paradox: the concept of equality, introduced at the intersection of the ethical and the political, creates a "double structure" that addresses the tension between the particular and the universal. The relation to the particular other, "an unequal, asymmetrical relation to a height that cannot be comprehended," turns into a "communal bond," a "symmetrical community of equals" (Critchley, *The Ethics of Deconstruction*, 226); the "non-coincidence of the Same and the Other in the ethical relation" generates, paradoxically perhaps, the "coincidence of beings in a community" (227).[19] In the best case, this shift retains and is founded on the ethical commitment to the other, so that the hardening of ethics into morality becomes, following the detour through the saying, a *"justified Said,"* as Critchley dubs it, informed by ethics, by proximity, by the sight of the other's face. If the ethical inscribes an "anarchic, pre-original relation to the Other," the need for justice, equality, and community calls for a supplementation of this relation "by the measure of the *archē*: of principles, beginnings, and origins" (234). It seems, then, that for Lévinas the introduction of *le tiers* is a way out of the potential dead end of particularism and relativism. It is a compromise of sorts, a concession of the need for the said alongside the utopian language of the saying. The task of philosophy is to speak both languages and constantly move between them, or—hoping that Critchley would not mind the irresistible pun—to do the polis in different voices.

Bakhtin triangulates his dialogic conception in an entirely different spirit. After decades of work on a dialogic conception of the human subject, a conception that went through several permutations, but has always retained its centrifugal, oppositional, anti-totalitarian thrust, Bakhtin introduces the "superaddressee" as a third element, which creeps into the later text and seems to hollow out or at least complicate the very conception of dialogue:[20]

> Any utterance always has an addressee (of various sorts, with varying degrees of proximity, concreteness, awareness, and so forth) whose responsive understanding the author of the speech work seeks and surpasses.[21] This is the second party. . . . But in addition to

this addressee (the second party), the author of the utterance, with a greater or lesser awareness, presupposes a higher *superaddressee* (third), whose absolutely just responsive understanding is presumed, either in some metaphysical distance or in a distant historical time (the loophole addressee). In various ages and with various understandings of the world, this superaddressee and his ideally true responsive understanding assume various ideological expressions (God, absolute truth, the court of dispassionate human conscience, the people, the court of history, science, and so forth). (PT, 126)

Each dialogue takes place as if against the background of the responsive understanding of an invisibly present third party who stands above all the participants in the dialogue. (126)

The entry of this new participant who is "higher" and "stands above" all other interlocutors, like a supreme principle of arbitration, may be read as a point of *aporia* in Bakhtin's work in its implicit introduction of hierarchy: it is hard to conceive of this ultimate listener as anything but the "supreme author" or "ultimate other" who stages his comeback through the back door, offering the consolation of metaphysical grounding, which seems to hollow out the very concept of the dialogue. Indeed, as many of Bakhtin's readers have felt, there is a distinct aura of religiosity about this new participant.[22] Apparently aware of the problematic implications of this new presence, Bakhtin immediately adds that the superaddressee, who is "a constitutive aspect of the whole utterance," is not "any mystical or metaphysical being (although, given a certain understanding of the world, he can be expressed as such)" (126).[23]

This disclaimer notwithstanding, the superaddressee still needs to be accounted for within the framework of Bakhtin's work, bearing in mind that the complexity of this move is probably due, at least to some extent, to the historical circumstances of his writing, which made it, on the one hand, immensely dangerous to articulate the concept of transcendence, and on the other hand, desperately important to do just that. Far from an isolated instance, this nostalgia for a higher level of arbitration also appears in Bakhtin's "Toward a Reworking of the Dostoevsky Book," originally written in the same notebook as "The Problem of the Text," in an oblique note on Dostoyevsky's conception of atheism as "a lack of faith in this sense, as indifference toward an ultimate value which makes demands on the whole man, as a rejection of the ultimate position." This is followed by an equally oblique comment on Dostoyevsky's "vacillations as regards the *content* of this ultimate value" (TRDB, 294). This has been, of course, the unresolved question of Western ethics throughout the process of secularization: how is one to choose that "ultimate value" without recourse to the ultimate authoritative other? It is the very same question that lies at the core of Dostoyevsky's work, for even the most radically polyphonic of his novels are never quite free of a deep metaphysical nostalgia and a desire for ethical grounding. Dostoyevsky's characters are all too aware of the axiological void that has opened up with the removal of the metaphysical anchor: "there is no virtue if there is no immortality" (*PDP*, 86), and "If God is dead, everything is allowed" (*The Brothers Karamazov*, 77–78, 156).

As we have already noted, the very conception of Dostoyevsky's polyphonic revolution becomes problematic in retrospect, when we are told that Bakhtin saw his book on Dostoyevsky as "morally flawed," because it could not openly deal with "the main questions . . . what Dostoevsky agonized about all his life—the existence of God" (Bocharov, "Conversations with Bakhtin," 1013). Have we come full circle, then? Can the introduction of the superaddressee be reconciled with the "centrifugal" Bakhtin, or is it a retraction of dialogism, an escape from freedom, as Erich Fromm might have put it? Does the recourse to the superaddressee denote a reversion to metaphysics? Is this ultimate listener a new version of the "supreme author" or ultimate transgredient other who has crept back and staged his comeback through the back door, offering the consolation of metaphysical grounding or "consummation"?

Not quite. Bakhtin's introduction of the superaddressee does seem to hark back both to "Author and Hero" and to his lectures of 1924–25. But having dealt with the former text extensively in previous chapters, let us now take a look at a later and less familiar text, "The Problem of Grounded Peace," a lecture given by Bakhtin in 1924 or 1925, which has survived as a set of notes taken by L. V. Pumpiansky. Needless to say, these notes are at several removes from the actual text of the lecture, being part of an ongoing conversation among members of the circle that we can only partially share. They relate to materials and issues to which we get no access and have the rather limited addressivity of notes taken by an auditor for mnemonic rather than expository purposes. If dialogism teaches us anything, it is precisely the essentiality of context to an understanding of the text, and the need to consider the dynamics of refraction through the receiver's understanding of the message. Conversely, there may be some advantage in the contemporaneity of these notes, where distinct echoes of Bakhtin's essays of the period are clearly audible, and some mutuality of illumination may be generated if we read these echoes as intertexts.

Given the overt religiosity of the lecture (which might have contributed to Bakhtin's arrest and sentence of exile a few years later), it is important to understand that, for Bakhtin, the desire for a state of "grounded peace" has nothing to do with religious dogma, theology, or moral laws. It is not "the tranquility of self-complacency or aesthetic mythologem" (PGP, 209), that is, the sense of oneself as a whole, aesthetically fabricated and contained by the transgredient authorial gaze, which is simply another term for being identical to oneself. Mythologem, in this context, is on the side of knowledge and aesthetics—it is a response to the need for totalization, or, in the early Bakhtinian idiom, the desire for "consummation." To borrow Richard A. Cohen's beautiful formulation from the Lévinasian context, mythos is the pearl secreted by the "irritation of knowledge over its fundamental incompleteness"—both logos and mythos are human constructions, and ethics, being neither the one nor the other, is "precisely what disrupts knowledge and myth" ("Introduction," in Cohen, ed., *Face to Face with Lévinas*, 4). Translated into the Bakhtinian idiom, that "irritation" is the sense of "disquietude" generated by the fundamental incompleteness of self-knowledge, the non-coincidence with oneself, the sense of "disquietude," of oneself as a task to be accomplished, yet-to-be. It is precisely the ethical drive, which is fundamentally a striving to be different from what one is and an acknowledgment of the "ought" that looms large ahead of the "is," that opens up the never-ending quest for "grounded peace":

> The true being of the spirit begins only when repentance begins, that is, essential and fundamental noncoinciding.... To get a feel of one's being and grasp it, finally, in a real way: to attain, finally,—attain in truth, the reality of one's personhood, rejecting all the mythologems

about it. I am infinitely bad, but Someone needs me to be good. In repenting, I specifically establish the One in Whom I posit my sin. And it is this that constitutes grounded peace, which does not make up or fabricate anything. Tranquility or peace of mind can be either the tranquility of self-complacency or that of trust; what must free me from the tranquility of self-complacency, that is, from the tranquility of an aesthetic mythologem, is precisely disquietude, which will develop, through repentance, into trust.—What is at issue is more serious than freedom, what is at issue (in faith) is something more than freedom, i.e. more than guarantees.

But at certain moments we will inevitably confront the problem of the *incarnated* God. (PGP, 209)

This is difficult. The distinction made here, apparently close to the time when "Author and Hero" was written, is between a fabricated aesthetic mythologem of self-adequacy, which leads to self-complacency, and an awareness of non-self-adequacy, the "disquietude" that sends the subject looking for the "Someone [who] needs me to be good," "One in Whom I posit my sin" (PGP, 209). But this kind of trust is not premised on any metaphysical guarantees. Like the fervent religiosity of Pascal and his wager, or Kierkegaard with the leap of faith, or—to take three examples much closer home—the embattled religiosity of Paul Tillich, Gabriel Marcel, and Karl Jaspers, it has nothing to do with systemic theological doctrine, with the powers of clericalism, or with set articles of faith.[24] We can go back to Bakhtin's own view of Dostoyevsky's religiosity, which "[was] not faith (in the sense of a specific faith in orthodoxy, in progress, in man, in revolution, etc.) but a *sense of faith*, that is, an integral attitude (by means of the whole person) toward a higher and ultimate value. Atheism is often understood by Dostoyevsky as a lack of faith in this sense, as indifference toward an ultimate value which makes demands on the whole man, as a rejection of an ultimate position in the ultimate whole of the world" (TRDB, 294).[25] Far from a guarantee of divine Providence or a cosmic order, the feeling of faith is an expression of metaphysical exile, a profound and incurable homesickness.

This need for "grounded peace," for a metaphysical anchor outside and above the self cannot be answered by the "immanentization of God" either. Juxtaposing the Publican and the Pharisee in Luke 18:9–14,

Bakhtin says that whereas the latter has "absorbed this Third consciousness *into himself*" and rendered "the justification of himself immanent," the former, the righteous one, has "unsealed the possible myth about his own personality" (PGP, 208). Whereas the "moral consciousness" recognizes only two participants in the ethical event, "for religious consciousness there is a *third* one: a possible someone who evaluates" (208). Recall here Bakhtin's earlier conception of ethics, initially articulated in *Toward a Philosophy of the Act*, which seems to anticipate this lecture: the ethical is not derived from a set of abstract a priori norms that are universally valid and should be implicitly followed by all; it is an "event" in which the singularity, the concrete position, and the context of the agent (i.e., "my unique place in being") are ineluctably inscribed. Likewise, religious consciousness relates not to dogma or to "dogmatic metaphysics," but to a "personal and intimate event" that involves "personal participation" (208). "The ought proceeds from unrepeatability or uniqueness alone, and one is tormented by conscience not for disobeying a law but as a result of proceeding from my once-occurrent position. Hence the impossibility of generalizing a religious norm" (208). Nearly forty years later, in "The Problem of the Text," Bakhtin recasts that third being "who needs me to be good," as the superaddressee: a silent participant in every interlocution, an addressee who converts responsiveness into responsibility, and offers the possibility of ethical grounding for the subject in terms of discourse.

To conclude, then, Bakhtin's "superaddressee" and Lévinas's "third" may both be read as belated escape clauses from the potential relativism of dialogics. In both there is at least a residual appeal to metaphysics. But whereas Lévinas's "third" remains at the level of an other to whom one owes, and the Lévinasian ethical subject remains in a state of invariable subjection, Bakhtin's superaddressee is explicitly defined in terms of discourse. For the superaddressee to exist, there has to be a conversation, an address, an addresser, and an addressee; there has to be some commonality that would enable the address and some potential convergence of the interlocutors' appeal to the superaddressee. The danger of relativism no longer looms large, as the evocation of the superaddressee is at least implicitly mutual: if two people turn to a third to resolve their conflict, the appeal has to carry a similar weight for both. The third party—whether God, future generations, or humanity at large—has to be recognized in its judicial capacity. Rather than an a priori metaphysical being, the superaddressee is called into being by the participants in discourse. If dialogism is not to be understood as a necessarily benign form of exchange, but as an intercalation that more often than not involves conflicting forces, it is the very existence of a bilateral conflict that generates the need for the third party. Even if the superaddressee is invoked by one of the participants as a loophole or a way around the dead end in the interaction with the concrete other, the very invocation suggests a sense of a higher or deeper truth.

Bakhtin's formulation is, in one sense, less ambitious and more orthodox than Lévinas's, in that it posits a standard of arbitration "beyond and above" the participants in the dialogue—that "Someone [who] needs me to be good." But it is also more viable, in that it posits that source of authority as implicit in the structure of discourse, rather than in the wholly other; and truly phenomenological, in that while it recognizes the constitutive role of the other, Bakhtin remains aware, at least from 1929 on, of both the benign and the malevolent aspects of this role. Given this emphasis, the ethical is no longer perceived as immanent in the constitution of subjectivity—it becomes a position, a stand, an attitude of "facing" the other in a dialogic relationship. Both Bakhtin and Lévinas develop an unsystemic, processual conception of ethics, predicated in both their cases on the non-coincidence of the subject with itself, its radical openness to the other. But it is Bakhtin's insistence on the discursive formation and the intra- rather than the intersubjective dynamics of subjectivity that enables the translation of these conceptions into an affirmation of agency, the recognition of commonality and reciprocity that is not in evidence in Lévinas's ethical postulate. Oscillating between vulnerability and resistance, navigating between the appeal of the needy other and the violence of the oppressive other, as we all do in the real world, this position is both all-too-human and thoroughly humane. It has to do with the making of choices, which is what ethics is all about.

CODA: A HOME AWAY FROM HOME

> There is nothing more whole than a broken heart.
>
> Rabbi Menachem Mendel of Kotzk (1787–1859)

IT IS TIME TO GET BACK TO THE SUBJECT IN QUESTION. But to do so on a firm note of conclusion would go against the very grain of the work done by Bakhtin and his fellow exiles: the subject that emerges from respective projects does not easily lend itself to complete thematization. It is reluctant to let its saying solidify into the said. Having disowned the certainties of the Cartesian heritage, the members of the exilic constellation need to go back to questions long submerged or sedimented under the weight of philosophical tradition, to retrace the "forgotten path," as Bakhtin calls it. This is not a default option in an attempt to get home through the back door. Theirs is an interrogative mode of philosophizing, "consonant," as Merleau-Ponty writes, "with the porous being which it questions and from which it obtains not an answer, but a confirmation of its astonishment" (*The Visible and the Invisible*, 102). This interrogation is neither an affirmation nor a negation, veiled or expected, "but an original manner of aiming at something, as it were a *question-knowing*, which by principle no statement or 'answer' can go beyond and which perhaps therefore is the proper mode of our relationship with Being, as though it were the mute or reticent interlocutor of our questions" (129).

Lévinas, too, is poignantly aware of the difficulty, if not the impossibility, of thematization. "The fact that philosophy cannot fully totalize the alterity of meaning in some final presence or simultaneity," he says, "is not for me a deficiency or fault.... The best thing about philosophy is that it fails" (Kearney, "Dialogue with Emmanuel Lévinas," in Cohen, ed., *Face to Face with Lévinas*, 22). That glorious failure has been the subject of this study, and if the thought of the exilic constellation with which we have engaged here is less than fully articulated and involves a great deal of philosophical stammering, it is because no other kind of thought would have been appropriate for the question of the subject.

Over a century since that point in time "in or about December 1910," when, as Virginia Woolf so quaintly and accurately observed, "human character changed," Western civilization seems to have come to a crossroads. The secularization process, believed to be all but accomplished at the turn of the twentieth century, has in the meantime set off a backlash far more lethal than anything known since Descartes: during the first half of the twentieth century, the irresistibility of the "centripetal" mode of being, galvanized by socioeconomic and political forces, was translated into the secular versions that generated the murderous fanaticism of Fascism, Stalinism, and Nazism. In the twenty-first century, apparently struck by historical amnesia, we seem to be once again in the grip of a similar desire for totalization, an eruption of quasi-religious fanaticism that may turn out to be more disastrous still.

At the "centrifugal" end of the spectrum, we have not fared much better: having lost our moorings in anything broader or higher than mere individuality; having—as Bakhtin would have it—quite rightly lost faith in an authorial other, we are subjected to and subjectified instead by floating, occasional, ever-changing desires. Far from being signs of autonomy, however, these ostensibly "centrifugal" desires are all too often yet another form of subjectification or interpellation by a transgredient other, an ideological apparatus unnamed and invisible and hence all the more powerful. In this arena of competing values with ostensibly equal claims to legitimacy, where economic or military might often turns to right; in the face of this "multiplicity of allergic egoisms which are at war with one another and are thus together," to borrow one of Lévinas's most astute phrases (*Otherwise than Being*, 4), the danger of relativism looms larger than ever.

But if the loss of onto-theological grounding has proven to be less liberating, and the state of metaphysical exile less comfortable than anticipated, it is quite clear that a simple reversion to foundational thinking is no longer impossible. There is no return to the naïveté of "consummation" by the authorial transgredient other and no recourse to a gift of grace descended from above. The task undertaken by philosophers like Rosenzweig, Bergson, Merleau-Ponty, Lévinas, and Bakhtin does not get accomplished in a philosophical homecoming. Feeling their way through the overgrown ruins of a civilization, they undertake the labor of bringing us to a different mode of transcendence, a place of exile that may become our home away from home.

We are not there yet. Between the Scylla of "pure loneliness within oneself," where the cocooned subject is a law unto itself, unable to bridge the distance that separates it from others, and the Charybdis of "the image *in absentia*," where the subject is wholly framed under and contained within the authorial gaze—two perspectives that never intersect or are, at most, "naively mixed (self-observation in a mirror)" ("Rhetoric," 68)—the subject faces an impossible axiological and psychological position. Confronting these impossible alternatives head on, Bakhtin recognizes the need to "search for a new plane on which I and the other can meet," where these two architectonic perspectives can intersect in an open process of becoming (68). Significantly, however, even in this ostensibly "centrifugal" fragment, Bakhtin concedes that the love it takes to enable this becoming may well be the love of God, who, being "simultaneously both within me and outside me," makes possible both the "belief in the proper reflection of oneself in the higher other" and "my inner infinitude and open-endedness" (68). God may be dead, but the "feeling for faith" is certainly alive.

Like Lévinas, Bakhtin can no longer resort to the hypothesis of the Auctor Mundi as an infrastructure for ethics. In their post-Holocaust, post-Stalinist world, the ethical imperative can no longer be thought to emanate from a divine Providence or an abstract system, and the transcendent can no longer be thematized and postulated as the supreme author. Lévinas, for one, is entirely uninhibited in expressing the need for an alternative path to transcendence. His work, he says, "does not seek to restore any ruined concept" of divinity. Fully aware of "the death of a certain god" (*Otherwise than Being*, 185), he sets out to recover "the transcendence that was lost or reified in metaphysics: the transcendence of the Other" (Critchley, *The Ethics of Deconstruction*, 114). The link between ethics and faith is reversed by Lévinas, who, in a traditionally Jewish manner responds to the question, "Is morality possible without God?" with another question: "Is divinity possible without relation to a human Other?" A purely dyadic relation with God is impossible, for "we are always a threesome: I and you and the Third who is in our midst. And only as a Third does He reveal Himself" ("Ideology and Idealism," 247). For Lévinas, then, the recovery of the religious dimension of human existence derives from the intersubjective constitution of the subject and its relationship with the concrete human other, but, as we have seen, he takes this sanctification of alterity to a point of complete, willing, and unconditional surrender to the other's demand. Notwithstanding its modification through the introduction of "the third," this is hardly a viable response to the question of "how to be."

Bakhtin's recovery of transcendence takes a different route. As already noted, the question of his religiosity, or rather, of the precise nature of his belief, has remained unresolved, like the question of the "disputed texts." However, unlike the latter issue which is mostly a matter of incomplete or conflicting biographical accounts, the question of religion runs much deeper.[1] As others have done before, we may begin with a brief reference to Bakhtin's "Toward a Reworking of the Dostoevsky Book," written at the time of his "rehabilitation," when he apparently felt more at liberty to deal with what the forbidden questions. Bakhtin's reading of Dostoyevsky's conception of atheism as "indifference toward the ultimate value," regardless of whether it is an accurate description of Dostoyevsky's religiosity, is crucial because of its obvious relevance to Bakhtin's own position. It is, in fact, entirely compatible with the accounts given by his younger disciples—Sergei Bocharov, Georgii Gachev, and Vadim Kozhinov—which seem to converge on this point. Bakhtin, Bocharov writes, "turned from the high road of Russian religious philosophy. All of the originality of Bakhtin-as-thinker is connected to this fundamental fact and conditioned by it," and "Author and Hero," though not a work of religious philosophy, is aesthetics "resolved in theological terms; aesthetics on the border of religious philosophy, without crossing that border" ("The Event of Being," 42).

A similar view is offered by Gachev in a wonderfully idiosyncratic passage (taking a great deal of poetic license, which, one cannot help feeling, would probably have earned the approval of Bakhtin as well): Bakhtin's work, Gachev writes, is not orthodox, "not even in its religiosity." It is not about God, but about "your neighbor" ("Bakhtin," 45). It has replaced the "long-standing Russian idea of 'communality,' which formerly was understood as the UNIfication [sic] of individuals in the gravitational pull of everything toward the Supreme: toward God, toward the Homeland, in which they are dissolved and differences become unimportant" with a conception of communality, where individuals do not "look up at Heaven, nor ahead at the priest or altar, but at each other, at our own, low, horizontal level" (46–47). Particularity rather than universality, concreteness rather than abstraction, horizontality rather than verticality—these are the ingredients of Bakhtin's "feeling for faith," as well as the seeds of what could have been a true revolution of the people.

Finally, Kozhinov, Bakhtin's literary co-executor, also testifies, in an interview with Nicolas Rzhevsky, that "Mikhail Mikhailovich was a deeply religious person" (Rzhevsky, "Kozhinov on Bakhtin," 56), but he, too, insists that "he thought faith to exist on the edge, that this is, if you like, the essence of the highest Christian freedom" (60). As Rzhevsky summarizes the interview, "the issue, given the biographical date, is not whether Bakhtin was religious—the evidence is too strong to suggest that he was not—but to what extent religion entered his philosophical concerns" (62). In response to this question, I would suggest that religion, or rather, the particular variety of Bakhtinian religiosity—an "exilic" mode of faith that has nothing to do with theology or vertical metaphysics—not only enters but actually structures and thoroughly saturates the Bakhtinian outlook.

How, then, does Bakhtin articulate this profound and apparently incurable religiosity when God appears to have finally accomplished his retreat into silence or death? In what form does the need for transcendence survive the demise of the transcendent? To answer these questions, we should first make an attempt to tidy up the conceptual muddle around this problematic term, which seems to bite its own tail: both *heimlich* and *unheimlich*, like Freud's Uncanny, it may refer to diametrically opposing notions. The traditional denotation of "the transcendent," whether Platonic or theological, points to an unconditioned and nondependent entity, a reference point that is not only outside and beyond the economies of human experience but actually serves to frame and unify it. In this sense, the transcendent is clearly a plausible construction of the Bakhtinian concept of "transgredience"—an authorial, aesthetic, epistemological, or divine vantage point that offers grounding and enables identity, coherence, and unification.

At the same time, however, there is another conception of transcendence, which denotes, as Calvin Schrag writes, a "radical alterity,"

> [a] stance or posture for a protest against aspirations toward hegemony and claims for ultimacy among the culture-spheres of science, morality, art, and religion itself. . . . curbing any absolutization of methodologies, conceptual frameworks, beliefs, creeds, and institutional practices. . . . It relativizes the culture-spheres and installs a vigilance over their claims and presuppositions, curtailing any temptations to achieve a God's–eye view of the panorama of human history. (*The Self After Postmodernity*, 124)

Transcendence in this sense, Schrag writes, provides the "requisite safeguards against ideological hegemony," whether in science, morality, art, or institutionalized religion (124). Bakhtin's "loophole out of anything given" certainly answers to this description. Aligned with the "yet-to-be" mode of existence, with the rejection of consummation or finalization, it defies, rather than conforms to, any and all transgredient frames.[2]

This kind of immanent transcendence is probably what Rosenzweig had in mind when he wrote that "'I' is always a nay become audible. 'I' always involves a contradiction, it is always underlines, always emphasized, always an 'I, however.' . . . 'I' is simple [sic] always willy-nilly subject in all sentences in which it occurs. It can never be passive, never object" (*The Star of Redemption*, 173). Rosenzweig's conception of subjectivity as pitted "against the All" serves as an introduction to a section structured like a glossary of terms, wherein "dialogue" is the first entry. This, Rosenzweig says, "accords with the wholly real employment of language, the center-piece as it were of this entire book," relating to discourse in terms, not of representation or systemic structure, but of "word and response" (174). The next entries, "Monologue," "The Question," and "The Address," not only anticipate the work of both Lévinas and Bakhtin, but are distinctly audible in it. Under "Monologue," for instance, Rosenzweig writes about the inauthenticity of the subject when it is not yet confronted by Thou:

> Only when the I acknowledges the Thou as something external to itself, that is, only when it makes the transition from monologue to

authentic dialogue, only then does it become that I which we have just claimed for the primeval Nay become audible. The I of the monologue is not yet an "I, however." It is an unemphatic I, an I that is also self-understood precisely because it is only self-addressed. It is thus an I concealed in the secret of the third person and not as yet a manifest I. (174–75)[3]

That the "language of love" is part of the chapter in *The Star of Redemption* on "Revelation or The Ever-Renewed Birth of the Soul" speaks for itself.

Having discarded the idea of a "secular conversion" in Bakhtin's thought somewhere between the writing of "Author and Hero" and *Problems of Dostoevsky's Poetics*, we need to find a more viable alternative to account for his deployment of transcendence in its two contradictory senses. To resolve this paradox, I would suggest that Schrag's distinction between transcendence as absolute externality and transcendence as a form of alterity inherent in the very constitution of the subject should be supplemented by the distinction between the nominal and the verbal aspects of transcendence. The former, often denoted as a noun phrase—"the transcendent"—indicates an entity, a substance that, however ineffable, is still thought of as a being; the latter, denoted as "transcendence," refers to an action, a process, or a movement that breaks through anything given, anything ready-at-hand and finalized. Bakhtin's superaddressee features in both the nominal and the verbal senses of transcendence: in the former sense, as the transcendent, it may be called God, the "transgredient" author, or the (capitalized) Other who features in "Author and Hero." In the latter, opposite sense, it would just as readily accept other names—such as the loophole, for instance—and be construed an invincible reaching-out of consciousness into the "yet-to-be"; a way out of anything given, anything ready-at-hand and finalized.[4]

Bakhtin's recovery of transcendence begins, like that of Lévinas, with an inversion of the metaphysics of presence, a shift from a *vertical-external* orientation toward the supreme Auctor Mundi as the source of the ethical command to a *lateral-immanent* relationship wherein human intersubjectivity (the opening up to alterity) is extrapolated into the realm of the divine. In Bakhtin's late notes, there are two enigmatic and apparently self-contradictory references to Christ and the truth. The first reference seems to be premised on a three-way equation of Christ, the Truth, and the Word: "The word as something personal. Christ as truth" and Dostoyevsky's "profound understanding of the personal nature of the word" (N70–71, 148). Only two pages later, however, there is a cryptic comment on "the juxtaposition [counterposition] of truth and Christ in Dostoevsky" (150), which is glossed in the editorial notes as a reference to "the famous letter from Dostoevsky to N. D. Fonivizina of February 1854, in which he says ' . . . if someone were to prove to me that Christ is outside the truth, then I would prefer to remain with Christ than with the truth'" (158n28).[5] What should we make of this apparent contradiction?

The question is immediately resolved by Bakhtin himself. Dostoyevsky, he argues, refers to an "impersonal objective truth, that is, truth from the standpoint of a third party. The court of arbitration is a rhetorical court. Dostoyevsky's attitude toward juries. Impartiality and *higher* partiality" (150). If we recall the two types of truth—the philosophical, abstract, and universal *istina* that Bakhtin juxtaposes with the literary, concrete, and singular *pravda* in *Toward a Philosophy of the Act* (37 and passim)—the apparent contradiction is resolved. The Grand Inquisitor with his "state power, rhetoric, and authority" (N70–71, 151) stands for the former; his truth is an "impersonal objective truth, that is, truth from the standpoint of a third party" (150). Christ with "his silence and his kiss" stands for the latter, personal truth (150). Dostoyevsky's choice to remain with Christ rather than with the truth is thus not the choice of a lie. It is the choice of love rather than knowledge in relation to the other, or perhaps it is the kind of supremely ethical knowledge that does not entail finalization and allows the other the freedom of loopholes and agency. The "small-scale Copernican revolution" that Bakhtin credits to Dostoyevsky may well have been his own. In this reversal of the onto-theological paradigm, it is not the human subject who aspires to imitate the infinite goodness of divinity, since the very concept of divinity (or the infinite, in Lévinas's terms) consists in the attainment of the ultimate level of interhuman subjectivity.[6]

Bakhtin, too, is metaphysically disinherited, and his superaddressee is not a poor man's substitute for the theological-metaphysical conception of God. Indeed, Bakhtin is explicitly hostile to the "sacred and authoritarian word in general with its indisputability, unconditionality, and unequivocality" (133). This mistrust of the rhetoric of clericalism, theology, or other human voices of authority that claim a superhuman status cannot be easily reconciled with any form of orthodoxy, religious or ideological, and stands opposed to any and all kinds of *doxa*. I would, therefore, suggest that, rather than an escape clause or a point of *aporia*, the late construct of the superaddressee offers an enhancement of Bakhtin's earlier articulation of ethics. It is, in fact, a *paradoxical* concept that rejects the either/or construction and accommodates both senses of transcendence.[7]

The very structure of the term is telling. It is both "vertical" ("super")[8] and lateral ("addressee"): its externality to the subject turns it into a valid principle of both inter- and intrasubjective coherence and unification, and the fact that the participants in the dialogue need to invoke (or invent) it as an implicit third participant turns it into a resource of arbitration (assuming a measure of commonality, which would allow it to be at least potentially shared by the participants in the dialogue), rather than judgment. If it is a figure for God, it is not the theological conception of God as a transgredient author outside and above his creation, but a conception of God as a *force within* the subject, which allows it to transcend any given *doxa* and any superimposed definition of its selfhood. This is the force that preempts any and all "last words," that disrupts the closure that is both desired (as "consummation") and dreaded (as "finalization"), because even the most authoritative frame of discourse can be transcended through loopholes.

To grasp the meaning of this conception of this unmetaphysical mode of transcendence for the subject of ethics, let us, once again, consult Rosenzweig:

> The concept of order of this world is thus not the universal, neither the *arche* nor the *telos*, neither the natural nor the historical unity, but rather the singular, the event, *not beginning or end, but center of the world*. From the beginning as well as from the end the world is "infinite," from the beginning, infinite in space toward the end, infinite in time. Only from the center does there arise a bounded home in the unbounded world, a patch of ground between four tent pegs, that can be posted further and further out. Only seen from this viewpoint do beginning and end change from a concept of the

boundedness of the infinite to cornerstones of our word-possession: the "beginning" becomes the creation, the "end" the redemption. Revelation is then capable of being a *center* point. ("Germ Cell," 57)

This is the point where the "defiant I" (57) insists on its freedom and its strength, an insistence that alone makes its obedience to ideals significant, where "That which is the Highest, instead of demanding our surrender, surrenders itself to us" (58).

On this reading, the Bakhtinian version of the sacred has nothing to do with systemic theological doctrine, with the powers of clericalism, with set articles of religious faith, with myth, or with absolute knowledge: rather than bow to the transcendent, in whatever theological or metaphysical guise, it is premised on transcendence, enabled only in and through the interaction of humans, and variously tagged as the superaddressee, the loophole or the "refraction" of the word. Rather than relate to universal, abstracted systems (the "All" or the "Essence," in Rosenzweig's terms), it adheres to the singular, the concrete, and the ever-changing. The centrality of language within this outlook is not to be equated with grammar, for it is in the defamiliarized and sometimes ungrammatical language of literature that truth can best be heard.

If we normally relate the religious sensibility to a "centripetal" drive, the Bakhtinian ultimate version of the sacred is "centrifugal" in that it allows for the resistance to the authorial word; it is "anarchic" in that it does not derive from the *archē*; it is, to return to David Carr, an unmetaphysical variety of transcendence that does not subject itself to a first principle. (If there is such a first principle, it is that of starting in the middle.) I believe it is this form of anarchic and deeply felt religiosity that underlies the wistful comment scribbled in Bakhtin's notebook: "New *philosophical wonder* at everything is needed. Everything could have been different" ("Rhetoric," 70).[9] So much could have been different, indeed, if we could find it in ourselves to give up the illusory enclosure of self-identity and sameness and live on our own borderlines; or if, rather than severing all links with the sacred, we could recognize the sacredness of the profane. It is not accidental that Rosenzweig should have written of "a bounded home in the unbounded world, a patch of ground between four tent pegs, that can be posted further and further out" ("Germ Cell," 57), and it is not only the deterritorialized history of the Jewish people that Rosenzweig may have had in mind:

the precariousness of the tent, the nomadic home of those who have no grounding in a sovereign territory of their own, may, in fact, make it more endurable than any seemingly solid edifice.

Living as we do in our exilic home away from home, Bakhtin's touching, almost childlike recognition that "Someone needs me to be good" does not offer "grounded peace." We are neither autonomous nor identical with ourselves and can no longer find a resting place either in the consolations of metaphysics, or in the certitude of Cartesian formulae. But our very heteronomy, our vulnerability to being authored by the other, is also the source of our potential resistance to narrative frames, to political systems, and to the grammar of ideology. It is this "disquietude," as Bakhtin calls it, that brings about the encounter with the sacred—the ineffable that lies not *beyond* but *within* the subject, that turns the human into the humane and enables the conversion of responsiveness to responsibility. It is, quite simply, that which allows us to pull ourselves up by our own bootstraps.

REFERENCE MATTER

NOTES

INTRODUCTION

1. Having borrowed the poignant phrase "homecoming festival" from TMHS, I was alerted by Sergeiy Sandler to the possibility that it is, in fact, a mistranslation of the Russian word *vozrozhdenie* (Bakhtin, *Sobraniie Sochinenii* [Collected Works], 6: 435), which actually means "revival," read by the translator as *vozvraschenie* ("return"). In this case, however, it seems to me that the mistranslation is actually felicitous and truer to Bakhtin, who, I feel, would have been willing to allow his translator and readers a considerable degree of poetic license in this case.

2. According to L. A. Gogotishvili, TMHS is actually a later compilation done by V. V. Kozhinov out of Bakhtin's fragmented notebooks. It now appears in its original form as part of Bakhtin's "Working Notes from the 1960s and Early 1970s" in *Sobraniie Sochinenii* (Collected Works), vol. 6. I am very grateful to Sergeiy Sandler for drawing my attention to this editorial issue.

3. The editors of *Speech Genres and Other Late Essays* indicate that Bakhtin is referring here to the collection of his works from various years on which he was working just before his death, which appeared as *Voprosi literaturi i estetiki*. It was, for the most part, subsequently translated into English as *The Dialogic Imagination* (1981).

4. Rzhevsky, "Kozhinov on Bakhtin," 429. For astute discussions of the issues at stake in the cross-cultural transmission of Bakhtin's work, see Emerson, *First Hundred Years*; Zbinden, *Bakhtin Between East and West*.

5. A general caveat is in order here: the chronology of Bakhtin's writings has been a persistent source of scholarly worry and debate, because there is some evidence suggesting that the dating of texts as "early" or "late" may, in fact, be inaccurate, not only due to Bakhtin's own revisions throughout his lifetime

and the complex publication history of his work, but also because the early editing of some texts involved "cutting and pasting." As the focus of the present study is not diachronic or evolutionary, I have retained much of the more conventional dating, as well as the editorial English titles, but the reservation regarding the chronology should be kept in mind.

6. For notable studies of Montaigne's contemporaneity, see Friedrich, *Montaigne*; Cave, *Cornucopian Text*; Starobinski, *Montaigne in Motion*; Screech, *Montaigne and Melancholy*; Bencivega, *Discipline of Subjectivity*.

7. The best discussion of the profound links between Rabelais and Montaigne is Cave, *Cornucopian Text*, which focuses on their shared conception of the performativity of discourse, the self-conscious, productive, open-ended practice of writing as opposed to codified theory, and their emphases on abundance, multiplicity, mutability, and singularity, noting: "The Rabelaisian quest, in which the final goal is always thus deferred is internalized in the *Essais* . . . [where] the narrator or 'subject' has now become the protagonist" (274). A focused discussion of paradox and ambiguity in the work of Rabelais and Montaigne is offered by Bowen, *Age of Bluff*.

THE ARCHITECTONICS OF SUBJECTIVITY

1. The dating of Bakhtin's texts is a complex issue, but if Brian Poole is right in arguing in "From Phenomenology to Dialogue" that the essay was actually concluded closer to (or even concurrently with) the writing of *PDP*, this would lend much support to a reading of these two texts as internally divided rather than neatly opposed to each other. I am grateful to Sergeiy Sandler for drawing my attention to the editorial comments in Bakhtin's *Sobraniie Sochinenii* (Collected Works), 1: 496–503, 505, and 2: 433–34, which suggest that both these texts could also, in fact, be dated to the early 1920s.

2. For the sake of authenticity, though not without some obvious misgivings, I have reproduced and followed Bakhtin's gender bias (and the choices of his translators) throughout this volume, whenever his work is cited or paraphrased.

3. Neither Holquist, "Introduction" to AA, 14–39, nor Morson and Emerson, *Mikhail Bakhtin: Creation of a Prosaics*, 176–79, 186, who have dealt with Bakhtin's "authored self," appear to be particularly troubled by this foundational analogy.

4. For a fuller discussion of this, see Erdinast-Vulcan, "Borderlines and Contraband."

5. For a thorough discussion of this "authored self," see Holquist, *Dialogism*, chap. 2; Morson and Emerson, *Mikhail Bakhtin: Creation of a Prosaics*, chap. 5. These accounts of Bakhtin's theory of the subject are both extremely valuable, not least for their differences of approach, but it seems to me that neither fully addresses the fundamental conflict between the aesthetic and the ethical vectors in the construction of the subject.

6. Given the proliferation of narrative identity theory over the past twenty-five years or so, it is both very difficult and redundant to offer anything like a survey of seminal positions and concepts here. For a fuller discussion of this issue, see Erdinast-Vulcan, "'The *I* That Tells Itself.'"

7. One cannot fully engage with this issue without due recognition of Ricœur's work, most notably vol. 3 of *Time and Narrative* and *Oneself as Another*, which intersect with Bakhtin's work at several points. For the present discussion, note Ricœur's insistence on the narrative agency of the subject and its ability to bring "innovation" into the "sedimentation" of received traditions, and to be the narrator, if not the author, of his/her life. "What sedimentation has contracted, narration can redeploy" (*Oneself as Another*, 122). My reading of Bakhtin's position would suggest that at least part of the "sedimentation" is due to the framing narratives superimposed on, rather than autonomously produced by, the subject.

8. In her note on the translation of *ja i drugoi*, Emerson writes: "Russian distinguishes between *drugoi* (another, other person) and *chuzhoi* (alien, strange; also, the other). The English pair 'I/other', with its intonations of alienations and opposition, has specifically been avoided here. The *another* Bakhtin has in mind is not hostile to the *I* but a necessary component of it, a friendly other, a living factor in the attempts of the *I* toward self-definition" (*PDP*, Appendix II, 302n15). In a later essay, Emerson takes up this point in an attempt to correct the skewed image of the "libertarian Baxtin" (based mainly on the essays from the 1930s), and presents him as "an apostle of constraints" who privileges the "outside perspective" as a source of value. Emerson argues, however, that it is this very privilege, the "deferment of one's self to the other for finalization [that] raises moral and ethical questions" concerning one's identity, the concept of responsibility, and personal morality ("Problems with Baxtin's Poetics," 507, 511, 512). Ann Jefferson also notes Bakhtin's problematic assumption of the essential benevolence of the authoring other, and uses the work of Sartre (whose initial formulations regarding the constitutive function of the other's gaze are often strikingly close to those of Bakhtin), as a critique of Bakhtin's benign construction (Jefferson, "Bodymatters," 152–77).

9. Residues of this philosophical embarrassment are visible even in the work of eminent Slavonic scholars like Morson and Emerson in discussing the transition from "Author and Hero" to *Problems of Dostoevsky's Poetics*: "The problematics of these manuscripts suggest why Bakhtin found it necessary to develop his theory of polyphony and its attendant concept of a 'wholeness of a higher order'" (*Mikhail Bakhtin: Creation of a Prosaics*, 190); "Bakhtin's fascination with the physicality of bodies (which somehow constricted his definition of aesthetic authorship and the whole of the hero) . . . gave way to other individualizing forces" with the conceptualization of the polyphonic novel" (196). For earlier discussions of this conceptual shift, see Erdinast-Vulcan, "Bakhtin's Homesickness" and "Borderlines and Contraband."

10. For a thoughtful attempt to reconcile the earlier essays with the "progressivist" Bakhtin and resolve its inherent ambivalence, see Godzich, "Correcting Kant." Godzich argues that while Kant's first and second Critiques are "grounded in the sovereign position of the subject and seek to ensure cognitive certainty for this subject," the third Critique turns to the constitution of the subject itself and shows that this constitution is, in fact, a form of alterity, or, in Godzich's own coinage, "altruity." Following this Kantian self-correction, Bakhtin shows, according to Godzich, that the constitution of the subject

> does not take place a priori but is always given in the realm of experience and in a position of dependency with respect to some givenness of the a posteriori. In other words, the constitution of the subject depends on precisely that which resists the theoretic pretensions of the subject, and it forces the subject to recognize itself as a historical being, constituted in time and space in relation to a preexisting givenness, and, as a historical being, it can only counterpose its own activity in time and space to the givenness it encounters. (14)

11. Erdinast-Vulcan, "Bakhtin's Homesickness," deals with this issue at greater length, suggesting that the fundamental rupture between the early and the late essays, reflected in a shift of attitude toward Dostoyevsky's work, is symptomatic of Bakhtin's ambivalence and anxiety about the process of secularization.

12. In their discussion of "Author and Hero," Morson and Emerson seem to be only intermittently sensitive to the conflict between the aesthetic and the ethical modalities, which they view as different phases along the "shifting ratio of finalizability to unfinalizability" in Bakhtin's work (*Mikhail Bakhtin: Creation of a Prosaics*, 217). At one point they seem to perceive the aesthetic relationship as an extension of the ethical one (178–79), but they do later refer—quite rightly, I believe—to "aesthetic escapes from responsibility" (182), to the fact that "selfhood is not a kind of text" (216), and to the opposition of "loophole and rhythm" (193), which they relate to a "shifting ratio of finalizability to unfinalizability" through the various phases of Bakhtin's work (217).

13. Holquist's engagement with the "biological" inspiration of Bakhtin's work is directly relevant to this point, because living systems, unlike mechanical ones, are unique, constantly responsive to, modifying and modified by their context, and—most important—indeterminate ("Dialogism and Aesthetics," 171–74).

14. The problematic role of the other in the constitution of the self is discussed by Emerson, "Problems with Baxtin's Poetics," 503–25.

15. Notably, this passage was added only in the second edition of *Problems of Dostoevsky's Poetics* (1963).

16. See the translator's note in *Art and Answerability*, 233, no. 6; and "Translators' Glossary" in *Bakhtin and Cultural Theory*, ed. Hirshkop and Shepherd, 193–94. It is noteworthy that in *The Formal Method in Literary Scholarship*, published under the name of P. N. Medvedev, but which, according to Rus-

sian sources followed by Clark and Holquist, may have been authored, co-authored, or influenced by Bakhtin, the word "finalization" (*zavershenie*) is used in reference to the distinctive quality of aesthetics: " . . . except for art, no sphere of ideological activity knows finalization in the strict sense of the word" (129); "Every [artistic] genre represents a special way of constructing and finalizing a whole, finalizing it essentially and thematically . . . and not just conditionally or compositionally" (130). Significantly, the only exception to the exclusive claim of art to "finalization" is religion, a claim that would be "impossible in any other sphere of ideological creation" (130). The conjunction of finalization, art, and religion may, of course, be perceived as evidence of diametrically opposing interpretations of Bakhtin's work, depending on one's view of the disputed texts. However, even with a strong measure of skepticism regarding the wholesale attribution of the book to Bakhtin, it is still highly probable that this aesthetic concept was common currency within the Bakhtin circle at the time.

17. In *Mikhail Bakhtin: Creation of a Prosaics*, Morson and Emerson relegate these two modes of being to two different phases in Bakhtin's work which they see as moving along a spectrum between "finalizabilty" and "unfinalizability." In "Author and Hero," they suggest, we have the highest degree of "finalizability," and in *Problems of Dostoevsky's Poetics*, there is a higher degree of "unfinalizability" (which will reach its highest point—a dead end, actually—in *Rabelais and His World*). I would take issue with Morson and Emerson on this point: Bakhtin's equation of the ethical mode of being with a sense of oneself as an "unframed," free agent—someone who "does not coincide with [an authorial definition] of himself"—is already evident in the earlier essay, from which I have just quoted. I suggest, rather, that these two modes of self-experience are co-existent and that their tensile interdependence (however uneasy) is precisely what Bakhtin has in mind in the conception of "architectonics."

THE POETICS OF SUBJECTIVITY

1. This reading of Bakhtin's response should, perhaps, be qualified, since the wording can also be understood as a reflection on the institutional structure of the university in Petrograd. And, once again, I am indebted to Sergeiy Sandler for this comment.

2. This is, of course, just one instance of a predominant theme in Heidegger's later work. For the fullest articulation of this philosophical contraband, see id., "Essence of Truth."

3. This conceptual and ethical horseshoe curve, which brings the pre- and postmodern too close together for comfort, may, in fact, be symptomatic of much of what goes under the name of postmodernism in the West.

4. The finely balanced account of Bakhtin's position in relation to formalism provided by Shaitanov, "Concept of the Generic Word," focuses mainly on questions of genre and relates only in passing to Shklovsky's concept of

ostranenie (defamiliarization, alienation, estrangement), which is vital for the present discussion.

5. Shklovsky's "Art as Technique" was also translated under the title "Art as Device" by Benjamin Sher, and partly retranslated by Caryl Emerson in "Shklovsky's *ostranenie*" (640).

6. As rendered by Emerson: "So, in order to return sensation to life, in order to make us feel things as objects, to make a stone feel stony, there exists that which is called art. The purpose of art is to impart sensation to an object as something seen rather than 'merely' recognized; the device of art is the device of the 'estrangement' of things and the device of defacilitated form, enhancing the difficulty and duration of perception, so that the perceptual process in art is an end in itself and should be prolonged: *art is a means for experiencing the making of a thing, but what is made in art is not important*" ("Shklovsky's *ostranenie*," 640).

7. Shklovsky's ethical concerns did not escape the contributors to *Poetics Today*'s issue *Estrangement Revisited* (Winter 2005). Svetlana Boym writes of the evolution of Shklovsky's concept of estrangement from a technique of art to "an existential art of survival and a practice of freedom and dissent" and relates his work to Arendt's writing on freedom (581); Michael Holquist and Ilya Kliger write about Shklovsky's "moral pathos" (629); and Galin Tihanov writes of Shklovsky's "hunger for substance" (684) and conception of "the socio-psychological mission of art" (673).

8. The question of the "disputed texts" (officially authored by members of the circle but sometimes attributed to Bakhtin) has not been resolved by Bakhtin scholarship at this point, and it is certainly beyond my own competence to make a contribution to this dispute. The issue certainly warrants some further in-depth historical and textual investigation in the framework of Slavonic studies. However, it seems to me that, having survived his associates, Bakhtin had numerous opportunities to identify himself as the author of these texts in the last decade of his life, when he was back in the public intellectual arena, and the fact that he chose not to claim authorship, at least not explicitly, is reason enough to relate to these texts as written by their nominal authors. Furthermore, when it comes to texts like *The Formal Method*, probably written with an eye to the dictates of hegemonic ideology, we should bear in mind that the philosophical contamination resulting from the circumstances of the writing may pose a problem even in the attribution of the text to its "real" historical author. We, as Westerners, "whose fate was made secure from the cradle to the grave by the perfected mechanism of democratic institutions," to quote Conrad's wry observation (*Under Western Eyes*, 175), should proceed with a great deal of caution and humility. It is not for us to judge.

That said, it is still noteworthy that—as I have gratefully learned from Sergeiy Sandler—in the recent Russian edition of Bakhtin's *Sobraniie Sochinenii* (Collected Works), 6: 434–35, the relevant fragment is not only more extensive than the translated note titled TMHS by the editors, but is also a nearly verbatim reproduction of the brief concluding chapter of *The Formal Method* and carries a more positive evaluation of the formalists' work.

9. Shklovsky's juxtaposition of prose and poetry is clearly not a distinction between different literary genres (Dostoyevsky's prose is thoroughly poetic on this account), but between different modes of being.

10. Emerson, "Shklovsky's *ostranenie*," 637, relates Shklovsky's "estrangement" (*ostranenie*) to Bakhtin's "outsideness" (*vnenakhodimos'*), suggesting that both concepts promote "acts of distancing over acts of identification, making this distance a prerequisite for genuine art." Taking an entirely different route, I would suggest that the Bakhtinian term analogous to Shklovsky's "estrangement," which may have been actually inspired by Shklovsky, is "loophole," the breach of the enframing "outsiderly" perspective of the authorial other.

11. Emerson notes that "an earlier reference to *ostranenie* in "Author and Hero" was edited out of the 1979 Russian text and is therefore not included in the Liapunov translation (p. 99, where the omission of a page is marked by an ellipsis). The full Russian text, she writes, "includes this enigmatic phrase: 'making strange and braking as a disconnection of the horizon'" (657n31). I suggest that this phrase is less enigmatic if we relate it to the phenomenological frame of reference that underlies "Author and Hero" and the focus on perception common to Bakhtin and Shklovsky: "estrangement" in this context is the disconnection, disruption, or halting (braking) of smooth habitual perception. Sergeiy Sandler informs me that Liapunov actually relates this comment to Shklovsky in Bakhtin's *Sobraniie Sochinenii* (Collected Works), 1: 682–83, and I am very grateful for this confirmation of my own intuitive understanding of the phrase here.

12. Given the sophistication of Voloshinov's theory of inner speech, developed in *MPL*, it may be surprising that he should fail to see the potential affinities between his own conception and Freud's emphasis on the cultural formation of the unconscious. But his reductive and sometimes downright vulgar representation of Freud may have been no more than one of the obligatory blind spots imposed by a regime of ideological state terrorism, which would not have been tolerant of anything but a wholesale condemnation of the bourgeois individualism represented by Freud.

13. This passage is translated slightly differently in Morson and Emerson, *Mikhail Bakhtin: Creation of a Prosaics*, 191–92: "A sense of *mine* in the experiencing of an object is something studied by psychology, but in complete abstraction from the value-generating weight of *I* and *other*, and from that which makes them singularly unique. Psychology knows only a 'hypothetical individuality.' . . . [in psychology,] inner givenness is not contemplated but rather studied [improperly] in a value-free context, in the posited unity of rule-governed psychological regularities."

14. The relation of Bakhtin's work to the Lacanian version of Freudianism is more complex and warrants a separate and lengthier discussion, which would also account for their apparent similarities. For present purposes, note that for

Lacan, too, the formula of desire vs. law is still operative, since the initiation of the subject into the symbolic order (which is the realm of the law) is set in motion by the entry of the Father's *Nom* (name) or *Non* (prohibition).

15. I believe that Morson and Emerson are right in saying that for Bakhtin, "the problem of the self was not strictly a psychological problem but more broadly and loosely a philosophical one" (*Mikhail Bakhtin: Creation of a Prosaics*, 174), founded on "a sense of people as free and morally responsible agents who are truly unfinalizable" (175), and closely related to Bakhtin's early interest in ethics and to the question of how the self is "constituted as an entity that performs responsible acts in the world" (176). But Morson and Emerson seem to concur in the separation of philosophy and psychology, relegating the latter to the category of "systems," to which Bakhtin was so adamantly opposed. My own argument here is that psychology in general and psychoanalysis in particular are far less "systemic" and "deterministic" than that, and that Bakhtin's objections to the discipline are based first and foremost on its view of ethics as a superstructure.

16. My understanding of the container-contained paradigm is indebted to Joan and Neville Symington's very helpful introduction to Bion's difficult thought in *The Clinical Thinking of Wilfred Bion*. I have also learned a great deal from Dana Amir's *Al ha'liriyut shel ha'nefesh* (On the Lyrical Aspects of the Psyche), which extends this meta-psychoanalytic theory to the reading of literature.

17. In Bion's conception, the very same forces and their correlative aspects are operative in the healthy psyche as well, and the very definition of mental health is the capacity to move along the axis between the continuous and the emergent senses of selfhood. Most notably, perhaps, Bion sees the artistic creative process as a constant (if not always conscious) enactment of this movement. It is a risk-fraught activity, punctuated by small-scale "catastrophes," but it is different only in degree from the workings of the healthy psyche (unlike the Freudian romantic view of artistic creation as compensatory and related to neurosis).

18. The first and ultimate container, or—to use Bakhtin's term—the prototype of the first authorial/other figure, is the mother. It is from her that the baby first receives the sense of its own integrity and continuity. She is, according to the Lacanian formula, the first mirror. If this mirroring is benign, if it holds the baby together while allowing it room for change, the child will develop the capacity to move between a continuous sense of selfhood and the sense of an emergent self that can move on and away, outgrowing its own former contours. For Bion, the role of the psychoanalyst is to take on the position of the environment-mother that first failed the child. Bakhtin makes the same analogy: "Just as the body is formed initially in the mother's womb (body), a person's consciousness awakens wrapped in another's consciousness. Only later does one begin to be subsumed by neutral words and categories, that is, one is defined as a person irrespective of *I* and *other*" (N70–71, 138).

19. Bion, "Container and Contained Transformed"; Britton, "Keeping Things in Mind," 112. Drawing on Bion's paradigm, Britton describes a pa-

tient's "fear of the containing object," which takes the form of "fear that one's nature is taken in by the other's devouring curiosity and somehow lost in the process; that one is comprehended by and nullified during the process." In the case described that fear was translated into a fear of entombment, incarceration in a coffin, being buried alive (Britton, "Keeping Things in Mind," 109).

20. While it seems clear that Bakhtin recognizes the potentially disabling effect of containment, the paralysis of the continuous self, it is difficult to tell whether he recognizes the kind of ethical relativism that emerges from it as a problem; or is fully aware of the potentially psychotic effect of an all-out rejection of containment in the psychological sphere. The carnivalesque, after all, is still ritualized, still confined to social regulation (and this has been, of course, a consistent note in the critique of the concept). In any case, it is clear that there is no place in the carnivalesque for subjective, individual interiority, and it also appears to be a dead end for Bakhtin, who does not pursue the concept in his subsequent work. This may be one of the reasons why *Rabelais and His World* is so difficult to reconcile with the rest of Bakhtin's work (see Emerson and Morson, *Mikhail Bakhtin: Creation of a Prosaics*, 223–26), although Bakhtin's engagement with the concept of the carnivalesque continues beyond the Rabelais book. The ethical relativism that has its roots in the dialogic and is taken to an extreme length in the carnivalesque may have been the reason for Bakhtin's introduction of the concept of the superaddressee in his later work: the superaddressee offers a form of triangulation, which may be necessary for both the psychic and ethical orientation of subjectivity.

21. Bollas also, misleadingly, to my mind, refers in *Being a Character* to the experiencing and the reflective modes of being as the "simple" and the "complex" selves, respectively. As I hope will have become clear in the course of the discussion, the attribution of simplicity or complexity, with its hierarchical or evolutionary implications, is problematic in that it does not allow for the full tug-of-war between these complementary modes of self-experience.

22. Bollas relates to pathology as a severe disruption of this balance, an extreme self-subjectification or self-objectification (*Being a Character*, 53), which brings him very close to Bion.

23. Morson and Emerson are undoubtedly fully justified in claiming that "'wholes'—all of them—are always transcended by our inner selves, and a recognition of such endlessly forward momentum is, in fact, constitutive of a healthy inner perspective" (*Mikhail Bakhtin: Creation of a Prosaics*, 184), but its seems to me that they stop short of pursuing the full implications of this insight.

THE SHATTERED MIRROR OF MODERNITY

1. On this conceptual trend, see Foucault, *Discipline and Punish*; id., "Eye of Power"; Irigary, *Speculum*. The most relevant and influential texts of the 1990s include Jay, *Downcast Eyes*, and Levin, ed., *Modernity*. The philosophical project of deconstruction, beginning with the exposure of the often violent hierarchies

that implicitly structure the discourse of the West, is profoundly concerned with the binary construction and identification of knowledge with light. Derrida argues that "the metaphysical domination of the concept of form cannot fail to effectuate a certain subjection of *sense* to seeing, of sense to the sense of sight" ("Form and Meaning," 108), and writes of the "ancient clandestine friendship between light and power" and of knowledge as vision that "assimilates the other to the same" ("Violence and Metaphysics," 96). Resistance to this ocular paradigm, which serves as a template to the "violent relationship of the West to its other" (id., "Ends of Man," 135), is—significantly for my concerns—evident in the works of both Lévinas and Merleau-Ponty.

2. A different and important corrective to "ocularphobic" conceptualizations of culture in relation to Bakhtin's work is offered by Gardiner, "Bakhtin and the Metaphorics of Perception." Gardiner persuasively argues that Bakhtin's work offers a more nuanced and holistic "post-ocularcentric" position, does not lend itself to any rigid valuational hierarchy of sensory experience, and posits a "dialogic specularity," based on the reversibility and multiplicity of perspectives, that enriches the encounter of self and other (58).

3. Bakhtin, Emerson observes, "visualizes voices, he senses their proximity and interaction as bodies. A voice, Bakhtin everywhere tells us, is not just words or ideas strung together: it is a 'semantic position', a point of view on the world, it is one personality orienting itself among other personalities within a limited field" ("Introduction," *PDP*, xxxiv).

4. Bruss, "V. N. Voloshinov," offers a thoughtful discussion of Voloshinov's discursive approach to subjectivity, relates his critique of Saussure in *Marxism and the Philosophy of Language* to the epistemological foundations of Lacanian thought, and suggests that Voloshinov anticipated the Lacanian evolution of Freud's premises. Indeed, whatever position one takes on the "disputed texts," it is impossible to overlook the affinities of this text with Bakhtin's "metalinguistic" theses. However, Bruss does not make any reference in "V. N. Voloshinov" either to Bakhtin's aversion to mirroring or to the Lacanian "stage of the mirror," which would have further reinforced his argument. For more immediate discussions of Bakhtin and Lacan, see Patterson, *Literature and Spirit*, 67–97; Etkind, *Eros*, 312–46; Stam, *Subversive Pleasures*, 51–55, 162–63; Handley, "Ethics of Subject Creation," 144–62; Pollard, *Discourse and Desire*. Insightful as these discussions are, however, they mostly seem to lean toward the "centrifugal" Bakhtin, to credit his work with a more monolithic consistency than it actually exhibits, and to gloss over the internal ambivalence that accounts for the liminality of his cultural position.

5. See Lacan, "Aggressivity in Psychoanalysis" and "Mirror Stage."

6. In *Lacan and Language*, 30, Muller and Richardson translate a passage from Lacan's article on "The Family" (1938), a transitional paper between his work on paranoia and the paper on the mirror stage, where Lacan extends the clinical observations from the developmental to the "ontological" sphere.

7. One wonders, however, whether this concept has anything to do with the actual reality of human growth and development. I believe that most people who have ever observed babies and infants as they begin to talk would testify to a completely different sense of their experience. The joy of being able to name things, of self-expression, and of speech, so much in evidence at this stage, is certainly a far cry from the Lacanian romanticized *angst* of the entry into the symbolic order. It seems that Lacan here reflects the *Freudian* Oedipal paradigm, offering an elaborate theoretical construct that simply does not work in real life.

8. The theme of the mirror also features in "Rhetoric" (68), "On the Questions of Self-Consciousness and Self-Evaluation" (72–73), and a later fragment included in N70–71 (*Speech Genres*, 146–47). According to Bocharov's commentary on this fragment, this theme is present in one form or another throughout most of Bakhtin's works (*Sobranie Sochinenii*, 5: 464). I am very grateful to Sergeiy Sandler for the translation of Bocharov's comment.

9. In "Next Hundred Years," 25n8, trans. Emerson notes that Bakhtin's "special animus against mirrors" offers

> only a reflection, which, although it does reproduce an image of the mobile face, must be untrue because it remains within the loop of a single consciousness. Others never see me as I see my passive reflection; likewise, I can never appear to myself as I appear to others. When I do try to see myself in that way, as when I peer into a mirror and grin vacuously, imagining the mirror image to be a benevolent other pleased to see me, all I can register on my own face is ghostliness and lack of definition because there is only one pair of eyes at work in this exchange and such a singularity is always static and false. To empathize with another person in any useful or enriching way, one must remain consciously alien to that person, specifically not a duplication. "What I look like," Bakhtin insists, is always conditioned by the response in me that you, a genuine other gazing at me, bring forth. Thus I can never (in any nontrivial way) see myself in a glass—although I can see an authentic image of myself reflected in the pupils of your eyes. (Emerson, "Next Hundred Years," 15)

I would suggest, however, that the predominant consciousness in the mirror is, in fact, that of the *other*. For an alternative translation of the "mirror" fragment, see Nikulin, "Man at the Mirror," 61. I am grateful to Sergeiy Sandler for having drawn my attention to this translation, which seems to support my reading of the conceptualization of mirroring in Bakhtin's work.

10. According to the translator's note in the glossary to *The Dialogic Imagination*, the concept of authorial refraction (*prelomlenie*) is "central to the light-ray metaphor Bakhtin uses to illustrate the complexity in reading a prose communication. Every word is like a ray of light on a trajectory to both an object and a receiver. Both paths are strewn with previous claims that slow up, distort, refract the intention of the word. A semantic 'spectral dispersion' occurs" (432).

11. The phrase "spectral dispersion" is a rendering of *prelomlenie*, which is

elsewhere translated as "refraction." I am grateful to Sergeiy Sandler for having checked and confirmed this for me.

12. The concept of refraction appears as early as the introduction to the 1929 edition of *PDP*, where Bakhtin tackles the formalist approach to literature:

> At the basis of our analysis lies the conviction that every literary work is internally and immanently sociological. Within it living social forces intersect; each element of its form is permeated with living social evaluations. For this reason a purely formal analysis must take each element of the artistic structure as a point of refraction of living social forces, as a synthetic crystal whose facets are structured and ground in such a way that they refract specific rays of social evaluations, and refract them at a specific angle. (Appendix I, "Three Fragments from the 1929 Edition of *Problems of Dostoevsky's Art*," 276)

The introduction to the 1963 edition has replaced the original introduction, but the term "refraction" is still present in the book itself.

13. In the editorial notes on the "Person at the Mirror" fragment, we are told that while revising his book on Dostoyevsky in 1961–62, Bakhtin scribbled a comment in the margins of page 185 of the manuscript: "Man at the mirror. To develop" (*Sobraniie Sochinenii* [Collected Works], 6: 507). This remark, the editors write, is related to Bakhtin's analysis of Dostoyevsky's *Notes from Underground*, and to "mirror possessedness" (that is, being possessed by the other while looking at the mirror), which appears in the discussion of confession in the Dostoyevskian novel in "Author and Hero."

14. This can be described, at the risk of being cute, as a transition from catoptrics—the branch of optics dealing with the formation of images by reflection in mirrors—to dioptrics, the branch of optics dealing with the formation of images by refraction through lenses.

15. That Derrida often sounds distinctly Bakhtinian is hardly surprising, given their underlying conceptual affinities, but it is only in its latest phase that Derrida's work becomes tinged with the Bakhtinian homesickness. I feel that this is when it becomes most pregnant with meaning.

16. For commentaries on Bakhtin's relation to Lukács throughout the various phases of their careers, see Pechey, *Mikhail Bakhtin*; Tihanov, *Master and the Slave*; Neubauer, "Bakhtin versus Lukács" (1996); Erdinast-Vulcan, "Narrative, Modernism." Notes from the early 1940s that Bakhtin titled "On Questions of the Theory of the Novel: The Problem of Dialogue, Letter, and Autobiography" directly engage in a polemic with Lukács and eventually led to the draft of "Epic and Novel" (*Sobraniie Sochinenii* [Collected Works], 3: 557–607). I am grateful to Sergeiy Sandler for having drawn my attention to this point.

17. Bakhtin was "profoundly unresponsive to the major works of twentieth-century modernism," Emerson notes ("Introduction" to *Bakhtin in Contexts*, ed. Mandelker, 17). For an illuminating discussion of this issue, see Burton, "Paradoxical Relations." Notes taken by a student at Bakhtin's course on world literature (*Saransk*, 1958–59) seem, however, to relate to Joyce, for instance,

in an appreciative, if cautious, spirit. I am grateful to Sergeiy Sandler, who has told me of these notes and alerted me to the need for qualification on this point.

18. A similarly conciliatory, narrativized view of death as that which rounds off a person's life in a way unattainable by the individual consciousness itself is expressed by Wittgenstein: "After someone has died we see his life in a conciliatory light. His life appears to us with outlines softened by a haze. There was no softening for *him* though. His life was jagged and incomplete. For him there was no reconciliation; his life is naked and wretched" (*Culture and Value*, 46e).

19. Bakhtin's approval of Shklovsky's book on Dostoyevsky is decidedly noteworthy in this context: "*'as long as a work remained multi-leveled and multi-voiced, as long as the people in it were still arguing, then despair over the absence of a solution would not set in*. The end of a novel signified for Dostoevsky the fall of a new Tower of Babylon'" (Shklovsky cited by Bakhtin in *PDP*, 39). The Tower of Babel failed to materialize because of God's wrath at the presumption of its builders. The means of its destruction was the plurality and diversity of languages, which, so the biblical story goes, supplanted the single language the builders had used. Bakhtin's implicit approval of this diversity in citing Shklovsky's reading of Dostoyevsky is evidently incompatible both with the spirit of the biblical narrative and with his homogenizing centripetal conception of the "aesthetic relations" in "Author and Hero."

THE EXILIC CONSTELLATION: INTRODUCTION

1. The omission of attribution is, perhaps, less of an embarrassment when seen in the appropriate cultural context. Cassirer's and Scheler's works may have been deemed to be common knowledge for the educated European reader at the time, so giving them credit could have been construed as redundant.

2. For seminal studies of Bakhtin's Western philosophical contexts, see Clark and Holquist, "Influence of Kant"; Emerson, "Making of M. M. Bakhtin"; Brandist, *Bakhtin Circle* and "Two Routes"; Tihanov, *Master and the Slave*; Brandist et al., eds., *Bakhtin Circle*. For the role played by Max Scheler, Nicolai Hartmann, and Ernst Cassirer in Voloshinov's and Bakhtin's work, see Poole, "Bakhtin and Cassirer" and "From Phenomenology to Dialogue."

3. It is arguable that Franz Rosenzweig, a hero of tragic stature, might have been comfortably included among the philosophers discussed in this part of the book. His work was certainly an acknowledged source of inspiration for Lévinas, and its echoes have undoubtedly found their way into Bakhtin's work as well. Unlike the "exilic" thinkers, however, Rosenzweig had openly embraced his own religiosity and created his own integral conception of the relation between man, world, and God in *The Star of Redemption*. As this study is primarily concerned with the process of thought rather than its fully completed product, I have chosen not to include Rosenzweig among the philosophical exiles discussed in this part, and settle for brief references to his work at relevant points throughout the discussion.

THE DEAD END OF OMNISCIENCE

1. In their comments on the direct Bergsonian references throughout Bakhtin's work, Morson and Emerson suggest that Bakhtin's familiarity with Bergson had been mediated through Nikolai Losskii's book *The Intuitive Philosophy of Bergson* (in Russian; Moscow: Put', 1914) and argue that while Bakhtin would have been sympathetic to Bergson as "the celebrator of open-ended flow, champion of intuition against the disembodied workings of 'spatialized' intellect, and proponent of the creative capacities of time" (Morson and Emerson, *Mikhail Bakhtin: Creation of a Prosaics*, 177), he would have been opposed to the view, attributed to Bergson, of the subject as "pure inner change and flow, the pure Heraclitian flux of self, the river one cannot step into twice. If the self is only such a flow, *who* is it that can be held morally responsible?" (179). The only problem with this succinct formulation of Bakhtin's position between these two extremes is that a celebration of pure "unfinalizability," pure flux, as it were, is not really compatible with the work of Bergson himself, and it is arguable that Bakhtin would have been much more sympathetic to Bergson if he had had first-hand knowledge of the philosopher's work. Be that as it may, our present concern is not with genealogy and influence, but with shared anxieties and fundamental philosophical affinities.

2. For some focused discussions of Bakhtin's relation to Bergson, see Rousseau, "Perpetual Crises," passim; Rudova, "Bergsonism in Russia," passim; Taylor, "Kanaev, Vitalism," passim. Oddly, though, most of these commentaries (with the partial exception of Rudova) do not relate to the issue of temporality, which is, arguably, Bergson's major contribution to Western philosophy. Rudova notes the fact that both thinkers worked at a time when "traditional systems of thought were being questioned" (185), but does not elaborate on the philosophical aspects of this observation. The treatment of their points of affinity in this brief article, valid though it is, does not give due credit and weight to the radical potential and the profoundly ethical aspects of Bergson's early works, which, I suggest, were inspirational for Bakhtin, either directly or through the mediation of the formalists.

3. Taylor, "Kanaev, Vitalism," 151, cites Nina Perlina's claim that much of the essay "Contemporary Vitalism" is derived from a work by the philosopher Nikolai Losskii that appeared under the same title in 1922.

4. See Holquist, "Dialogism and Aesthetics" and "Bakhtin and Beautiful Science."

5. Another articulation of the same dilemma in ancient Jewish tradition is cited by Lévinas in "Bad Conscience and the Inexorable," quoting the talmudic sage Reb Hanina, who says that "everything is in the hands of God, except for the fear of God" (*Berakhot* 33B; quoted in Cohen, ed., *Face to Face with Lévinas*, 40).

6. To the best of my knowledge, these fragments, from Bakhtin's *Sobraniie Sochinenii* (Collected Works), vol. 5, have not yet been published in English translation. Since they are relatively inaccessible and unfamiliar to Western

readers, I have quoted them at some length. I am most grateful to Professor S. G. Bocharov for permission to have them translated here, and to Victoria Clebanov and Sergeiy Sandler for their thoughtful and responsible translations of these notes.

7. In a subsequent essay, "Sideshadowing and Tempics," Morson offers a theory of "tempics" as a subsection of "prosaics," a cultural-ethical approach founded on Bakhtinian principles.

8. While the cross-Atlantic convergence of James and Bergson on this point is not surprising in view of the correspondence between them and their mutual and sincerely sympathetic recognition of each other's work, it seems more likely, as far as can be gathered from the explicit references in Bakhtin's work, that it was Bergson who was his source of philosophical inspiration.

9. See also "The Problem of Speech Genres," where dialogicity becomes the foundational premise of Bakhtin's metalinguistics, although the term itself appears for the first time only in "The Problem of the Text."

10. I am very grateful to Professor S. G. Bocharov for permission to publish this fragment in translation, and to Victoria Clebanov and Sergeiy Sandler for their respective translations of this passage, which I have synthesized and slightly modified for the purpose of this discussion.

11. This sentence was added to the second edition of *Problems of Dostoevsky's Poetics* and is probably drawn from Bakhtin's notebooks of the 1940s. I am very grateful to Sergeiy Sandler for this comment.

IN THE BEGINNING WAS THE BODY

1. Bakhtin did, apparently, know of Merleau-Ponty's work, at least enough to list two of his works—*Signs* and *Phenomenology of Perception*—in "Notebook 2" of the "Working Notes from the 1960s and early 1970" (*Sobraniie Sochinenii* [Collected Works], 6: 365). I am very grateful to Sergeiy Sandler and to the anonymous reader who have drawn my attention to this, noting that the bibliographical list may have been culled from Otto Friedrich Bollnow's book *Mensch und Raum* (Stuttgart: Kohlhammer, 1963). But be that as it may, there is no evidence that Bakhtin had actually read or responded to Merleau-Ponty or vice versa, and it is impossible to attribute their almost uncanny resemblances to anything but a profound temperamental affinity. For the most thorough investigation of this virtual relationship, see Gardiner, "'The Incomparable Monster'" (1998). For brief references to this affinity, see Holquist's introduction to Bakhtin, *Art and Answerability*, xxxv; Jung, "Bakhtin's Body Politics" / "Bakhtin's Dialogical Body Politics." Merleau-Ponty is not mentioned in Bernard-Donals, *Mikhail Bakhtin*, apart from a brief footnote claiming that Bakhtin and Merleau-Ponty had not read each other's works (2). It seems to me that if we take Merleau-Ponty (rather than Husserl) as the more significant figure for a phenomenological reading of Bakhtin, Bernard-Donals's Marxist reading loses much of its grounding.

2. The reading of Merleau-Ponty in this study is synchronic rather than diachronic. Undoubtedly, we thus cannot deal with the evolution of his work through its various phases, which a close diachronic reading would have enabled us to follow, but as in the case of Bakhtin, the focus of the present discussion is Merleau-Ponty's response to the challenge of writing on the ruins of Cartesian philosophy, which is consistent throughout the trajectory of his life's work.

3. Though not immediately visible or explicit, the implications of Merleau-Ponty's work for ethics have been recognized and articulated by some readers. Drawing on "The Chiasm," the elusive and haunting last chapter of the unfinished last manuscript, for his reconstruction of a Merleau-Pontyan ethics, Gary B. Madison suggests that Merleau-Ponty's later work offers a universalist, rational ethics, whose ground (*principium*) is the "reversibility of the flesh," and whose focus is the communicative process and the alterity that is at the very core of the subject itself: intersubjectivity, he writes, is "as primordial as subjectivity itself, for subjectivity is, at its roots, an *intercorporeity*" ("Ethics and Politics of the Flesh," 165). Another relevant reconstruction is offered by Glenn Edwards McGee who recognizes the nonsystemic nature of the philosopher's thinking about value theory and suggests that rather than ethical taxonomies, the focus of his work is on the embodied, situated "moral actor." In traditional ethics, the subject is held to be a rational moral actor who is, in essence, "the same entity through time," transcendent to the body, to circumstances, to feelings and inclinations at the moment of choice, and can thus be held responsible for the choices of the past. Ethics, on this account, is the making of rational adjudication between alternatives (rules, goals, etc.), and the good is universal ("Merleau-Pontyan Ethics," 199). In Merleau-Ponty's alternative thinking of ethics, individuation takes place in and through an intersubjective relationship, values are "synthesized" through shared meaning and language (204), and "the most salient notions in responsibility are grounded in *context*, that is, the degree to which one acts from within one's possibilities, and in the *social*, that is, the relation of one to one's other" (206).

4. Emerson's translation of the same passage is somewhat different, but suggests the same conception of subjectivity: "I am conscious of myself and become myself only while revealing myself for another, through another, and with the help of another . . . every internal experience ends up on the boundary, encounters another, and in this tension-filled encounter lies its entire essence. . . . The very being of man (both external and internal) is the *deepest communion. To be means to communicate.* . . . To be means to be for another, and through the other, for oneself" (TRDB, 287).

5. Merleau-Ponty's posthumously published *The Prose of the World* is another unfinished fragment, dating from the early 1950s. It was part of a planned work, which was to include *The Origin of Truth*, eventually entitled *The Visible and the Invisible*.

6. The analogous reversibility of the visual, the tactile, and the discursive is extensively discussed by Froman, *Merleau-Ponty*.

7. The ethical implications of this transition have not been lost on Merleau-Ponty's readers. Duane H. Davis argues that "speech, written discourse, and gesture all permit some sort of transcendence whereby I can be said to 'get outside of myself'" and that "an examination of language ought to reveal a great deal about this transcendence, and thereby make room for a discussion of such ethical implications of transcendence" ("Reversible Subjectivity," 31); Gary B. Madison articulates a Merleau-Pontyan "universal, rational ethics" whose ground is the "reversibility of the flesh" and whose focus is the "communicative process" ("Ethics and Politics of the Flesh," 165).

8. There are additional indications of Merleau-Ponty's budding discursive orientation in *The Visible and the Invisible* (175) and in the earlier incomplete manuscript of *The Prose of the World*, where discourse and gesture are explicitly correlated:

> Speech is a gesture which suppresses itself as such and goes beyond itself toward a meaning.... It is therefore necessary to conceive the operation of speech as outside any previously institutionalized signification, as a unique act.... Speech is peculiarly my own, my productivity, and yet speech is so only to make meaning out of my productivity and to communicate that meaning. The other who listens and understands joins with me in what is most singular in me. (141)

9. See also Hirschkop, *Mikhail Bakhtin*, 174.

10. Sergeiy Sandler has suggested that the Russian term *oveschestvlenie*, translated as "materialization" in this context, should have been rendered as "reification." If this is the case, it lends some additional support to my own reading.

11. Holquist makes a similar point in claiming that "the condition of being in a body is similar to the condition of being in a language insofar as in both cases the relation between one and many, self and other, us and them, is primary" ("Bakhtin and the Beautiful Science," 225).

12. In his introduction to Brandist et al., eds., *Bakhtin Circle*, David Shepherd expresses skepticism regarding the attribution of the "disputed texts" to Bakhtin (with the exception of the article on vitalism, where the attribution is supported by Kanaev's own testimony), but acknowledges the "collaborative ethos" of the circle (19), which seems to me a good way of getting around this thorny issue. For a very sound discussion of the degree of collaboration in this case, see ibid., 157–85. It seems to me that Brandist's reading of "the utterance" as being "on the borderline between the domain of the linguist and that of the literary critic" (157) is particularly apt.

13. For the two most recent and relevant contributions to the discussion of the Voloshinov-Bakhtinian philosophy of language, see Holquist and Kliger, "Minding the Gap," and Seifrid, *Word Made Self*.

14. Saussure is the obvious target of Merleau-Ponty's reference to "congealed relations" and the "reduction to synchrony" in his "Working Notes for *The Visible and the Invisible*," 181.

15. As the structuralist flavor of the term "oppositional" may be misleading here, it would have been more in keeping with Merleau-Ponty's approach to render it as "differential."

16. Low, *Merleau-Ponty's Last Vision*, makes a very good case for Merleau-Ponty's view of perception as a meaning-producing interaction and of praxis as the "original domain" (75) and highlights the analogy between body and speech in Merleau-Ponty's work (21). But whereas Low still relates to an "ontological priority granted to the body" and to speech as "sublimated bodily gesture" (22), I would suggest that the radical potential of Merleau-Ponty's thought lies precisely in its openness to an inversion of this ontological priority, where bodily perception is conceived of as sublimated language. It is this two-way flow between the somatic and the semiotic that makes his work so illuminating for a reading of Bakhtin.

17. Benveniste, *Problems in General Linguistics*, consisting of essays written between 1939 and 1964, is the first of a two-volume collection of Benveniste's essays, *Problèmes de linguistique générale*, the second of which (a collection of essays written between 1965 and 1972) was published in French in 1974, but has not been translated into English.

18. Oddly, Merleau-Ponty himself refers to formalism critically, saying that it

> is certainly correct to condemn formalism, but it is usually forgotten that formalism's error is not that it overestimates form but that it esteems form so little that it abstracts it from meaning. In this regard formalism does not differ from a "thematic" literature which also separates the meaning and structure in a work. The true opposite of formalism is a good theory of speech which distinguishes speech from any technique or device. Speech is not a means in the service of an external end. It contains its own ebbing, its own rule of usage and vision of the world, the way a gesture reveals the whole truth about a man. (*Visible and the Invisible*, 89)

The evident injustice of this critique, based on little more than the popular connotations of the label, is less interesting than the fact that Merleau-Ponty seems to be utterly oblivious to the profound resemblance between his own philosophical quest and the aesthetic project of formalism.

19. This thoroughly modernist conception of aesthetics needs no further testimony than T. S. Eliot's description of the poetic undertaking as an attempt to "dislocate language into meaning" ("Metaphysical Poets," 289).

20. Notably, Heidegger's articulation of his nonpropositional sense of truth in "On the Origin of the Work of Art" is also predicated on estrangement, an opening into what is "other than usual" (72–73, 78).

21. For readers of poetry, this would hardly count as news, since the "heresy of paraphrase," to use Cleanth Brooks's coinage, has long been a commonplace of literary studies. A poem, Brooks argues, cannot be read as an idea "wrapped in emotion" or a "prose-sense decorated by sensuous imagery" (187), and any attempt to abstract its "prose meaning," "statement," or "argument" is bound to result, not only in an impoverished reading, but in a total distortion of the

experience of reading. The New Critics of the 1940s, and Brooks as one of their founding fathers, have served as convenient straw figures for a wide range of poststructuralist literary and cultural theories, and some of the criticism leveled at their work is undoubtedly sound, but one would be hard put to find more subtle, articulate, and responsive readers of poetry. Elitist, ensconced in their ivory towers of culture, and rather deaf to the voices of history they may have been, but their writings on poetry are still classics, and Brooks's "heresy of paraphrase" is a good case in point.

22. Heidegger's "Essence of Truth" is, of course, highly relevant on this point.

FROM DIALOGICS TO TRIALOGICS

1. For some interesting discussions of these affinities, which place both Bakhtin and Lévinas within the philosophy of alterity, see Ponzio, "Relation of Otherness"; Patterson, *Literature and Spirit*; Gardiner, "Alterity and Ethics"; Nealon, "Ethics of Dialogue"; Eskin, *Ethics and Dialogue*.

2. On the conception of exile in the work of Lévinas, see Wyschogrod, "Autochthony and Welcome."

3. Derrida, too, focuses on the concept of the signature as that which inscribes the "here-and-now" of the signatory, but also the "repeatability, recognizability, and reproducibility" of the signature. The event of the signature cannot be subjective—it always answers to another subject, and "there is always another who countersigns" (Derrida, *Acts of Literature*, 18). This is yet another instance of the mutually constitutive nature of the singular and the general.

4. Lévinas also uses the term "nonindifference" to describe the relationship of the subject with the other. The editors of *TPA* trace the etymological relation of the Bakhtinian concept of "participative thinking" to this nonindifference: "*uchastnoe myshlenie*—engaged, committed, involved, concerned, or interested thinking: unindifferent thinking (I [i.e., Holquist] occasionally add 'unindifferent' in parentheses after 'participative')" (*TPA*, 86n29). May we legitimately speculate that Lévinas's use of the term is likewise related to his own Russian origins?

5. This commentary is fully substantiated both by Lévinas's own insistence on the nonvisual character of the face and by the fact that the Hebrew verbal root of *panim* also denotes an "address," which clearly points to a discursive rather than a visual context, but I believe that the face, which looms so large in Lévinas's work, is still unavoidably embedded in a spatial and visual context.

6. Notably, Hannah Arendt cites the etymology of the word "persona" as "sounding through," noting that in ancient Rome, in the mask that covered an actor's face, there was "a broad opening at the place of the mouth through which the individual, undisguised voice of the actor could sound. It is from this sounding through that the word *persona* was derived: *per-sonare*, 'to sound through', is the verb of which *persona*, the mask, is the noun" (Arendt, *Responsibility and Judgment*, 12). I am very grateful to Anniken Greve for this reference.

7. For illuminating discussions of the glaring incongruity of Lévinas's antipathy to art and his persistent references to literary works, see Eaglestone, *Ethical Criticism*, and Robbins, *Altered Reading*. It seems to me that the productivity of these contributions lies, not only in their respective attempts to resolve this apparent contradiction, but in their broader implications for literature and ethics.

8. Notwithstanding Lévinas's own Platonic allusion to the poet who "exiles himself from the city" ("Reality and Its Shadow," 141), I would take issue with Wyschogrod's reading of Lévinas at this point (*Emmanuel Lévinas*, 73–74).

9. Much has been written by Derrida and subsequent readers, of Lévinas's derogation of vision that stands for the violence of the economy of selfhood. For one instance of this position, see Lévinas, *Difficult Freedom*, 6, 8. As suggested earlier, the transition from the spatial-visual to the temporal-auditory in Bakhtin's work is less clear-cut than it seems, and the present discussion will not follow this seductive analogy with Lévinas beyond this brief observation.

10. Recall Merleau-Ponty's similar hostility to the ocular regime and his objection to the "paradigm of visuality" (*Visible and the Invisible*, 83).

11. For thoughtful discussions of Lévinas's conception of literature and its relation to the juxtaposition of the saying and the said, see Critchley, *Ethics of Deconstruction*.

12. Lévinas's references to the "amphibology of being" (*Otherwise than Being*, 19 and passim) may well refer to a similar architectonic relation underlying the dynamics of subjectivity, but the distinction between self and other, the insistence on the irreducible alterity of the other, has a nearly axiomatic position in his work.

13. Though often cited and quoted in Lévinas's work (see, e.g., *Totality and Infinity*, 217, 236; *Ethics and Infinity*, 98, 101), this phrase is not explicitly attributed to Dostoyevsky, which may testify to a degree of internalization or assimilation precluding the need for explicit attribution.

14. See Robbins, *Altered Reading*, 147–50. The statement is first articulated in *The Brothers Karamazov* by Father Zosima's elder brother, Markel, on his deathbed; it is later repeated by Father Zosima in his recounting of his own conversion; and recounted by his disciple, Alyosha Karamazov. As Robbins notes, this assertion occurs about a dozen times in Lévinas's work (148).

15. For a different evaluation of this fundamental difference between Lévinas's and Bakhtin's conceptions of the relation between the subject and the other, see Eskin, *Ethics and Dialogue*, who writes that "[w]hile Levinas reiterates the priority of the other, who interpellates *me* (in the accusative case), thus enabling me to become an agent, an 'I' (in the nominative case), Bakhtin takes the 'I' as the most fundamental moment in co-existence for granted. . . . In other words, Bakhtin does not problematize the initial emergence of the active 'I' by way of the other . . . the self is always already an *actively experiencing* self. . . . Semethically [*sic*], I indeed owe my existence to an interlocutor; co-existentially,

I am always already an actively experiencing agent" (78). Nealon is even more critical of the Bakhtinian conception of subjectivity, which, he suggests, is ultimately "approporiative" and "voracious" (*Alterity Politics*, 42) in that it does not allow the same primacy to the other as does Lévinas's (41–42).

16. Note, however, that the Hebrew verbal root of "face" (*panim; pana*) means not only bodily "turning," as Handleman points out, but also an "addressing," as in a request or a question. But Lévinas does not follow up this rich allusiveness, which seems to have motivated his initial choice of the term. His insistence on the "speaking face" notwithstanding, it seems that the visual sense of this metaphor has taken over, after all, obscuring the discursive, dialogic, and—yes, reciprocal—nature of the ethical relationship.

17. As Schrag, *Self After Postmodernity*, which often intersects with the concerns of the present study, puts it in another context, while "responsivity" is a descriptive term, "responsibility" is related to an ethical stance. In response to the challenge of this conversion from the phenomenal to the axiological level, Schrag offers the "ethic of the fitting response," which aligns the ability to respond with the "moral injunction to do so in the proper way" (91). But the question remains. Even if we take into account the intersubjective constitution of subjectivity, the formative role of the "we-experience" within which the "I-experience" is embedded; even if we problematize the distinction between facts and values, as Schrag does, arguing that facts, too, are based on interpretative constructs (98); even if we relegate the either-or conception to theory and turn to the praxis of communal life—the issue of ethics is far from resolved, and it may well be the case that any transition from that which is factually the case with all human beings (be it their somatic, linguistic, or communal constitution) cannot be simply converted into ethics. If this were possible, there would not be any need for ethics in the first place.

18. Cf. Lévinas, *Otherwise than Being*, 157–62, 158, 160; id., *Totality and Infinity*, subsection 6, "The Other and the Others" (212–14); id., "Ego and Totality."

19. On the significance of "third" and the question of justice in Lévinas's thought, see also Peperzak, *To the Other*, 174–78.

20. This new turn coincided with a relative relaxation in state censorship in the Soviet Union, and Bakhtin might have felt he could now introduce this new factor, which would act as a centripetal ballast and counter the centrifugal, potentially relativistic pull of his earlier work.

21. Rather than "surpasses," a more accurate rendering might be "anticipates," according to Sergeiy Sandler.

22. In one of the earliest responses to the introduction of the superaddressee, Zavala, "Bakhtin and the Third," 51, argues for a Bakhtinian triadic model of communication, a model for responsive understanding between social subjects, where the listener or the "third" has a regulatory role that affects meaning and closure. Significantly, notwithstanding her suggestion that the "third" is, in fact, an "emancipatory totality," an anticipation of discursive understanding

or resistance, Zavala (quite rightly, I believe) relates this construct to Saint Augustine's third "I," who is "the intended moral effect of a closing down of the enunciatory gap; the complete individual (collective to Bakhtin), which will be called upon to hold in place the circuit of guarantees between subject and knowledge" (57). Morson and Emerson relate to the superaddressee (*nadadresat*) as "a principle of hope" that is constitutive in every utterance, a perfect listener who "is not an ideological but a metalinguistic fact." Quite rightly, I think, they choose to overlook Bakhtin's deliberate blurring of the theological overtones of this new conception, and conclude that "God may be dead, but in some form the superaddressee is always with us" (*Mikhail Bakhtin: Creation of a Prosaics*, 136). Holquist writes that "poets who feel misunderstood in their lifetimes, martyrs for lost political causes, quite ordinary people caught in lives of quiet desperation—all have been correct to hope that outside the tyranny of the present there is a possible addressee who will understand them" (*Dialogism*, 38). Brandist sees the superaddressee as "a sort of guarantor against the degeneration of plurality of perspectives into meaningless relativism" (*Bakhtin Circle*, 169):

> The Marburg School principle that it is the idea of God that is important in human society, rather than God as a being with attributes, returns in the idea of the superaddressee . . . [who] is thus, for Bakhtin, a direction of consciousness determined by feeling rather than intellect, it is an object of will not of knowledge. . . . The superaddressee is an "infinitely remote" but "validly posited" point of direction. Consciousness strives towards its infinite goal, co-creating the world as an object of cognition as it goes. However, the superaddressee also constitutes the juridical strand within Bakhtin's thought, which also derived from the Marburg School. It is the eternally deferred supreme judge who views the social world from without. (170–71)

Pechey sees the superaddressee as a hypothetical but invariably implicit premise of a "Habermassian ideal speech situation" ("Eternity and Modernity," 361). Farmer, "'Not Theory . . . ,'" in *Mikhail Bakhtin*, ed. Gardiner, 363 and passim, links the superaddressee to the "contexts of Eden." Dop, " Dialogic Epistemology," 31, translates the concept into a Hegelian universal, "presupposed metaphysical 'center'."

23. See also: "Understanding is never a tautology or duplication, for it always involves two and a potential third" (PT, 115); "The word is a drama in which three characters participate (it is not a duet, but a trio)"; "The relationship to others' utterances . . . is a living tripartite unity. But the third element is still not usually taken into account" (122).

24. While this reference was suggested by my own reading of these philosophers and the intuitive sense of linkage between their and Bakhtin's temperamental religiosity, I was gratified to hear after the completion of this study that Bakhtin had actually read and wrote extensive notes on Gabriel Marcel's *Being and Having*, and that he had read or planned to read Karl Jaspers (whose name

appears in the bibliographical lists in the late notebooks). Once again, I am grateful to Sergeiy Sandler for generously sharing his knowledge of Russian sources with me.

25. It is noteworthy, then, that Felch and Contino subtitled their anthology of articles on Bakhtin and religion *A Feeling for Faith* in recognition of the fact that "Bakhtin was careful to distinguish between 'faith', which he identified as an abstract codification of a belief system, and 'a feeling for faith'. The latter involves both the preparation for personal encounters—the adoption of a proper attitude—and the actual living engagement of persons, both human and divine" ("Introduction," 1).

CODA: A HOME AWAY FROM HOME

1. Clark's and Holquist's 1984 biographical portrayal of Bakhtin as profoundly religious, substantiated by a great deal of historical detail concerning the religious associations with which Bakhtin was probably involved, initially came under heavy attack from I. R. Titunik, Gary Saul Morson, and Caryl Emerson, who objected to what they saw as the circumstantial nature of Holquist's evidence, and to what they argued was a reading of Bakhtin's works as "a kind of theology in code" (*Mikhail Bakhtin: Creation of a Prosaics*, 114). These objections notwithstanding, Morson and Emerson also note that at times "Bakhtin's prophetic tone verges on the theological.... [His] theology, to the extent he had one, is not of resurrection but of incarnation," suggesting that it is not a monologic doctrine but a *"conversation* with Christ" (61–62). Several nuanced, though often divergent, conceptions of the character of Bakhtin's religious affiliations were offered in the late 1990s and early 2000s by Mihailovic, *Corporeal Words*; Coates, *Christianity in Bakhtin*; the various contributors to *Bakhtin and Religion*, ed. Felch and Contino; and Felch, "'In the Chorus of Others'"—all trying to disclose the religious template on which Bakhtin's philosophy is founded. A different conception of this issue has been proposed by Hirschkop, who in "The Sacred and the Everyday" reads Bakhtin's relation to the sacred as similar to that of his contemporaries Benjamin and Wittgenstein and suggests that it is premised on his non-Saussurean conception of language as discourse, where the superaddressee is "the ideal interlocutor." As I earlier indicated, I believe that this construction, notwithstanding its congeniality, is still embedded in a secular sensibility and does not do full justice either to Bakhtin's temperamental religiosity or to his profound ambivalence about it. More problematically still, it does not take on board Bakhtin's awareness of and anxiety about the immanent relativism ("indifference," as he sometimes puts it) of any approach to ethics that has no recourse to that which lies over and above the constructions of the participants in dialogue. Regrettably, I have not been able to trace a published version of Hirschkop's paper "The Sacred and the Everyday," presented at the Eleventh International Bakhtin Conference in Curitiba, Parana, Brazil, on 22 July 2003.

2. In an attempt to subsume the two opposed senses of transcendence, Schrag, *Self After Postmodernity*, cites Félix Guattari's conception of "transversality," a unity that is not underwritten by foundational epistemological principles or metaphysical guarantees. It is "a dimension that tries to overcome both the impasse of pure verticality and that of mere horizontality" (132), and dissolves the opposition between unification and plurality. It is not "driven by a nostalgia for a primordial and unblemished *archē*, an untrammeled beginning, and an appetition for a fixed and universal *telos*" (129), but is, on the contrary, "an achievement of communication as it visits a multiplicity of viewpoints, perspectives, belief systems, and regions of concern" (133). Attractive as this formulation is, it seems to me that it still remains within the field of semantics. Like many compromise formations replacing the "either-or" with a "both-and" paradigm, it does not have the compelling power of choice that underlies the ethics of real life.

3. Recall here that Merleau-Ponty, too, makes a brief reference to the same underlying principle of subjectivity: "I am a general refusal to be anything, accompanied surreptitiously by a continual acceptance of such and such a qualified form of being. *For even this general refusal is still one manner of being and has its place in the world*" (*Phenomenology of Perception*, 452).

4. Coates notes that "the term used by Bakhtin to denote the human subject's responsible act of transcending his or her own boundaries to engage with the world is *iskhozhdenie*, or 'going out'. Clearly, this is closely linked semantically and axiologically with Christ's act of Incarnation, described by Bakhtin with the term *niskhozhdenie*, or 'going down'" (Coates, *Christianity in Bakhtin*, 34; see also 49, 179n10, 95–98, 120–21, 128–51). My own view is that the kind of religiosity in evidence in Bakhtin's work is not specifically bound to any theological version of divinity, but the link between human and divine transcendence is compelling.

5. Bakhtin also quotes this letter in *PDP*, 97–98.

6. In "Russian Orthodoxy and the Early Bakhtin," Emerson reads the adaptation of the relational aspects of Trinitarian theology as a rejection of the Cartesian split between body and mind. "If there is an Ideal in Bakhtin's otherwise passionately quotidian philosophy, it is here in the intimate individuating reciprocity promised by the embodied image of Christ" (19).

7. It is, of course, no accident that "paradoxical" is precisely the adjective used by David Carr to describe Kant's theory of subjectivity. Carr makes a persuasive case against the conflation of Kant's work with the Cartesian metaphysics of the subject, suggesting that the "transcendent tradition," inaugurated by Kant, is, in fact, a critique of the Cartesian position, and focuses two "equally necessary and essentially incompatible" descriptions of both self and self-consciousness (*Paradox of Subjectivity*, 135). Bakhtin's neo-Kantian inspiration, extensively discussed by Holquist, Brandist, and other scholars, can easily be discerned in the dynamics of I-for-myself and I-for-the-other, easily translat-

able into the terms of this "paradox of subjectivity," but what Bakhtin offers in his own Copernican revolution is not only an echo of the Kantian paradox but an attempt to resolve it by transposing it into the dynamics of discourse.

8. The translation "vertical" seems to be most felicitous in this case, since I'm told that the morpheme *nad* in the Russian word *nadadresat* also indicates verticality.

9. This may be an echo of Rosenzweig's *Understanding the Sick and the Healthy*, which predicates the "sickness" of philosophy on its translation of "wonder" into a search for a timeless, motionless "essence," detached from the stream of life and change and dissociated from the particularity of all living things. This type of philosophical wonder, which leaves no room for everyday life, is at the heart of the state of "utter paralysis" that afflicts the traditional philosophical project, Rosenzweig says (40–59).

BIBLIOGRAPHY

BAKHTIN'S WRITINGS

Bakhtin's writings are cited in this list under their familiar English titles, but one should bear in mind that some of these were supplied in the process of translation, compilation, and editing; that some of the texts were put together from surviving fragments and notes; and that the accurate periodization of the various texts is still in progress. The year(s) given following the title refer to the approximate time of the writing, with the (often much later) year(s) of the text's first publication in Russian following after a solidus.

"Art and Answerability." 1919. In *Art and Answerability: Early Philosophical Essays by M. M. Bakhtin*, trans. Vadim Liapunov, ed. Michael Holquist and Vadim Liapunov, 1–3. Austin: University of Texas Press, 1990.

"Author and Hero in Aesthetic Activity." 1922–24/1977–78. In *Art and Answerability: Early Philosophical Essays by M. M. Bakhtin*, trans. Vadim Liapunov, ed. Michael Holquist and Vadim Liapunov, 4–256. Austin: University of Texas Press, 1990.

"The *Bildungsroman* and Its Significance in the History of Realism." 1936–38/1979. In M. M. Bakhtin, *Speech Genres and Other Late Essays*, trans. Vern E. McGee, ed. Caryl Emerson and Michael Holquist, 10–59. Austin: University of Texas Press, 1986.

The Dialogic Imagination: Four Essays. Translated by Michael Holquist and Caryl Emerson. Edited by Michael Holquist. Austin: University of Texas Press, 1981.

"Discourse in the Novel." 1930–36/1972. In M. M. Bakhtin, *The Dialogic Imagination: Four Essays*, trans. Michael Holquist and Caryl Emerson, ed. Michael Holquist, 259–422. Austin: University of Texas Press, 1981.

"Epic and Novel: Toward a Methodology for the Study of the Novel." 1941/1970. In M. M. Bakhtin, *The Dialogic Imagination*, trans. Michael Holquist and Caryl Emerson, ed. Michael Holquist, 447–83. Austin: University of Texas Press, 1981.

"Forms of Time and the Chronotope in the Novel." 1937–38/1975. In M. M. Bakhtin, *The Dialogic Imagination*, trans. Michael Holquist and Caryl Emerson, ed. Michael Holquist, 84–258. Austin: University of Texas Press, 1981.

"From Notes Made in 1970–1971." 1961–74/1979. In M. M. Bakhtin, *Speech Genres and Other Late Essays*, trans. Vern E. McGee, ed. Caryl Emerson and Michael Holquist, 336–60. Austin: University of Texas Press, 1986.

"On the Questions of Self-Consciousness and Self-Evaluation." Ca. 1943–46/1992. First published, ed. V. I. Slavetzky, by V. V. Kozhinov in *Literaturnaya Ucheba* [Literary Studies], no. 5–6 (1992): 156. Repr. in M. M. Bakhtin, *Sobranie Sochinenii* [Collected Works], ed. S. G. Bocharov and L. A. Gogotishvili, 5 (1940–ca. 1960): 72–79. Moscow: Russkie Slovari, 1996. Translated by Victoria Clebanov and Sergeiy Sandler.

"The Person at the Mirror." Ca. 1943/1992. First published, ed. V. I. Slavetzky, by V. V. Kozhinov in *Literaturnaya Ucheba* [Literary Studies], no. 5–6 (1992): 156. Repr. in M. M. Bakhtin, *Sobranie Sochinenii* [Collected Works], ed. S. G. Bocharov and L. A. Gogotishvili, 5 (1940–ca. 1960): 71. Moscow: Russkie Slovari, 1996. Translated by Caryl Emerson in id., "The Next Hundred Years of Mikhail Bakhtin," *Rhetoric Review* 19, no. 1–2 (Autumn 2000): 25n8.

"The Problem of Content, Material, and Form in Verbal Art." 1924/1975. In *Art and Answerability: Early Philosophical Essays by M. M. Bakhtin*, trans. Vadim Liapunov, ed. Michael Holquist and Vadim Liapunov, 257–325. Austin: University of Texas Press, 1990.

"The Problem of Grounded Peace: A Lecture by M. M. Bakhtin." 1924–25/1992. In "M. M. Bakhtin's Lectures and Comments of 1924–1925: From the Notebooks of L. V. Pumpiansky," edited by N. I. Nikolaev. First published in *Bakhtin kak filosof*, ed. L. A. Gogotishvili and S. Gurevich. Moscow: Nauka, 1992. English introduction and translation by Vadim Liapunov in *Bakhtin and Religion: A Feeling for Faith*, ed. Susan M. Felch and Paul J. Contino, 207–9. Evanston, Ill.: Northwestern University Press, 2001.

"The Problem of Speech Genres." 1953–54/1978. In M. M. Bakhtin, *Speech Genres and Other Late Essays*, trans. Vern E. McGee, ed. Caryl Emerson and Michael Holquist, 60–102. Austin: University of Texas Press, 1986.

"The Problem of the Text in Linguistics, Philology, and the Human Sciences." 1959–61/1979. In M. M. Bakhtin, *Speech Genres and Other Late Essays*, trans. Vern E. McGee, ed. Caryl Emerson and Michael Holquist, 103–31. Austin: University of Texas Press, 1986.

Problems of Dostoevsky's Art. In Russian. 1929. Revised and retitled *Problems of Dostoevsky's Poetics*, 1963. Translated and edited by Caryl Emerson and introduced by Wayne C. Booth under the title *Problems of Dostoevsky's Poetics*. Minneapolis: University of Minnesota Press, 1984.

Rabelais and His World. 1940/1965. Translated by Helen Iswolsky. Prologue by Michael Holquist. Cambridge, Mass.: MIT Press, 1984.

"Rhetoric, insofar as it is false . . ." 1943/1992. First published, ed. V. I. Slavetzky, under the title "On Love and Knowledge in the Artistic Image" (in Russian) by V. V. Kozhinov in *Literaturnaya Ucheba* [Literary Studies], no. 5–6 (1992): 153–56. Repr. in M. M. Bakhtin, *Sobranie Sochinenii* [Collected Works], ed. S. G. Bocharov and L. A. Gogotishvili, 5 (1940–ca. 1960): 63–70. Moscow: Russkie Slovari, 1996. Translated by Victoria Clebanov and Sergeiy Sandler.

Sobranie Sochinenii [Collected Works]. Edited by S. G. Bocharov and L. A. Gogotishvili. 7 vols. Moscow: Russkie Slovari, 1996–2003.

Speech Genres and Other Late Essays. Translated by Vern E. McGee. Edited by Caryl Emerson and Michael Holquist. Austin: University of Texas Press, 1986.

Toward a Philosophy of the Act. 1921–22/1986. Translation and notes by Vadim Liapunov. Edited by Michael Holquist and Vadim Liapunov. Austin: University of Texas Press, 1993.

"Toward a Reworking of the Dostoevsky Book." 1961/1979. In M. M. Bakhtin, *Problems of Dostoevsky's Poetics*, trans. from the 2nd Russian edition (1963), ed. Caryl Emerson, Appendix II, 283–302. Minneapolis: University of Minnesota Press, 1984.

"Towards a Methodology for the Human Sciences." 1974. In M. M. Bakhtin, *Speech Genres and Other Late Essays*, trans. Vern E. McGee, ed. Caryl Emerson and Michael Holquist, 159–72. Austin: University of Texas Press, 1986.

"Towards the Philosophical Foundations of the Human Sciences." Ca. 1940–43/1979. Repr. in M. M. Bakhtin, *Sobraniie Sochinenii* [Collected Works], ed. S. G. Bocharov and L. A. Gogotishvili, 5 (1940–ca. 1960): 7–10. Moscow: Russkie Slovari, 1996. Translated by Sergeiy Sandler.

OTHER SOURCES

Adlam, Carol, Rachel Falconer, Vitalii Makhlin, and Alastair Renfrew, eds. *Face to Face: Bakhtin in Russia and the West*. Sheffield, UK: Sheffield Academic Press, 1997.

Adorno, Theodor. *Negative Dialectics*. New York: Continuum, 1970.

Amir, Dana. *Al ha'liriyut shel ha'nefesh* [On the Lyrical Aspects of the Psyche]. Haifa: University of Haifa Press, 2008.

Arendt, Hannah. *Responsibility and Judgment*. New York: Schocken Books, 2003.

Aucouturier, Michel. "The Theory of the Novel in Russia in the 1930s: Lukacs and Bakhtin." In *The Russian Novel from Pushkin to Pasternak*, ed. John Garrard, 227–40. New Haven, Conn.: Yale University Press, 1983.

Augustine, Saint, bishop of Hippo. *Confessions*. Translated by R. S. Pine-Coffin. Harmondsworth, UK: Penguin Books, 1961.

Austin, J. L. *How to Do Things with Words*. Cambridge, Mass.: Harvard University Press, 1962.
Bencivenga, Ermanno. *The Discipline of Subjectivity: An Essay on Montaigne*. Princeton, N.J.: Princeton University Press, 1990.
Benjamin, Walter. "The Storyteller: Reflections on the Works of Nikolai Leskov." 1936. In id., *Illuminations*, trans. Harry Zohn, ed. Hannah Arendt. New York: Schocken Books, 1969.
Benveniste, Émile. *Problems in General Linguistics*. 1966. Translated by Mary Elizabeth Meek. Coral Gables, Fla.: University of Miami Press, 1971.
Bergson, Henri. *Creative Evolution*. 1907. Translated by Arthur Mitchell. New York: Random House, 1944.
———. *Matter and Memory*. 1896. Translated by N. M. Paul and W. S. Palmer. New York: Zone Books, 1991.
———. *Time and Free Will: An Essay on the Immediate Data of Consciousness*. 1889. Translated by F. L. Pogson. London: George Allen & Unwin; New York: Macmillan, 1910.
Bernard-Donals, Michael F. *Mikhail Bakhtin: Between Phenomenology and Marxism*. Cambridge: Cambridge University Press, 1994.
Bion, Wilfred R. "Container and Contained Transformed." In id., *Attention and Interpretation: A Scientific Approach to Insight in Psycho-Analysis and Groups*, 72–82. 1970. London: Karnac Books, 1984.
Bocharov, Sergei. "Conversations with Bakhtin." Translated by Stephen Blackwell. Introduction and translation ed. Vadim Liapunov. *PMLA* 109 (1994): 1009–24.
———. "The Event of Being: On Mikhail Mikhalovitch Bakhtin." 1995. Translated by Thomas Cunningham. In *Critical Essays on Mikhail Bakhtin*, ed. Caryl Emerson, 29–44. New York: G. K. Hall, 1999.
Boethius. *The Consolation of Philosophy*. ca. 524 CE. Translated and edited by P. G. Walsh. Oxford: Oxford University Press, 1999.
Bollas, Christopher. *Being a Character: Psychoanalysis and Self Experience*. New York: Hill & Wang, 1992.
Bowen, Barbara C. *The Age of Bluff: Paradox and Ambiguity in Rabelais and Montaigne*. Urbana: University of Illinois Press, 1972.
Boym, Svetlana. "Poetics and Politics of Estrangement: Victor Shklovsky and Hannah Arendt." *Poetics Today* 26, 4 (Winter 2005): 581–611.
Brandist, Craig. *The Bakhtin Circle: Philosophy, Culture, and Politics*. London: Pluto Press, 2002.
———. "Two Routes 'to Concreteness' in the Work of the Bakhtin Circle." *Journal of the History of Ideas* 63, 3 (2002): 521–37.
Brandist, Craig, David Shepherd, and Galin Tihanov, eds. *The Bakhtin Circle: In the Master's Absence*. Manchester, UK: Manchester University Press, 2004.
Brandist, Craig, and Galin Tihanov, eds. *Materializing Bakhtin: The Bakhtin Circle and Social Theory*. Basingstoke, UK: Palgrave Macmillan, 2000.

Britton, Ronald. "Keeping Things in Mind." In *Clinical Lectures on Klein and Bion*, ed. Robin Anderson, 102–13. Foreword by Hanna Segal. London: Routledge, 1992.
Brooks, Cleanth. "The Heresy of Paraphrase." In id., *The Well Wrought Urn: Studies in the Structure of Poetry*, 176–96. London: Dennis Dobson, 1947.
Bruss, Neal H. "V. N. Voloshinov and the Structure of Language in Freudianism." In V. N. Voloshinov, *Freudianism: A Marxist Critique* (1927), trans. I. R. Titunik, ed. Neal H. Bruss and I. R. Titunik, Appendix II, 101–48. New York: Academic Press, 1976.
Burton, Stacy. "Paradoxical Relations: Bakhtin and Modernism." *Modern Language Quarterly* 61, 3 (2000): 519–43.
Burwick, Frederick, and Paul Douglass, eds. *The Crisis in Modernism: Bergson and the Vitalist Controversy*. Cambridge: Cambridge University Press, 1992.
Carr, David. "Narrative and the Real World: An Argument for Continuity." *History and Theory* 25, 2 (May 1986): 117–31.
———. *The Paradox of Subjectivity: The Self in the Transcendental Tradition*. New York: Oxford University Press, 1999.
———. *Time, Narrative, and History*. Bloomington: Indiana University Press, 1991.
Carr, Herbert Wildon. *Henri Bergson: The Philosophy of Change*. London: T. C. & E. C. Jack; New York: Dodge, 1911.
Carroll, David. *The Subject in Question: The Language of Theory and the Strategies of Fiction*. Chicago: University of Chicago Press, 1982.
Cave, Terence. *The Cornucopian Text: Problems of Writing in the French Renaissance*. Oxford: Clarendon Press of Oxford University Press, 1979.
Clark, Katerina, and Michael Holquist. "A Continuing Dialogue." In *Rethinking Bakhtin: Extensions and Challenges*, ed. Gary Saul Morson and Caryl Emerson, 96–102. Evanston, Ill.: Northwestern University Press, 1989.
———. "The Influence of Kant in the Early Work of M. M. Bakhtin." In *Literary Theory and Criticism: Festschrift Presented to René Wellek in Honor of His Eightieth Birthday*, ed. Joseph Strelka, 1: 299–314. New York: Peter Lang, 1984.
———. *Mikhail Bakhtin*. Cambridge, Mass.: Belknap Press of Harvard University Press, 1984.
Clarkson, Carrol. "Embodying 'You': Levinas and the Question of the Second Person." *Journal of Literary Semantics* 43, 2 (2005): 95–105.
Coates, Ruth. *Christianity in Bakhtin: God and the Exiled Author*. Cambridge: Cambridge University Press, 1998.
Cohen, Richard A., ed. *Face to Face with Lévinas*. Albany: State University of New York Press, 1986.
Conrad, Joseph. *Under Western Eyes*. 1911. London: Dent, 1923.
Critchley, Simon. *The Ethics of Deconstruction: Derrida and Levinas*. Oxford: Blackwell, 1992.
Crowell, Steven G. "Kantianism and Phenomenology." In *The Ethical*, ed. Edith Wyschogrod and Gerald P. McKenny, 15–32. Oxford: Blackwell, 2003.

Curtis, James M. "Bergson and Russian Formalism." *Comparative Literature* 28, 2 (Spring 1976): 109–21.

Davis, Duane H. "Reversible Subjectivity: The Problem of Transcendence and Language." In *Merleau-Ponty Vivant*, ed. M. C. Dillon, 31–46. Albany: State University of New York Press, 1991.

Derrida, Jacques. *Acts of Literature*. Edited by Derek Attridge. New York: Routledge, 1992.

———. "Deconstruction in America: An Interview with Jacques Derrida," by James Creech, Peggy Kamuf, and Jane Todd. *Critical Exchange* 17 (Winter 1985): 1–32.

———. "Difference." In id., *Margins of Philosophy*, trans. Alan Bass. Chicago: University of Chicago Press, 1982.

———. *The Ear of the Other*. Translated by Avital Ronell. New York: Schocken Books, 1985.

———. "The Ends of Man." 1972. In id., *Margins of Philosophy*, 108–36. Chicago: University of Chicago Press, 1982.

———. "Form and Meaning: A Note on the Phenomenology of Language." Translated by David B. Allison. In id., *Speech and Phenomena and Other Essays on Husserl's Theory of Signs*. Evanston, Ill.: Northwestern University Press, 1973.

———. *Positions*. Translated by Alan Bass. Chicago: University of Chicago Press, 1981.

———. "Qual Quelle: Valéry's Sources." In id., *Margins of Philosophy*, trans. Alan Bass, 273–306. Chicago: University of Chicago Press, 1982.

———. "This Strange Institution Called Literature: An Interview with Jacques Derrida." In id., *Acts of Literature*, ed. Derek Attridge, 33–75. New York: Routledge, 1992.

———. "The Time of a Thesis." In id., *Acts of Literature*, ed. Derek Attridge. New York: Routledge, 1992.

———. "Violence and Metaphysics: An Essay on the Thought of Emmanuel Levinas." In id., *Writing and Difference*, trans. and ed. Alan Bass, 79–153. London: Routledge & Kegan Paul, 1978.

Descartes, René. *The Philosophical Works of Descartes*. Translated by E. S. Haldane and G.R.T. Ross. Cambridge: Cambridge University Press, 1969.

Dillon, M. C. "Am I a Grammatical Fiction? The Debate over Ego Psychology." In *Merleau-Ponty's Later Works and Their Practical Implications: The Dehiscence of Responsibility*, ed. Duane H. Davis, 309–24. New York: Humanity Books, 2001.

———. "*Ecart*: Reply to Claude Lefort's 'Flesh and Otherness'." In *Ontology and Alterity in Merleau-Ponty*, ed. Galen A. Johnson and Michael B. Smith, 14–26. Evanston, Ill.: Northwestern University Press, 1990.

———, ed. *Merleau-Ponty Vivant*. Albany: State University of New York Press, 1991.

Dop, Erik. "A Dialogic Epistemology: Bakhtin on Truth and Meaning." *Dialogism* 4 (2002): 7–33.

Dostoyevsky, Fyodor. 1881. *The Brothers Karamazov*. Translated by David Magarshack. Harmondsworth, UK: Penguin Books, 1958.

Eaglestone, Robert. *Ethical Criticism: Reading After Levinas*. Edinburgh: Edinburgh University Press, 1997.

Eliot, T. S. "The Metaphysical Poets." 1921. In id., *Collected Essays*, 2nd ed., 281–91. London: Faber & Faber, 1934.

Emerson, Caryl. "Bakhtin at 100: Art, Ethics, and the Architectonic Self." *Centennial Review* 39, 3 (1995): 397–418.

——— . "Editor's Preface" to *Problems of Dostoevsky's Poetics*. 1929; 2nd ed. 1963. Translated and edited by Caryl Emerson. Introduction by Wayne C. Booth. Minneapolis: University of Minnesota Press, 1984.

——— . *The First Hundred Years of Mikhail Bakhtin*. Princeton, N.J.: Princeton University Press, 1997.

——— . "Introduction: Dialogue on Every Corner, Bakhtin in Every Class." In *Bakhtin in Contexts: Across the Disciplines*, ed. Amy Mandelker, 1–32. Evanston, Ill.: Northwestern University Press, 1995.

——— . "Isaiah Berlin and Mikhail Bakhtin: Relativistic Affiliations." *Symploke* 7, 1–2 (1999): 139–64.

——— . "Keeping the Self Intact During the Culture Wars: A Centennial Essay for Mikhail Bakhtin." *New Literary History* 27, 1 (1996): 107–26.

——— . "The Making of M. M. Bakhtin as a Philosopher." In *Russian Thought After Communism: The Recovery of a Philosophical Heritage*, ed. James P. Scanlan, 206–26. Armonk, N.Y.: M. E. Sharpe, 1994.

——— . "The Next Hundred Years of Mikhail Bakhtin." *Rhetoric Review* 19, 1–2 (Autumn 2000): 12–27.

——— . "The Outer Word and Inner Speech: Bakhtin, Vygotsky, and the Internalization of Language." *Critical Inquiry* 10, 2 (1983): 245–64.

——— . "Problems with Baxtin's Poetics." *Slavic and East European Journal* 32, 4 (1988): 503–25.

——— . "Prosaics and the Problem of Form." *Slavic and East European Journal* 41, 2 (Spring 1997): 16–39.

——— . "Russian Orthodoxy and the Early Bakhtin." *Religion and Literature* 22, 2–3 (1990): 109–31.

——— . "Shklovsky's *ostranenie*, Bakhtin's *vnenakhodimost'* (How Distance Serves an Aesthetics of Arousal Differently from an Aesthetics Based on Pain)." *Poetics Today* 26, 4 (Winter 2005): 637–64.

——— , ed. *Critical Essays on Mikhail Bakhtin*. New York: G. K. Hall, 1999.

Emerson, Caryl, and Gary Saul Morson. *Mikhail Bakhtin: Creation of a Prosaics*. Stanford, Calif.: Stanford University Press, 1990.

——— . "Penultimate Words." In *The Current in Criticism*, ed. Clayton Koelb and Virgil Lokke, 43–64. West Lafayette, Ind.: Purdue University Press, 1984.

———. *Rethinking Bakhtin: Extensions and Challenges*. Evanston, Ill: Northwestern University Press, 1989.

Erdinast-Vulcan, Daphna. "Bakhtin's Homesickness: A Late Reply to Julia Kristeva." *Textual Practice* 9, 2 (Summer 1995): 223–42.

———. "Between the Face and the Voice: Bakhtin Meets Levinas." *Continental Philosophy Review* 41, 1 (2008): 43–58.

———. "Borderlines and Contraband: Bakhtin and the Question of the Subject." *Poetics Today* 18, 2 (1997): 251–69.

———. "'The *I* That Tells Itself': A Bakhtinian Perspective on Narrative Identity." *Narrative* 16, 1 (2008): 1–15.

———. "Narrative, Modernism, and the Crisis of Authority: A Bakhtinian Perspective." *Science in Context* 7, 1 (1994): 143–58.

———. "That Which Has No Name in Philosophy: Merleau-Ponty and the Language of Literature." *Human Studies* 30, 4 (2007): 395–409.

Eskin, Michael. *Ethics and Dialogue in the Works of Levinas, Bakhtin, Mandel'shtam, and Celan*. Oxford: Oxford University Press, 2000.

Etkind, Alexander. *Eros of the Impossible: The History of Psychoanalysis in Russia*. 1993. Translated by Noah and Maria Rubins. Boulder, Colo.: Westview Press, 1997.

Farmer, Frank M. "'Not Theory . . . but a Sense of Theory': The Superaddressee and the Contexts of Eden." *Symploke* 2, 1 (1994): 87–101. Repr. in *Mikhail Bakhtin*, ed. Michael Gardiner, 2: 363–76. Thousand Oaks, Calif.: SAGE, 2003.

Felch, Susan. "'In the Chorus of Others': M. M. Bakhtin's Sense of Tradition." In *The Force of Tradition*, ed. Donald G. Marshall, 55–78. Lanham, Md.: Rowman & Littlefield, 2005.

Felch, Susan M., and Paul J. Contino, eds. *Bakhtin and Religion: A Feeling for Faith*. Evanston, Ill.: Northwestern University Press, 2001.

Foucault, Michel. *Discipline and Punish: The Birth of the Prison*. 1975. Translated by Alan Sheridan. New York: Pantheon Books, 1977.

———. "The Eye of Power." In *Power/Knowledge: Selected Interviews and Other Writings 1972–1977*, trans. Colin Gordon, Lev Marshall, John Mapham, and Kate Soper, ed. Colin Gordon. New York: Pantheon Books, 1980.

———. *The Order of Things: An Archeology of the Human Sciences*. 1966. Translated by Alan Sheridan. London: Routledge, 2001.

Friedrich, Hugo. *Montaigne*. 1968. Translated by Dawn Eng. Berkeley: University of California Press, 1991.

Froman, Wayne Jeffrey. *Merleau-Ponty: Language and the Act of Speech*. Lewisburg, Pa.: Bucknell University Press; London: Associated University Presses, 1982.

Gachev, Georgii. Extract from "Bakhtin." 1991. Translated and annotated by Thomas Cunningham. In *Critical Essays on Mikhail Bakhtin*, ed. Caryl Emerson, 45–51. New York: G. K. Hall, 1999.

Gardiner, Michael. "Alterity and Ethics: A Dialogical Perspective." *Theory, Culture & Society* 13, 2 (1996): 121–43.

———. "Bakhtin and the Metaphorics of Perception." In *Interpreting Visual Culture: Explorations in the Hermeneutics of the Visual*, ed. Ian Heywood and Barry Sandywell, 57–73. New York: Routledge, 1999.

———. *Critiques of Everyday Life*. New York: Routledge, 2000.

———. *The Dialogics of Critique: M. M. Bakhtin and the Theory of Ideology*. London: Routledge, 1992.

———. "'The Incomparable Monster of Solipsism': Bakhtin and Merleau-Ponty." In *Bakhtin and the Human Sciences: No Last Words*, ed. Michael Mayerfeld Bell and Michael Gardiner, 128–44. Thousand Oaks, Calif.: SAGE, 1998.

———. "'A Very Understandable Horror of Dialectics': Bakhtin and Marxist Phenomenology." In *Materializing Bakhtin: The Bakhtin Circle and Social Theory*, ed. Craig Brandist and Galin Tihanov, 119–41. Basingstoke, UK: Palgrave Macmillan, 2000.

———, ed. *Mikhail Bakhtin*. 4 vols. Thousand Oaks, Calif.: SAGE, 2003.

Gardiner, Michael, and Michael Mayerfeld Bell, eds. *Bakhtin and the Human Sciences: No Last Words*. Thousand Oaks, Calif.: SAGE, 1998.

Gasché, Rodolphe. *The Tain of the Mirror: Derrida and the Philosophy of Reflection*. Cambridge, Mass.: Harvard University Press, 1986.

Godzich, Wlad. "Correcting Kant: Bakhtin and Intercultural Interactions." *Boundary 2*, 18, 1 (1991): 5–17.

Handleman, Susan. "Facing the Other: Levinas, Perelman, and Rosenzweig." In *Summoning: Ideas of the Covenant and Interpretive Theory*, ed. Ellen Spolsky, 47–70. Albany: State University of New York Press, 1993.

Handley, William R. "The Ethics of Subject Creation in Bakhtin and Lacan." In *Bakhtin: Carnival and Other Subjects*, ed. David Shepherd, 144–62. Amsterdam: Rodopi, 1993.

Heidegger, Martin. "The End of Philosophy and the Task of Thinking." In id., *Basic Writings, 1927–1964*, ed. David Farrell Krell, 427–48. New York: Harper & Row, 1977; 2nd ed., 1993.

———. "The Essence of Truth." In id., *Basic Writings, 1927–1964*, ed. David Farrell Krell, 111–38. New York: Harper & Row, 1977; 2nd ed., 1993.

———. "Letter on Humanism." In id., *Basic Writings, 1927–1964*, ed. David Farrell Krell, 213–66. New York: Harper & Row, 1977; 2nd ed., 1993.

———. "The Origin of the Work of Art." 1950. In id., *Poetry, Language, Thought*, trans. and ed. Albert Hofstadter, 15–86. New York: Harper & Row, 1971; Colophon ed., 1975.

Hirschkop, Ken. "Bakhtin's Linguistic Turn." *Dialogism* 5, 6 (2001): 21–34.

———. *Mikhail Bakhtin: An Aesthetic for Democracy*. Oxford: Oxford University Press, 1999.

———. "The Sacred and the Everyday: Attitudes to Language in Bakhtin, Benjamin and Wittgenstein." Paper presented at the Eleventh International Bakhtin Conference in Curitiba, Parana, Brazil, on 22 July 2003.

Hirschkop, Ken, and David Shepherd, eds. *Bakhtin and Cultural Theory.* Manchester, UK: Manchester University Press, 1989.
Holquist, Michael. "Answering as Authoring: Mikhail Bakhtin's Translinguistics." In *Bakhtin: Essays and Dialogues on His Work,* ed. Gary Saul Morson, 59–71. Chicago: University of Chicago Press, 1986.
———. "Bakhtin and Beautiful Science: The Paradox of Cultural Relativity Revisited." In *Dialogue and Critical Discourse: Language, Culture, Critical Theory,* ed. Michael Macovsky, 215–36. New York: Oxford University Press, 1997.
———. *Dialogism: Bakhtin and His World.* London: Routledge, 1990.
———. "Dialogism and Aesthetics." In *Late Soviet Culture: From Perestroika to Novostroika,* ed. Gene Kuperman and Thomas Lahussen, 155–76. Durham, N.C.: Duke University Press, 1993.
———. "Introduction." In *Art and Answerability: Early Philosophical Essays by M. M. Bakhtin,* trans. Vladimir Liapunov, ed. Michael Holquist and Vladimir Liapunov, ix–xlix. Austin: University of Texas Press, 1990.
———. "The Role of Chronotope in Dialog." In *Proceedings of the Second International Interdisciplinary Conference on Perspectives and Limits of Dialogism in Mikhail Bakhtin, Stockholm University, Sweden, 3–5 June, 2009,* 9–17. Stockholm: Stockholm University Department of Scandinavian Languages, 2010.
———. "The Surd Heard." In *Literature and History: Theoretical Problems and Russian Case Studies,* ed. Gary Saul Morson, 137–56. Stanford, Calif.: Stanford University Press, 1986.
Holquist, Michael, and Katerina Clark. "A Continuing Dialogue." In *Rethinking Bakhtin: Extensions and Challenges,* ed. Gary Saul Morson and Caryl Emerson, 96–102. Evanston, Ill.: Northwestern University Press, 1989.
———. "The Influence of Kant in the Early Work of M. M. Bakhtin." In *Literary Theory and Criticism: Festschrift Presented to René Wellek in Honor of His Eightieth Birthday,* ed. Joseph Strelka, 1: 299–314. New York: Peter Lang, 1984.
———. *Mikhail Bakhtin.* Cambridge, Mass.: Harvard University Press, 1984.
Holquist, Michael, and Ilya Kliger. "Minding the Gap: Toward a Historical Poetics of Estrangement." *Poetics Today* 26, 4 (Winter 2005): 613–46.
Irigaray, Luce. *Speculum of the Other Woman.* 1974. Translated by G. C. Gill. Ithaca, N.Y.: Cornell University Press, 1992.
Jabès, Edmund. *The Book of Questions.* Vol. 2: *Yaël; Elya; Aely; El, or the Last Book.* Translated by Rosemary Waldrop. Hanover, N.H.: Wesleyan University Press; University Press of New England, 1991.
Jay, Martin. *Downcast Eyes: The Denigration of Vision in Twentieth-Century French Thought.* Berkeley: University of California Press, 1993.
Jefferson, Ann. "Bodymatters: Self and Other in Bakhtin, Sartre and Barthes." In *Bakhtin and Cultural Theory,* ed. Ken Hirschkop and David Shepherd, 152–77. Manchester, UK: Manchester University Press, 1989.
Johnson, Galen, and Michael B. Smith, eds. *Ontology and Alterity in Merleau-Ponty.* Evanston, Ill.: Northwestern University Press, 1990.

Judovitz, Dalia. *Subjectivity and Representation in Descartes: The Origins of Modernity*. Cambridge: Cambridge University Press, 1988.
Jung, Hwa Jol. "Bakhtin's Body Politics: A Phenomenological Dialogics." *Man and World* 23 (1990): 85–99. Repr. as "Bakhtin's Dialogical Body Politics" in *Bakhtin and the Human Sciences: No Last Words*, ed. Michael Meyer Bell and Michael Gardiner, 95–111. Thousand Oaks, Calif.: SAGE, 1998.
Kanaev, I. I. [/ M. M. Bakhtin?]. "Contemporary Vitalism." 1926. Originally published under Kanaev's name in *Chelovek i Priroda* [Man and Nature], 1: 33–42 and 2: 9–23. Translated by Charles Byrd in *The Crisis in Modernism: Bergson and the Vitalist Controversy*, ed. Frederick Burwick and Paul Douglass, 76–96. Cambridge: Cambridge University Press, 1992.
Kearney, Richard. *Continental Philosophy in the 20th Century*. London: Routledge, 1993.
Kearney, Richard, and Emmanuel Lévinas. "Dialogue with Emmanuel Levinas." In *Face to Face with Lévinas*, ed. Richard Cohen, 13–33. Albany: State University of New York Press, 1986.
Kermode, Frank. *The Sense of an Ending*. New York: Oxford University Press, 1967.
Kołakowski, Leszek. *Bergson*. Oxford: Oxford University Press, 1985.
———. *Metaphysical Horror*. Oxford: Blackwell, 1988.
Kozhinov, Vadim. "Bakhtin and His Readers." 1993. Translated and annotated by Craig Cravens. In *Critical Essays on Mikhael Bakhtin*, ed. Caryl Emerson, 67–80. New York: G. K. Hall, 1999.
Kristeva, Julia. "From One Identity to an Other." 1969. In id., *Desire in Language: A Semiotic Approach to Literature and Art*, trans. Thomas Gora, Alice Jardine, and Leon S. Roudiez, ed. Leon S. Roudiez, 124–47. New York: Columbia University Press, 1980.
———. "The Ruin of a Poetics." 1970. In *Russian Formalism*, ed. Stephen Bann and John E. Bowlt, 102–19. Edinburgh: Scottish Academic Press, 1973.
———. "Word, Dialogue and Novel." 1969. In id., *Desire in Language: A Semiotic Approach to Literature and Art*, trans. Thomas Gora, Alice Jardine, and Leon S. Roudiez, ed. Leon S. Roudiez, 64–91. New York: Columbia University Press, 1980.
Lacan, Jacques. "Aggressivity in Psychoanalysis." 1948. In id., *Écrits: A Selection*, trans. Alan Sheridan, 8–29. London: Tavistock Publications, 1977.
———. "The Mirror Stage as Formative of the Function of the *I* as Revealed in Psychoanalytic Experience." 1949. In id., *Écrits: A Selection*, trans. Alan Sheridan, 4–7. London: Tavistock Publications, 1977.
Lakoff, George, and Mark Johnson. *The Metaphors We Live By*. Chicago: University of Chicago Press, 1981.
Lefort, Claude. "Flesh and Otherness." In *Ontology and Alterity in Merleau-Ponty*, ed. Galen A. Johnson and Michael B. Smith, 3–13. Evanston, Ill.: Northwestern University Press, 1990.

Levin, David Michael. "Justice in the Flesh." In *Ontology and Alterity in Merleau-Ponty*, ed. Galen A. Johnson and Michael B. Smith, 35–44. Evanston, Ill.: Northwestern University Press, 1990.

———, ed. *Modernity and the Hegemony of Vision*. Berkeley: University of California Press, 1993.

Lévinas, Emmanuel. "Bad Conscience and the Inexorable." In *Face to Face with Lévinas*, ed. Richard A. Cohen, 35–40. Albany: State University of New York Press, 1986.

———. *Collected Philosophical Papers*. Translated by Alphonso Lingis. Dordrecht: Martinus Nijhoff, 1987.

———. *Difficult Freedom: Essays on Judaism*. Translated by Seán Hand. Baltimore: Johns Hopkins University Press, 1997.

———. "The Ego and the Totality." In id., *Collected Philosophical Papers*, trans. Alphonso Lingis, 25–45. Dordrecht: Martinus Nijhoff, 1987.

———. *Entre-Nous: On Thinking-of-the-Other*. 1991. Translated by Michael B. Smith and Barbara Harshav. New York: Columbia University Press, 1998.

———. *Ethics and Infinity: Conversations with Philippe Nemo*. Translated by Richard A. Cohen. Pittsburgh: Duquesne University Press, 1985.

———. *Existence and Existents*. 1947. Translated by Alphonso Lingis. The Hague: Martin Nijhoff, 1978.

———. "God and Philosophy." In id., *Collected Philosophical Papers*, trans. Alphonso Lingis, 153–73. Dordrecht: Martinus Nijhoff, 1987.

———. "Humanism and An-archy." 1968. In id., *Collected Philosophical Papers*, trans. Alphonso Lingis, 127–39. Dordrecht: Martinus Nijhoff, 1987.

———. "Language and Proximity." In id., *Collected Philosophical Papers*, trans. Alphonso Lingis, 109–25. Dordrecht: Martinus Nijhoff, 1987.

———. *Of God Who Comes to Mind*. 1982. Translated by Bettina Bergo. Stanford, Calif.: Stanford University Press, 1998.

———. *Otherwise Than Being, or, Beyond Essence*. 1974. Translated by Alphonso Lingis. Dordrecht: Kluwer Academic, 1978.

———. *Outside the Subject*. 1987. Translated by Michael B. Smith. Stanford, Calif.: Stanford University Press, 1993.

———. "Philosophy and the Idea of Infinity." In id., *Collected Philosophical Papers*, trans. Alphonso Lingis, 47–59. Dordrecht: Martinus Nijhoff, 1987.

———. "Reality and Its Shadow." 1948. In id., *Collected Philosophical Papers*, trans. Alphonso Lingis, 1–13. Dordrecht: Martinus Nijhoff, 1987.

———. "Signature." Translated by Mary Ellen Petrisko. *Research in Phenomenology*, ed. Adrian Peperzak, 8 (1978): 175–89.

———. *Time and the Other*. Translated by Richard Cohen. Pittsburgh: Duquesne University Press, 1987.

———. *Totality and Infinity: An Essay on Exteriority*. Translated by Alphonso Lingis. Pittsburgh: Duquesne University Press, 1969.

———. "The Trace of the Other." 1963. Translated by Aphonso Lingis. In

Deconstruction in Context: Literature and Philosophy, ed. Mark C. Taylor, 345–59. Chicago: University of Chicago Press, 1986.
———. "The Transcendence of Words." 1949. Translated by Seán Hand. In *The Levinas Reader*, ed. Seán Hand. Oxford: Blackwell, 1989.
Lévinas, Emmanuel, and Richard Kearney. "Dialogue with Emmanuel Lévinas." In *Face to Face with Lévinas*, ed. Richard A. Cohen, 13–33. Albany: State University of New York Press, 1986.
Low, Douglas. *Merleau-Ponty's Last Vision: A Proposal for the Completion of "The Visible and the Invisible."* Evanston, Ill.: Northwestern University Press, 2000.
Lukács, Georg. *The Theory of the Novel*. Translated by Anna Bostock. Cambridge, Mass.: MIT Press, 1971.
MacIntyre, Alasdair. *After Virtue: A Study in Moral Theory*. 1981. 2nd ed., London: Duckworth, 1985.
Madison, Gary B. "The Ethics and Politics of the Flesh." In *The Ethics of Postmodernity: Current Trends in Continental Thought*, ed. Gary B. Madison and Marty Fairbairn. Evanston, Ill.: Northwestern University Press, 1998. Repr. in *Merleau-Ponty's Later Works and Their Practical Implications: The Dehiscence of Responsibility*, ed. Duane H. Davis, 161–85. New York: Humanity Books, 2001.
———. "Flesh as Otherness." In *Ontology and Alterity in Merleau-Ponty*, ed. Galen A. Johnson and Michael B. Smith, 27–34. Evanston, Ill.: Northwestern University Press, 1990.
Mandleker, Amy, ed. *Bakhtin in Contexts: Across the Disciplines*. Evanston, Ill.: Northwestern University Press, 1995.
McGee, Glenn Edwards. "Merleau-Pontyan Ethics: Intimations of a Different Phenomenology of Value." In *Rereading Merleau-Ponty: Essays Beyond the Continental-Analytic Divide*, ed. Lawrence Hass and Dorothea Olkowski, 197–207. New York: Humanity Books, 2000.
Medvedev, P. N. [/M. M. Bakhtin?]. *The Formal Method in Literary Scholarship*. 1928. Translated by Albert Wehrle. With a foreword by Wlad Godzich. Cambridge, Mass.: Harvard University Press, 1985.
Melehy, Hassan. *Writing Cogito: Montaigne, Descartes, and the Institution of the Modern Subject*. Albany: State University of New York Press, 1997.
Merleau-Ponty, Maurice. "Indirect Language and the Voices of Silence." 1952. In id., *Signs*, trans. with an introduction by Richard C. McCleary, 39–83. Evanston, Ill.: Northwestern University Press, 1964.
———. "On the Phenomenology of Language." 1960. In id., *Signs*, trans. with an introduction by Richard C. McCleary, 84–97. Evanston, Ill.: Northwestern University Press, 1964.
———. *Phenomenology of Perception*. 1945. Translated by Colin Smith. London: Routledge Humanities Press, 1962.
———. "The Philosopher and His Shadow." 1960. In id., *Signs*, trans. with an introduction by Richard C. McCleary, 159–81. Evanston, Ill.: Northwestern University Press, 1964.

———. *The Prose of the World*. Translated by John O'Neill. Evanston, Ill.: Northwestern University Press, 1973.

———. "Reading Montaigne." In id., *Signs*, trans. with an introduction by Richard C. McCleary, 198–211. Evanston, Ill.: Northwestern University Press, 1964.

———. *Sense and Non-Sense*. 1948. Translated by Herbert L. Dreyfus and Patricia Allen Dreyfus. Evanston, Ill.: Northwestern University Press, 1964.

———. *Signs*. 1960. Translated with an introduction by Richard C. McCleary Evanston, Ill.: Northwestern University Press, 1964.

———. *The Visible and the Invisible*. 1964. Translated by Alphonso Lingis. Edited by Claude Lefort. Evanston, Ill.: Northwestern University Press, 1968.

———. "Working Notes for *The Visible and the Invisible*." 1964. In id., *The Visible and the Invisible*, trans. Alphonso Lingis, ed. Claude Lefort. Evanston, Ill.: Northwestern University Press, 1968.

Mihailovic, Alexandar. *Corporeal Words: Mikhail Bakhtin's Theology of Discourse*. Evanston, Ill.: Northwestern University Press, 1997.

Misch, Georg. *A History of Autobiography in Antiquity*. 1907; 2nd ed. 1931; 3rd ed. 1949–50. Translated in collaboration with the author by E. W. Dickes. London: Routledge & Kegan Paul, 1950.

Montaigne, Michel Eyquem de. *Essays*. 1533–92. Translated by Donald Murdoch Frame. Stanford, Calif.: Stanford University Press, 1965.

Morson, Gary Saul. "Bakhtin, Genres, and Temporality." *New Literary History* 22, 4 (1991): 1071–92.

———. *Narrative and Freedom: The Shadows of Time*. New Haven, Conn.: Yale University Press, 1994.

———. "Prosaic Bakhtin: Landmarks, AntiIntelligtsialism, and the Russian Countertradition." In *Bakhtin in Contexts: Across the Disciplines*, ed. Amy Mandelker, 33–78. Evanston, Ill.: Northwestern University Press, 1995.

———. "Sideshadowing and Tempics." *New Literary History* 29, 4 (1998): 599–624.

———. "Strange Synchronies and Surplus Possibilities: Bakhtin and Time." *Slavic Review* 52, 3 (Autumn 1993): 477–93.

Morson, Gary Saul, and Caryl Emerson. "Extracts from a *Heteroglossary*." In *Dialogue and Critical Discourse: Language, Culture, Critical Theory*, ed. Michael Macovski, 256–72. Oxford: Oxford University Press, 1997.

———. *Mikhail Bakhtin: Creation of a Prosaics*. Stanford, Calif.: Stanford University Press, 1990.

Muller, John P., and William J. Richardson. *Lacan and Language*. New York: International Universities Press, 1982.

Natanson, Maurice. "The Schematism of Moral Agency." *New Literary History* 15, 1 (Autumn 1983): 13–23.

Nealon, Jeffrey T. *Alterity Politics: Ethics and Performative Subjectivity*. Durham, N.C.: Duke University Press, 1998.

———. "The Ethics of Dialogue: Bakhtin and Levinas." *College English* 59, 2 (1997): 129–48.

Neubauer, John. "Bakhtin Versus Lukács: Inscriptions of Homelessness in Theories of the Novel." *Poetics Today* 17, 4 (Winter 1996): 531–46.
Nielsen, Greg Marc. "The Norms of Answerability: Bakhtin and the Fourth Postulate." In *Bakhtin and the Human Sciences: No Last Words*, ed. Michael Gardiner and Michael Mayerfeld Bell, 214–30. Thousand Oaks, Calif.: SAGE, 1998.
———. *The Norms of Answerability: Social Theory Between Bakhtin and Habermas.* Albany: State University of New York Press, 2002.
Nikulin, Dmitry. "The Man at the Mirror (Dialogue with Oneself)." *Iris: European Journal of Philosophy and Public Debate* 13 (April 2011): 61–79.
Patterson, David. "Bakhtin and Levinas: Signification, Responsibility, Spirit." *Cithara: Essays on the Judeo-Christian Tradition* 26, 2 (1987): 5–19.
———. *Literature and Spirit: Essays on Bakhtin and His Contemporaries.* Lexington: University Press of Kentucky, 1988.
Pechey, Graham. "Eternity and Modernity: Bakhtin and the Epistemological Sublime." In *Critical Essays on Mikhail Bakhtin*, ed. Caryl Emerson, 355–78. New York: G. K. Hall, 1999.
———. *Mikhail Bakhtin: The Word in the World.* New York: Routledge, 2007.
Peperzak, Adriaan. *To the Other: An Introduction to the Philosophy of Emmanuel Levinas.* West Lafayette, Ind.: Purdue University Press, 1993.
Phelan, James. "Who's Here? Thoughts on Narrative Identity and Narrative Imperialism." Editor's Column, *Narrative* 13, 3 (October 2005): 205–10.
Pirog, Gerald. "Bakhtin and Freud on the Ego." In *Russian Literature and Psychoanalysis*, ed. Daniel Rancour-Laferriere, 401–16. Amsterdam: John Benjamins, 1989.
———. "The Bakhtin Circle's Freud: From Positivism to Hermeneutics." *Poetics Today* 8, 3–4 (1987): 591–610. Repr. in *Mikhail Bakhtin*, ed. Michael Gardiner, 1: 151–69. Thousand Oaks, Calif.: SAGE, 2003.
Pollard, Rachel. *Discourse and Desire: Mikhail Bakhtin and the Linguistic Turn in Psychotherapy.* London: Karnac Books, 2008.
Ponzio, Augusto. "The Relation of Otherness in Bakhtin, Blanchot, Levinas." *RSSI (Recherches sémiotiques/Semiotic Inquiry)* 7, 1 (1987): 1–18.
Poole, Brian. "Bakhtin and Cassirer: The Philosophical Origins of Bakhtin's Carnival Messianism." *South Atlantic Quarterly* 97 (1998): 579–98.
———. "From Phenomenology to Dialogue: Max Scheler's Phenomenological Tradition and Mikhail Bakhtin's Development from 'Toward a Philosophy of the Act' to His Study of Dostoevsky." In *Bakhtin and Cultural Theory*, ed. Ken Hirschkop and David Shepherd, 109–35. Manchester, UK: Manchester University Press, 2001.
Poulet, Georges. *Human Time.* New York: Harper & Brothers, 1956.
Priel, Beatriz. "Bakhtin and Winnicott: On Dialogue, Self, and Cure." *Psychoanalytic Dialogues* 9 (1999): 487–503.
Ricœur, Paul. "Life: A Story in Search of a Narrator." Translated by J. N. Kraay

and A. J. Scholten. In *Facts and Values*, ed. M. C. Doeser and J. N. Kraay, 121–32. Dordrecht: Martinus Nijhoff, 1986.

———. "Narrative Identity." *Philosophy Today* 35 (Spring 1991): 73–81.

———. "Narrative Time." In *On Narrative*, ed. W.J.T. Mitchell, 165–86. Chicago: University of Chicago Press, 1981.

———. *Oneself as Another*. Translated by K. Blamey. Chicago: University of Chicago Press, 1992.

———. *Time and Narrative*, vol. 3. 1985. Translated by K. Blamey and David Pellauer. Chicago: University of Chicago Press, 1988.

Riley, Patrick. *Character and Conversion in Autobiography: Augustine, Montaigne, Descartes, Rousseau, and Sartre*. Charlottesville, Va.: University of Virginia Press, 2004.

Robbins, Jill. *Altered Reading: Levinas and Literature*. Chicago: University of Chicago Press, 1999.

Rorty, Richard. "Analytic and Conversational Philosophy." In *A House Divided: Comparing Analytic and Continental Philosophy*, ed. C. G. Prado, 17–31. Amherst, N.Y.: Humanity Books, 2003.

Rosenzweig, Franz. "'Germ Cell' of *The Star of Redemption*." Letter to Rudolf Ehrenberg, 18 November 1917. In *Franz Rosenzweig's "The New Thinking,"* ed. and trans. Alan Udoff and Barbara E. Galli, 45–66. Syracuse, N.Y.: Syracuse University Press, 1999.

———. "The New Thinking." 1925. In *Franz Rosenzweig's "The New Thinking,"* ed. and trans. Alan Udoff and Barbara E. Galli, 67–102. Syracuse, N.Y.: Syracuse University Press, 1999.

———. *The Star of Redemption*. 1921. Translated by William W. Hallo. London: Routledge & Kegan Paul, 1970.

———. *Understanding the Sick and the Healthy: A View of World, Man, and God*. 1921. Translated by Nahum Glatzer. 1953. Cambridge, Mass.: Harvard University Press, 1999.

Rousseau, George. "The Perpetual Crises of Modernism and the Traditions of Enlightenment Vitalism: With a Note on Mikhail Bakhtin." In *The Crisis in Modernism: Bergson and the Vitalist Controversy*, ed. Frederick Burwick and Paul Douglass, 15–69. Cambridge: Cambridge University Press, 1992.

Rudova, Larissa. "Bergsonism in Russia." *Neophilologus* 80 (1996): 175–88.

Rzhevsky, Nicholas. "Kozhinov on Bakhtin." *New Literary History* 25 (1994): 429–44.

Schrag, Calvin O. *The Self After Postmodernity*. New Haven, Conn.: Yale University Press, 1997.

Screech, M. A. *Montaigne and Melancholy: The Wisdom of the Essays*. 1983. 2nd ed. with a foreword by Marc Fumaroli. London: Duckworth, 2000.

Seifrid, Thomas. *The Word Made Self: Russian Writing on Language, 1860–1930*. Ithaca, N.Y.: Cornell University Press, 2005.

Shaitanov, Igor. "The Concept of the Generic Word: Bakhtin and the Russian

Formalists." In *Face to Face: Bakhtin in Russia and the West*, ed. Carol Adlam, Rachel Falconer, Vitalii Makhlin, and Alastair Renfrew, 233–53. Sheffield, UK: Sheffield Academic Press, 1997.

Shklovsky, Victor. "Art as Technique." 1917. In *Russian Formalist Poetics: Four Essays*, trans. and ed. Lee T. Lemon and Marion J. Reis, 3–24. Lincoln: University of Nebraska Press, 1965.

———. "The Resurrection of the Word." 1914. Translated by Richard Sherwood. In *Russian Formalism*, ed. Stephen Bann and John E. Bowlt, 41–47. New York: Barnes & Noble, 1974.

Shotter, John. "Bakhtin and Vygotsky: Internalization as a Boundary Phenomenon." *New Ideas in Psychology* 11, 3 (1993): 379–90.

———. "The Social Construction of Our Inner Selves." *Journal of Constructivist Psychology* 10, 1 (1997): 7–24.

Shotter, John, and Michael Billig. "A Bakhtinian Psychology: From Out of the Heads of Individuals and into the Dialogues Between Them." In *Bakhtin and the Human Sciences: No Last Words*, ed. Michael Meyer Bell and Michael Gardiner, 13–29. Thousand Oaks, Calif.: SAGE, 1998. Repr. in *Mikhail Bakhtin*, ed. Michael Gardiner, 4: 321–38. Thousand Oaks, Calif.: SAGE, 2003.

Stam, Robert. *Subversive Pleasures: Bakhtin, Cultural Criticism, and Film*. Baltimore: Johns Hopkins University Press, 1989.

Starobinski, Jean. *Montaigne in Motion*. 1982. Translated by Arthur Goldhammer. Chicago: University of Chicago Press, 1985.

Steiner, John. "The Equilibrium Between the Paranoid-Schizoid and the Depressive Positions." In *Clinical Lectures on Klein and Bion*, ed. Robin Anderson, with a foreword by Hanna Segal, 46–58. London: Routledge, 1992.

Symington, Joan, and Neville Symington. *The Clinical Thinking of Wilfred Bion*. New York: Routledge, 1996.

Taylor, Ben. "Kanaev, Vitalism and the Bakhtin Circle." In *The Bakhtin Circle: In the Master's Absence*, ed. Craig Brandist, David Shepherd, and Galin Tihanov, 150–66. Manchester, UK: Manchester University Press, 2004.

Theunissen, Michael. *The Other: Studies in the Social Ontology of Husserl, Heidegger, Sartre, and Buber*. 1977. Translated by Christopher Macann, with an introduction by Fred R. Dallmayr. Cambridge, Mass.: MIT Press, 1984.

Tihanov, Galin. "The Body as a Cultural Value: Brief Notes on the History of the Idea and the Idea of History in Bakhtin's Writings." *Dialogism: An International Journal of Bakhtin Studies*, no. 5–6 (October 2000–April 2001): 111–21.

———. "Culture, Form, Life: The Early Lukacs and the Early Bakhtin." In *Materializing Bakhtin: The Bakhtin Circle and Social Theory*, ed. Craig Brandist and Galin Tihanov, 43–69. Basingstoke, UK: Palgrave Macmillan, 2000.

———. *The Master and the Slave: Lukács, Bakhtin, and the Ideas of Their Time*. Oxford: Oxford University Press, 2000.

———. "The Politics of Estrangement: The Case of the Early Shklovsky." *Poetics Today* 26, 4 (Winter 2005): 665–96.

Titunik, I. R. "The Baxtin Problem." *Slavic and East European Journal* 30, 1 (Spring 1986): 91–95.
Todorov, Tzvetan. *The Dialogical Principle*. Translated by Wlad Godzich. Manchester, UK: Manchester University Press, 1984.
Toulmin, Stephen. *Cosmopolis: The Hidden Agenda of Modernity*. New York: Free Press, 1990.
Trilling, Lionel. "On the Teaching of Modern Literature." In id., *Beyond Culture*, 3–30. New York: Viking Press, 1965.
Voloshinov, V. N. *Freudianism: A Marxist Critique*. 1927. Translated by I. R. Titunik. London: Academic Press, 1976.
Voloshinov, V. N. [/Bakhtin?]. *Marxism and the Philosophy of Language*. 1929. Translated by Ladislav Matejka and I. R. Titunik. New York: Seminar Press, 1973.
Wall, Anthony. "A Broken Thinker." *South Atlantic Quarterly* 97, 3–4 (Summer–Fall 1998): 669–98.
Winnicott, D. W. "Ego Distortion in Terms of True and False Self." In id., *The Maturational Processes and the Facilitating Environment*, 140–52. New York: International Universities Press, 1965.
Wittgenstein, Ludwig. *Culture and Value*. Translated by Peter Winch. Edited by G. H. von Wright in collaboration with Heikki Nyman. Oxford: Blackwell, 1980.
Wyschogrod, Edith. "Autochthony and Welcome: Discourses of Exile in Lévinas and Derrida." *Journal of Philosophy and Scripture* 1, 1 (Fall 2003): 36–42.
———. *Emmanuel Lévinas: The Problem of Ethical Metaphysics*. New York: Fordham University Press, 2000.
Zavala, Iris M. "Bakhtin and the Third: Communication as Response." *Critical Studies* 1, 2 (1989): 43–63.
Zbinden, Karine. *Bakhtin Between East and West: Cross-Cultural Transmission*. Oxford: Legenda, 2006.

INDEX

Addressivity, 150–151, 170, 186, 192
Adorno, Theodor, 102
Aesopean discourse, 3, 50, 51, 74
Aesthetics, 4, 25–69, 74–94 passim, 114, 117, 120–132 passim, 140, 147–148, 162, 170–202 passim
Alibi, 141, 139, 168, 169. *See also* Answerability
Alterity (otherness), 6, 31, 58, 61, 70, 78, 80, 86, 88–89, 91, 93, 96, 141–143, 146, 150, 161, 166–176, 181–182, 197, 200–203, 229n1
Amir, Dana, 219n16
Answerability, 24–25, 56, 128, 170, 185. *See also* Alibi
Architectonics of subjectivity, 11, 15, 23–49, 64, 70–74, 90, 139, 142, 146, 153, 181–182, 187
Arendt, Hannah, 230n6
A-topia of subjectivity, 170
Augustine, 6–10 passim, 32, 232n22
Austin, J. L., 155
Autobiography, 10, 15, 28–32, 38, 222n16
Autonomy, 10–11, 27, 40–41, 78, 88, 110, 121, 125, 132, 135, 166, 170, 172, 198, 207, 213n7. *See also* Heteronomy

Benjamin, Walter, 94–95, 102, 216, 233n1

Benveniste, Emile, 30, 133, 155–157, 228n17
Bergson, Henri, 14, 16, 18, 19, 107–134, 158, 167, 176, 199, 224nn1,2, 225n8
Bernard-Donals, Michael F., 225n1
Billig, Michael, 65
Bion, Wilfred, 16, 68–70, 74, 218nn16–19
Bocharov, Sergeiy, 34, 45, 191, 200, 221n8, 225n6
Boethius, 111–112, 126
Bollas, Christopher, 16, 72–75, 145, 219nn21,22
Borderlines, 2, 15, 21–96 passim, 126–134 passim, 143–172 passim, 178, 206. *See also* Contraband; Liminality
Boym, Svetlana, 74, 216n7
Brandist, Craig, 223n2, 227n12, 232n22, 234n7
Britton, Ronald, 69, 218–219n19
Brooks, Cleanth, 163, 228–229n21
Bruss, Neal, 220n
Burton, Stacy, 222n17

Carnivalesque, the, 4, 14, 33, 43, 48, 69, 76, 94, 109, 121, 122, 219n20
Carr, David, 28, 206, 234n7
Carr, Herbert Wildon, 107
Carroll, David, 91

INDEX

Cartesian divide, 7, 12–14, 16, 52–53, 64, 136. *See also* Descartes
Cassirer, Ernst, 102
Cave, Terence, 212nn6,7
Centrifugal (vector of subjectivity), 4, 14–16, 25, 36, 39–49 passim, 54, 62, 67–68, 76, 83, 152, 177, 186–191, 198–199, 206. *See also* Centripetal (vector of subjectivity)
Centripetal (vector of subjectivity), 4, 14–16, 25–26, 33–49 passim, 61–62, 67–68, 83, 110, 116, 152, 176, 186, 198. *See also* Centrifugal (vector of subjectivity)
Chomsky, Noam, 70
Chronotope, 119–134
Clark, Katerina, 109, 184, 215n16, 223n2, 233n1
Clarkson, Carrol, 183
Coates, Ruth, 233n1, 234n4
Cohen, Hermann, 101
Cohen, Richard A., 115, 170, 180–181, 188, 192, 198, 224n5
Coherent deformation, 160, 163. *See also* Defamiliarization; Estrangement (making-strange)
Conrad, Joseph, 91–92, 216n8
Consummation, 26, 28, 32–37 passim, 41, 48, 79, 81–93 passim, 140, 176–177, 191–192, 199–205 passim. *See also* Containment; Finalization; Framing
Containment, 15, 32–37 passim, 41, 68–69, 74, 81–93 passim, 127, 131, 170, 172, 178, 186, 219n19. *See also* Consummation; Finalization; Framing
Contino, Paul J., 233
Continuous self, 68–69, 219n20. *See also* Emergent self
Contraband, 15, 21–96 passim, 158, 163. *See also* Borderlines
Copernican revolution, 40–45 passim, 76, 79, 126, 143, 176, 184, 204, 235n7
Critchley, Simon, 172, 179, 189, 199, 130
Crowell, Steven G., 184
Curtis, James, 115

Davis, Duane H., 227n7

Deconstruction, 49, 53–55, 58, 72, 89, 148, 154, 179, 189, 199, 219n1
Defamiliarization, 57, 58, 160, 106, 216nn4,7. *See also* Estrangement; Formalism
Derrida, Jacques, 11, 22, 43, 53–55, 89, 96, 167, 220n1, 222n15, 229n3, 230n9
Descartes, René, 1, 6–16, 19, 23–35 passim, 43–47 passim, 53–54, 80, 88–90, 96, 103, 106–107, 111, 123, 135–141, 144, 158, 168, 172, 185, 197–198, 207, 226n3, 234n7. *See also* Cartesian divide
Determinism, 65, 107, 108, 110, 111, 112, 113, 119, 124. *See also* Free will
Diachronicity, 127, 129, 132, 172, 173, 181. *See also* Synchronicity
Dialogism, 33, 43, 50, 56, 57, 119, 143, 142, 158, 191, 192, 195
Dop, Eric, 232n22
Dostoyevsky, Fyodor, 4, 15, 17, 35–46, 49, 56, 67, 78–79, 84, 86, 90, 92, 93, 96, 118, 120–124, 147, 148, 151, 162, 164, 166, 169, 175–177, 182–184, 190, 194, 204, 214n15, 222n12, 223n19, 230n13, 233n1
Driesch, Hans, 109, 110
Durée, 111, 114, 116
Duvakin, Viktor, 51

Eaglestone, Robert, 230n7
Eichenbaum, Boris, 117
Eliot, T. S., 166
Embodiment, 6–14, 24–27, 48–47 passim, 65, 67, 85, 88, 129, 137–162 passim, 185, 226n6
Emergent self, 69, 74, 218n17
Emerson, Caryl, 5, 14, 49, 51, 65–66, 80–81, 122, 140, 146, 211n4, 212nn3,4, 213nn8,9, 214nn12,14, 215n17, 216nn5,6, 217nn10,11,13, 218n15, 219nn20,23, 220n3, 221n9, 222n17, 223n2, 224n1, 226n4, 232n22, 233n1, 234n6
Enlightenment, 11, 29, 32, 80, 89, 112, 114
Énoncé, 30, 157
Énonciation, 30, 157
Eskin, Michael, 229n1, 230n15
Estrangement (making-strange), 60–61,

74, 81, 115, 119, 127, 133, 160, 165, 181, 216nn4,6,7, 217nn10,11, 228n20. See also Defamiliarization
Ethics, 1, 2, 14–16, 23–24, 36, 45–74 passim, 89, 106, 111–205 passim, 218n15, 220n4, 226n3, 227n7, 229n1, 230nn7,11,13,15, 231n17, 233n1, 234n2
Exile, 1–3, 16–20, 36, 49, 54, 60, 89, 99, 101–201 passim, 207, 223n3, 229n2, 230n8

Face, 87, 170, 171–172
Farmer, Frank, 232n22
Faulkner, William, 91–92, 118
Felch, Susan, 233n25
Finalization, 41–42, 87, 176–178, 202–205, 213n8, 215n16. See also Consummation; Containment; Framing
Formalism, 16, 57–59, 63, 115–117, 160, 165, 215n4, 228n18
Foucault, Michel, 11, 219n1
Framing, 29, 49, 54, 78–79, 92, 127–128, 132, 170, 173, 177, 213n7. See also Consummation; Containment; Finalization
Free will, 37, 38, 108–119, 122–134. See also Determinism; Freedom
Freedom, 6, 37–41, 49, 51, 108–119, 122–134, 158, 173–176, 186, 191–193, 201, 204, 206, 216n6, 230n8. See also Determinism; Free will
Freud, Sigmund, 64–72, 201, 217nn12,14, 218n17, 220n4, 221n7
Froman, Wayne Jeffrey, 144, 226n6
Futurity, 110–113, 115–116, 123, 127–134, 138, 172–178, 181

Gachev, Georgii, 200–201
Gardiner, Michael, 135, 220n1, 225n1, 229n1, 232n22
Gasché, Rodolphe, 88–89
Greve, Anniken, 229n6
Grounded peace, 191–193, 207
Grounding, 7–10, 14, 16, 32–35, 45–49, 96–97, 104–106, 190–194, 198, 207

Handleman, Susan, 171, 172, 231n16

Handley, William, 220n4
Heidegger, Martin, 11, 53–55, 215n2, 228n20, 230n22
Heteroglossia, 4, 33, 29, 76, 78, 85
Heteronomy, 30–31, 119, 207. See also Autonomy
Hirschkop, Ken, 46, 146, 227n9, 232n1
Holquist, Michael, 17, 47, 60–61, 109, 119–23, 141–142, 150, 212nn3,5, 214n13, 215n16, 216n7, 223n2, 224n4, 225n1, 227nn11,13, 229n4, 232n22, 233n1, 234n7
Homesickness (metaphysical), 1, 15, 19, 21, 26, 49, 97, 105–106, 133, 193, 113–114, 222n15. See also Nostalgia
Humanism, 5, 7, 11–14, 18, 167
Husserl, Edmund, 18, 112, 114, 138, 148, 225n1

I-for-myself, 26–27, 30–32, 36–39, 47, 55, 62–67 passim, 72, 81, 93, 125, 131–132, 140, 153, 170, 181, 234n7
I-for-the-other, 27, 32, 77, 125, 132, 140, 175, 234n7
Image, 79, 81–84, 177, 221n9
Inner speech, 65–66, 74, 149, 217n12
Intersubjectivity, 15, 53–66, 74, 104, 106, 131–146 passim, 151, 156, 158, 163, 169, 173, 183, 185, 195, 200, 203, 226n3, 231n17
Intertextuality, 43, 53, 104
Intrasubjectivity, 15, 55, 61, 64, 74, 131, 142, 151, 158, 173, 205

James, William, 108, 124, 225n8
Jaspers, Karl, 193, 232–233n24
Jay, Martin, 114
Joyce, James, 91–92, 118, 222n17
Judovitz, Dalia, 8–13, 31, 88
Jung, Hwa Jol, 225n1

Kanaev, I. I., 109, 227n12
Kant, Immanuel, 14–15, 23–24, 27, 47, 52, 55–56, 60–61, 67, 101, 106, 111, 120, 128–129, 132–133, 141, 164, 184–185, 214n10, 223n1, 235n7
Karamazov, The Brothers (Dostoyevsky), 46, 191, 230n14

258   INDEX

Kearney, Richard, 50, 53, 104, 170, 173, 180–181, 188, 198
Kermode, Frank, 92–93
Kierkegaard, Søren, 8, 102–103, 193
Kliger, Ilya, 60–61, 216n7, 227n13
Kołakowski, Leszek, 23, 101, 111, 113, 127
Kozhinov, Vadim, 200, 201
Kristeva, Julia, 3–4, 43–47, 76

Lacan, Jacques, 67, 81–83, 154, 163, 217n14, 218n18, 220nn4–6, 221n7
Laplace, Pierre-Simon, 10, 112
Lateral transcendence, 20, 184, 187–188, 203, 205. *See also* Transcendence; Vertical transcendence
Lévinas, Emmanuel, 2, 16, 18–19, 50, 66, 101–105, 109, 115, 166–189, 192, 195, 197–204, 220n1, 223n3, 224n5, 229nn1,2,4,5, 230nn7–9,11–14, 231nn15,16,18
Liminality, 14, 19, 51, 54, 61, 64, 105, 119, 120–123, 130, 135, 142–149 passim, 151, 158–159, 169, 205, 220n4
Linguistic turn, 145–149, 172, 179
Literariness, 55, 57, 117, 155
Loophole, 38–39, 46–49, 62–63, 70–75, 83, 87, 115, 122, 127–132, 157, 163, 175, 181, 186, 188, 190, 195, 202–206, 214n12, 217n10
Low, Douglas, 228n16
Lukács, Georg, 90, 94, 222n16

MacIntyre, Alasdair, 28
Madison, Gary B., 226n3, 227n7
Marcel, Gabriel, 193, 232n22
McGee, Glenn Edwards, 226n3
Medvedev, P. N., 59–60, 63, 214n16
Melehy, Hassan, 8
Merleau-Ponty, Maurice, 2, 16, 18, 66, 101–103, 109, 115, 135–167, 179–181, 197, 199, 220n1, 225n1, 226nn2,3,5,6, 227nn7,8,14, 228nn15,16,18, 230n10, 234n3
Metaphysics, 1, 7–15, 19–20, 23–26, 32–36, 40–49, 53–54, 60, 77–81, 87–90, 96–97, 101, 104–106, 110–111, 134, 166, 183, 188–207, 220n1, 234n7
Mihailovic, Alexandar, 233n1

Mirror, 16, 76–97, 112, 125, 199, 218n18, 220nn4–6, 221nn8,9, 222nn13,14
Misch, Georg, 29
Modernists, 16, 36, 89–93, 96, 106, 114, 118, 228n19
Modernity, 12, 16, 76–97, 103, 106, 114, 219n1, 231n17, 232n22, 234n2
Montaigne, Michel Eyquem de, 6–9, 12–14, 25, 31–32, 38, 39, 104, 112, 136–137, 181, 212n7
Morson, Gary Saul, 5, 14, 66, 122–124, 140, 146, 212nn3,5, 213n9, 214n12, 215n17, 217n13, 218n15, 219nn20,23, 224n1, 225n7, 232n22, 233n1

Naïveté, 35–36, 45, 62, 83–84, 95–96, 146, 199
Narrative, 4, 9–10, 14–15, 28–29, 33, 35–39, 47–48, 62, 66, 71–72, 75, 83, 91–96, 114, 120, 123–124, 186, 207, 213nn6,7, 222n16, 223n19
Natanson, Maurice, 6
Nealon, Jeffrey T., 229n1, 231n15
Neubauer, John, 222n16
Nietzsche, Friedrich, 11, 16, 36, 54, 84, 89–92, 103, 134
Nikulin, Dmitry, 221n9
Nostalgia, 6, 14, 19, 39, 44, 46, 96, 106, 167, 190–191, 234n2. *See also* Homesickness (metaphysical)

Omniscience, 19, 27, 32, 107, 109, 111, 113, 115, 117, 119, 121, 123, 125, 127, 129, 130, 131, 132, 133, 134
Ontological hunger, 8, 32, 36
Ortega y Gasset, José, 92
Oversignification, 159

Pascal, Blaise, 8, 10, 11, 103, 193
Patterson, David, 222n1
Pechey, Graham, 222n16, 232n22
Performativity, 133, 155, 156, 157, 158, 161, 163, 165, 179, 180, 212n7
Phenomenology, 19, 24, 29, 53, 73, 88, 104, 106, 115, 124–170, 184–187, 195, 212n1, 217n11, 222n2, 225n1, 234n1
Pirog, Gerald, 65–66

Polyphony, 4, 33, 39, 50, 76, 78, 123, 129, 130, 213n9
Ponzio, Augusto, 229n1
Poole, Brian, 212n1, 223n2
Postmodernism, 4–6, 14, 16, 43, 73, 76, 80, 83, 106, 168
Postmodernity, 4, 33, 80, 88, 198, 202, 231n17
Poulet, Georges, 114
Priel, Beatriz, 70–71
Proust, Marcel, 91, 118
Psychoanalysis, 16, 64–72, 163, 218n15
Pumpiansky, L. V., 191

Rabelais, François, 4, 14, 69, 94, 109, 121–122, 212n7, 215n17, 219n20
Re-accentuation, 84–86, 89
Refraction, 16, 84–89, 96, 192, 206, 221n10, 222n11
Relational ethics, 25, 27, 34, 52, 67, 77, 140, 148, 156, 157, 158, 165
Relativism, 15, 19, 25, 49, 141–142, 186–189, 194, 198, 219n20, 232n22, 233n1
Rhythm, 26, 37–39, 47–49, 62–63, 68–75, 83, 93, 113, 115, 122, 132, 172–175, 214n12
Ricoeur, Paul, 28, 92, 183, 213n7
Riley, Patrick, 9
Robbins, Jill, 182–184
Rosenzweig, Franz, 101, 104–105, 113–114, 135, 171, 188–189, 199, 202, 205–206, 223n3, 235n9
Rousseau, George, 224n2
Rudova, Larissa, 224n2
Rzhevsky, Nicholas, 4, 201, 211n4

Said, the (*le dit*), 179, 180, 181, 187, 188, 189, 197, 230n11. See also Saying, the (*le dire*)
Sandler, Sergeiy, 211nn1,2, 213n1, 215n1, 216n8, 217n11, 221nn8,9, 222nn11,16, 223n17, 225nn6,10,11,1, 227n10, 231n21, 233n24
Saussure, Ferdinand de, 69, 148, 150, 152, 163, 220n4, 227n14, 233n1
Saying, the (*le dire*), 179, 180, 181, 187, 188, 189, 230n11. See also Said, the (*le dit*)

Schrag, Calvin, 186, 202, 204, 231n17, 234n2
Secularization, 1, 7, 9, 33, 36, 41–47 passim, 60, 78, 79, 99, 90, 94, 105, 168, 186, 191, 198, 203, 214n11
Seifrid, Thomas, 227n13
Self-representation, 15, 32, 35, 140
Semiotic, the, 19, 54, 135–161 passim, 228n16. See also Somatic, the
Shaitanov, Igor, 215n4
Shepherd, David, 214n16, 227n12
Shklovsky, Victor, 57–61, 63, 70, 115–117, 160, 215n4, 216n5, 217nn9–11, 223n19
Shotter, John, 65
Signature, 67, 168, 185, 229n3
Singularity, 12–15 passim, 24, 53, 105, 119, 122, 128–129, 138–146 passim, 165–169, 185, 194, 212n7, 221n9
Somatic, the, 19, 54, 135–148 passim, 158, 161, 228n16, 231n17. See also Semiotic, the
Speech-thinking, 178–179
Stam, Robert, 220n4
Starobinski, Jean, 8, 32, 38, 212n6
Subiectum (ethical, moral), 24–39 passim, 62–63, 138, 168, 173, 181
Superaddressee, 46–49 passim, 87, 187–195, 203–206, 219n20, 231–232n22, 233n1. See also Third, the
Surplus (excess) of knowledge, 26, 67, 126, 134
Surplus (excess) of vision, 26, 41, 79, 93, 134, 140, 147–148
Symington, Joan and Neville, 218n16
Synchronicity, 118–119, 123, 126–132 passim, 148, 173, 181, 226n2, 227n14

Taylor, Ben, 109, 224n2
Temporality, 19, 24, 27–32 passim, 52, 81, 91, 93, 103–127, 132–140 passim, 172–178 passim, 230n9
Theoreticism, 3, 23, 51, 56, 137, 167
Theunissen, Michael, 2
Third, the, 46, 84, 87, 115, 151, 166, 183–195 passim, 200–205 passim, 231n22. See also Superaddressee
Tihanov, Galin, 216n7, 222n16, 223n2

Tillich, Paul, 193
Titunik, I. R., 233n1
Todorov, Tzvetan, 143
Tolstoy, Lev, 58–59, 64, 78
Toulmin, Stephen, 12–13
Transcendence, 9–10, 14–17, 19–20, 26, 28, 35, 44–62 passim, 75, 93, 111, 113, 120, 132, 139, 143, 146, 152, 158, 164, 177–190, 199–206, 219, 226–227, 234. See also Lateral transcendence; Vertical transcendence
Transgredience, 26, 28, 33–55 passim, 62, 77–83 passim, 93–96, 147, 176–177, 184, 191–192, 198–205
Triangulation, 20, 70, 87–89, 219. See also Superaddressee; Third, the

Unconscious, the, 29, 57, 64–66, 72–73, 101, 105, 119

Universal singularity, 14, 141–146 passim
Utterance, 30, 46–47, 56, 63, 69–70, 84, 86, 99, 148–152, 155, 180, 185, 189–190, 227n12, 232nn22,23

Vertical transcendence, 187–188, 201, 203–205, 234n2, 235n8. See also Lateral transcendence; Transcendence
Voloshinov, V. N., 65–66, 148–150, 155, 217n12, 220n4, 223n2, 227n13
Vygotsky, L. S., 64

Wall, Anthony, 5
Winnicott, D. W., 16, 70–72, 74
Wittgenstein, Ludwig, 223n18, 233n1
Woolf, Virginia, 91–92, 118, 198
Wyschogrod, Edith, 172, 229n2, 230n8

Zavala, Iris, 231–232n22

The authorized representative in the EU for product safety and compliance is:
Mare Nostrum Group
B.V Doelen 72
4831 GR Breda
The Netherlands

www.ingramcontent.com/pod-product-compliance
Lightning Source LLC
Chambersburg PA
CBHW030533230426
43665CB00010B/866